Lessons of the Inca Shamans

Part 2

Beyond the Veil

Deborah Bryon, PhD

with forewords by Adolfo Ttito Condori
and Rodolfo Ttito Condori

Pine Winds Press
An imprint of Idyll Arbor, Inc.
39129 264th Ave SE, Enumclaw, WA 98022
www.PineWindsPress.com

Cover Design: Tom Blaschko
Pine Winds Press Editors: Sand Swenby, JoAnne Dyer

Author photos: Perry Edwards
Cover photo: Frances Marron at FrancesPhotography.com

paper ISBN 9780937663363
e-book ISBN 9780937663370

Library of Congress Cataloging-in-Publication Data
Bryon, Deborah.
  Lessons of the Inca Shamans, part 2 : beyond the veil / Deborah Bryon, PhD.
     pages cm
  Includes index.
  ISBN 978-0-937663-36-3 (trade paper) -- ISBN 978-0-937663-37-0 (e-book)
  1. Shamanism--Peru. 2. Incas--Rites and ceremonies. 3. Quero Indians--Religion. 4. Spirituality. 5. Self-actualization (Psychology) I. Title.
  GN475.8.B79 20147
  299.8'83230144--dc23
                                                        2013051098

*I want to thank my husband Perry, who has been on this journey
with me from the beginning, for his passion, vision, and
willingness to walk with me in other realms.*

*I also want to thank all of the wonderful paqos I have worked with,
my teachers Jose Luis and Adolfo, and my publisher Tom, Carol,
and medicine brother Rodolfo for their help and editorial support.*

*Finally, and most importantly, I would like to dedicate this book to
Chupícuaro, Huascaran, Ausangate, Alankoma, Pachatusan,
Pachamama, and all of the mountains spirits who provided their
insight and many of the words written on these pages. They are the
reason this book was written — this book is theirs.*

Contents

Forewords

Firstly, I give infinite thanks to the Apus and Pachamamas, who afford all our brothers and sisters the opportunity of Tupay [reigniting the eternal fire in ourselves] in the Ayllu K'anchaq Qoyllur (AKQ). The spirits connect all of us and let us open ourselves in mutual confidence to create a sacred space where the spirits of the mountains can travel to the edge of the veil. Here our brothers and sisters reading this book have the privilege of finding the teachings and practices contained in this book, which will be useful for both students and teachers.

Today mankind has realized its needs and, for that reason, has set forth on a search for new spiritual horizons. Even though insecurities and conflicts abound in these times, many people in Peru and other countries have begun the same quest for spirituality and at the same time have again started to find the strength in themselves to appreciate the sacred cosmos.

In the study of the Andean cosmos there are sources and secrets of Andean wisdom, in relation to Pachamama and the Apus, and in the other celestial beings that manifest themselves and inspire man by their connection to Kausay [the energy of creation]. At the same time the study of the Andean cosmos offers us a rich wisdom and practice we can share with the brother Paqos in real experiences that let us powerfully embrace and discover the magical mysteries of the cosmic mother. Here each teacher experiments and manifests his Kausay. From this understanding comes the search for cosmic knowledge. Sister

Deborah has been inspired to continue along the journey of the Paqos, which has been no easy task. Challenges and difficulties have presented themselves in her learning, training, and spiritual life, yet she fights to keep moving forward.

In this book, *Lessons of the Incas Shamans, Part 2*, she addresses a part of her spiritual experiences during her journeys to the sacred places and sacred mountains of the Andes. Sister Deborah describes her experiences and acquired understanding of the cosmos and of the Andean masters as a psychologist and Jungian analyst, describing them with passion and freely integrating them with her Western understanding, which is a part of Kausay. She made a firm decision about her connection, confidence, love, and choice to explain the tradition and customs of Andean coexistence to the world. To succeed in this, sister Deborah Bryon had to stay at the forefront of the Andean knowledge and practice that she received from her teachers. Only in this way could she overcome the challenges of a modern world and make her knowledge and desires to transmit this work her top priority. Because of this, one can say that this book is a gift for readers who have minds and hearts open enough to enjoy reading its pages; here you can receive a drop of wisdom and spiritual nourishment coming from the hearts of the Andean teachers.

In this sense, it is right to give additional congratulations to sister Deborah, for her complete confidence in ayni [right relationships] within the Andean spiritual cosmos and with the Paqos. In this book she courageously demonstrates her abilities and beliefs according to what she has learned from her teachers. She has captured their understanding like a psychologist in the fulfillment of the teachings of Tukuy: Yachay, Munay, Llank'ay. The spirits stay by her side; they have always blessed her to support her sacrifices and experiences. Because of this one can see the spiritual essence in every stage of the process as sister

Deborah rises to the level of an Andean teacher as a Yachacheq Paqo.

Adolfo Ttito Condori
Paqo Alto Misayoq.

Since the ancient times of the Incas, and the Andean cultures that came before them, the Andean teaching and customs have remained engraved in the hearts and minds of the teachers who originated them; those who developed the teachings and practices, little by little, have perfected them for the good of mankind.

The teacher's knowledge, in the past, was not written on paper or on a computer, as it is in our time. Instead, it was written in the sacred cosmos, in nature, and in everything that surrounds us. Now some Andean teachers like the Paqos and Hmaut'as read and decipher the mysteries of the Andean consciousness that was left by the ancestors. Andean men and Andean spirits continue to promote this sacred knowledge, by way of intermediary instructors on the earth, because the cosmos is the supreme manifestation of knowledge for mankind.

The spiritual secrets of the Andean teachers and students have been managed and disseminated by a select few, who maintained the knowledge over millennia and generations. Also, during various periods of that time, the line of teachers and the knowledge have been interrupted or even broken for a time by persons who had harmful intentions or were poorly informed. But we clearly know that Andean knowledge has not been and will not be erased from the memories of the teachers and the cosmos. Because of this, there exists an Inca prophecy named "Yachay Kutimuy," which means "the return of wisdom and the sacred Andean practices." The spiritual knowledge, integrated by the Andean masters, despite any intent to desecrate or suppress it, will always be present in the life of man and will be heard by all mankind, because it was not just planned by Andean men. It came from the direction and guidance of superior beings.

On the sacred Andean journey, many teachers and students have accepted and recognized the sacred task of collaborating in teaching and disseminating this knowledge: the wisdom, the practices, the ceremonies, the rites, and all the spiritual activity that is related to what it means to be Andean. We do this for the world in which we live, with the mission of supporting and changing modern society; awakening and fulfilling the Andean prophecy through the performance of these sacred Andean duties.

The motives and reasons of each teacher or student are powerful and it is inevitable, I assume for these and other reasons, that sister Deborah Bryon has accepted her task of writing down some of the teachings and customs of the master Paqos, also referred to as shamans. With the publication of this book entitled *Lessons of the Inca Shamans, Part 2*, sister Debora Bryon has undertaken a part of her task and the mission of spreading this Andean knowledge. In the same way, many other brothers and sisters are starting out on this task, from different perspectives, from different places, from different points of view, for different reasons, and using different ways of describing the knowledge, all of which are necessary for our modern age.

In the present, the Andean knowledge that is practiced and taught is scattered across all of Tawantinsuyu, the territory of the Inca Empire. For that reason, each master from each geographic location conserves only a part of the knowledge. But the reintegration of that sacred wisdom will occur one day, without fail, because it is part of the Andean prophecy, something we should consider seriously when we read and try to understand.

Because primitive cultures originated this sacred knowledge before 9,000 – 2,000 BC and these important cultures united in the time of the Incas to plan and propose to the world a new integration of the wisdom of the diverse traditions and cultures, to convert into a sole culture which was that of the Incas of Tawantinsuyu, we refer to the years after 1,100 AD when the Incas come forth into a new period and give a new future to the Andean world. The Andean spiritual practices and teachings are the summation of the knowledge of thousands of years during which many masters participated at different times to meet different needs.

To enter into the world of wisdom and customs of the Paqos is to give yourself the opportunity to make a self-discovery of who you are. It is to understand a new, beneficial reality for your life — to learn to discover other options for your life. It is to learn the intimate knowledge of the Hmaut'as. It is to learn the specific practices of the Paqos. It is to learn to build your own life. Because if you are able to build yourself, then together we can rebuild this world for the better.

Rodolfo Ttito Condori

NUNA HMAUT'A

Inka – Qanchi

Introduction

Above everything, we are children of the land. And the basic understanding is that we've always been children of the land, and as children of the land we need to, to remember the old way of dialoguing with that that supports us and nurtures us. Everything around us has kausay, *is infused with life force.*

—Don Hilario

As I grow older, it becomes clearer to me that human beings have an inherent need to find meaning in their lives. Based upon my experience as a psychologist and a Jungian analyst, working with people in the process of deep soul searching, this is what brings people a sense of well-being. In the West, many of us attempt to find meaning through discovering new ideas, establishing and achieving individual goals, and by developing our personal and professional identities. These formulate our individual belief systems as a function of our personalities. Our personalities are created from our genetic makeup and temperament as well as from our experience and subjective interpretation of our life events. The combination of all of these variables together makes a template that defines who we are — as we are living in this lifetime. Our understandings and perceptions of our individual life events influence our approach to making meaning, bringing us to our own conclusions of what is important to us.

1

Beyond our personal development in our outer world, making meaning can also come through connecting with something that is bigger than we are in both our inner and outer worlds. Most of us have a certain tendency towards introversion or extroversion, which will effect what we consider meaningful. Feeling a sense of meaning may emerge in creative expression and play, being in nature, and through spirit connection.

Of course, all our meaningful conclusions can change at just a moment's notice because, as living beings, we are energy, and energy movement is a fluid process running through the template of our personality. The flow of energy may alter the personality template as it comes in contact with it — and vice versa — and this can potentially change who we are. By being in close relationship with family, friends, animals, and nature, we connect and we change. We change through contact and connection. Q'ero *paqos* (shamans) experience the connection of *kausay* (life force) with Pachamama (Mother Earth), the energy of life that is everywhere. As Westerners, we tend to only access small parts of the vast energy source that is available to all of us, because our culture has forgotten what it is like to live in connection. We are all part of the living energy which Inca shamans call *kausay*.

With an appetite for the inner world, my own personal quest for meaning led me down the path of first becoming a stockbroker, then an artist, then psychologist and Jungian analyst using my mind. Finally, my search for meaning led me to the jungles and mountaintops of Peru, to work with indigenous *paqos* in the Andes Mountains. My own journey into Peruvian shamanism began a decade ago after hearing an introductory talk given by Jose Luis. This book is a continuation of my personal story of traveling down the shaman's, or *paqo's*, path. In this book, I will usually refer to shamans as *paqos* because this is the term used by the Incan medicine people. *Paqo* literally means

Figure 1. Jose Luis (photo by Carol Dearborn)

"doorway" in Quechua, the native language of the Incan medicine people.

My journey of becoming a *paqo* synchronistically began the same month I started my training as a Jungian analyst. This narrative is a continuation of *Lessons of the Inca Shamans* — of the teachings I received under the care of the Q'ero *paqos* as well as others encountered along the way. In exchange for receiving their lineage through initiation I promised to bring the sacred knowledge back to Western culture. Since feeling a Heart connection is more powerful and accessible through shared experience, I am using the context of my own experience and the experience of others as the underpinnings, to weave the tale of the lessons of the Inca shamans and the great mountain spirits together. A portion of the proceeds from this writing will be donated to Andean Research Institute (ARI), to help preserve the ancient Incan teachings and traditions, in the hope that we will begin to remember what is quickly becoming forgotten.

This narrative covers my fourth initiatory journey back to Peru, in July 2011. I will include an overview of Inca cosmology, and shamanism being practiced in the Andes Mountains today, interlaced with pages from my diary describing the series of events that took place. Many of the words printed on these pages are those given to me by Inca *paqos* that I have worked with and grown to love. These pages also contain the words and knowledge of the great *apus*, the winged beings who continue to offer wisdom and strength to those of us who agree to partake on this mystical journey. Last but not least, I have included many experiences shared by my husband, Perry, in sections intertwined throughout my text along with his notes, observations, and comments. What is written here is my best understanding at this time. My understanding has changed as I have made this journey and I expect it to change again as I continue to learn.

A significant portion of this book is from actual verbatims with the *paqos* and from recorded notes taken during dialogues with the *apu* mountain spirits during ceremony. I have also worked with *altomesayoq* Adolfo Ttito Condori and his brother Rodolfo who, although they were not with me on this particular journey, generously helped clarify some of the information in order to deepen my understanding.

If the idea that "winged beings" can actually communicate with us using words we can hear with our ears seems too difficult to accept — then don't. Put that question on the shelf for now. Later, when you are ready, you can decide for yourself if there is meaning in the words I have written. I have learned that the best way to resolve what you believe about the world must come from your own experiences — not from what someone tells you. I believe that learning and remembering come from within and lead to inner truth. To have any substance, your personal beliefs must resonate with you on a gut level. When I began my journey down this shamanic path, it took me several years to accept that what I was seeing and experiencing was actually real. If this material is new to you, you may find yourself wrestling with some of the same questions that I initially had. I hope you will consider the possibility that the world has more in it than we currently acknowledge.

1. Overview of Inca Shamanism

This work sets the stage for the next seven generations. The veil between worlds is thinner now — the way is the rites of passage. It is time to return to where we rightfully belong — the land. Like striking a match. Unless we want to have uneventful lives, like sheep. Live like jaguars instead.

—Asunta

In 2003, I began studying with the Q'ero medicine people who are the descendants of the Inca shamans living in Peru today. A *paqo's* approach to the world is very different from what we learn growing up in the "Western world" in the United States.

Rather than encouraging people to learn to "stand on their own two feet" as we do in the West, medicine people develop a very different understanding of their exterior world because they live close to nature. Instead of placing value on personal achievements and individualism, *paqos* develop a strong bond with Pachamama (Mother Earth) through serving their community, or *ayllu*. Because most Inca shamans grow up in small villages high in the Andes, they depend on Pachamama for their survival. By maintaining a physical and spiritual relationship with Pachamama through the daily activities of raising corn and herding llamas, they learn and grow. In the *paqo's* world, everything in life begins, exists, and ends with Pachamama.

Unlike those of us raised in the modern world of Western culture, shamans serve their experience rather than trying to make meaning from it. Trying to understand everything using our logical mind is not necessary. It can sometimes even hinder our growth because we miss things. *Paqos* have identified three centers that need to be considered in making meaning of the world: Belly, Heart, and Mind. Growing up in a village, or *ayllu*, *paqos* learn to rely on their Hearts and Bellies, in addition to their Minds, to make sense of the world. Depending on their feeling senses provides them with a broader range of perception because there are things that exist in the natural and spiritual world that cannot be understood using reason. As Westerners, we sometimes throw the baby out with the bathwater when we count on our logical minds to determine what is real. The medicine people believe that thinking about something brings separation while a Heart-centered focus of *kausay* brings connection. Shamans believe that feeling connected through the Heart leads to truth.

The *paqos' kausay* energy connection with Pachamama flows throughout their lives as the primary force. *Paqos* live their lives by tending to *kausay* and learning from the abundance in nature. *Kausay* is the building block of shamanism and Incan medicine. It is the fuel, life force, and the energy of creation, experienced in the Belly as a vibration, and in the Heart as a feeling of universal love. In the Mind, *kausay* is often seen as an intense light, or experienced as clarity, bringing a sense of all-knowing wisdom. It is also experienced in altered states of ecstasy when *paqos* enter into the spirit world of energy. Medicine people learn to source, or draw on, the life energy of *kausay* from Pachamama because Pachamama is constant and always there.

Sometimes a manifestation of *kausay* comes as an unexplainable event that, as Westerners, we would identify as strange, weird, or magic. You may remember times when you invariably experienced the flow of *kausay* energy through you if you think about it — a time when you felt very alive and "in the flow," a time when things were clicking.

The expression of *kausay* occurs by being in *ayni*, in an open reciprocal relationship with Pachamama. What is taken from the land is returned to the land in gratitude so that it can be born again. Everything in nature, and all living things, occurs in the order of "right relationship" — Kausay Pacha. Everything comes from and returns to Pachamama.

According to Inca cosmology, being in *ayni* (right relationship) comes as an expression of *munay* (unconditional, universal love) with the collective. In Inca shamanism, the definition of collective is much broader than in modern Western culture. Instead of using the term to refer to mass culture and society, shamans use the word collective to speak of the energetic relationship existing between all living things. For *paqos*, this consists of plants, animals, humans, and anything belonging to the physical and/or energetic realm of the natural world.

Exercise 1. Building *Kausay* in Connection with Pachamama

Find a comfortable place to sit cross-legged in a meditation position. If you are seated on a chair, make sure your feet are placed firmly on the ground. Take a few deep breaths, inhaling and exhaling from your Belly and close your eyes. As you exhale, feel yourself sinking deeper into your body, moving further with each breath into a receptive and peaceful state. As your attention gradually shifts more fully into what you are experiencing in your core, your breathing will become easy and relaxed, falling into a gentle rhythm. As you continue breathing from your Belly, feel your awareness dropping even farther into your interior, as you are sensing through your body.

Now, using your intention imagine a star of light located in the deepest part of your interior and visualize it growing, becoming stronger and larger. Using your intent, imagine feeling the energetic rays reaching down through your legs, through the bottoms of your feet, and deep into the earth. Again, using your intention, allow the rays of light to carry your focus, moving deep into the earth with the light.

From the place of sensing deep within the earth, sense your connection with the earth and with all living things. Feel yourself held and nourished in the loving and powerful presence of Pachamama, as the energy exchange begins to strengthen and expand between you and the earth. Give Pachamama rays of light emanating from the light star in your Belly and in exchange receive the nourishing energy from Pachamama in an exchange of *ayni*, of right relationship.

Using your intention, fully receive Pachamama's gift of energy by allowing it to move up through the bottoms of your feet, through your legs, into your Belly, throughout your entire body.

You may experience Pachamama's nourishing energy as an orange energy vibration, or as warm sunlight, or golden honey. Allow yourself to be fed by her energy, while making connection with her through the light emanating from the star in your Belly. Breathe the energy in and breathe it out through exhaling, directing it back, deep into the earth.

When you feel complete, open yourself to the feeling of gratitude for Pachamama. Thank her for her gift and for being present. When you are ready, in your own time, gradually bring yourself to your outer awareness and open your eyes.

For *paqos*, the expression of the collective in the spirit world includes the *apus* (the collective mountain spirits) and *santa tierras* (feminine spirits residing in the earth that are an aspect of Pachamama). Adolfo has told me that Pachamama gave birth to all of the *apus* and is the mother of everything that exists in our world. In my writing, I will refer to the energetic state of non-ordinary reality, in which all living things are connected, existing outside of the time/space continuum as the "energetic collective."

The energy of the collective manifests at different levels ranging on a continuum between physical and energetic states of ordinary and non-ordinary reality. Ordinary reality has to do with physical reality, while non-ordinary reality pertains to the energetic, spiritual world. *Paqos* move into altered states of consciousness between states in ordinary and non-ordinary reality through shifting between the levels of perception using their intention.

In the Western world, we access and perceive from these levels without consciously realizing it. It is not uncommon to hear people talk about feeling the protective presence of guardian angels or guides that on occasion save their lives. Many of us have had the experience of doing or avoiding something "by the skin of your teeth," or "knowing" something ahead of time without understanding how or why. Then, when we are trying to explain what happened, we say things like "I don't even know how I did that." Westerners frequently struggle with linking these levels together and recognizing their existence because they are beyond the physical and symbolic levels of perception.

Levels of Perception in Peruvian Shamanism

In Peruvian shamanism, there are four levels of psychic engagement, or states of perception.

Level 1. The Literal

The first level of perception is the literal level, taking place in ordinary reality. The literal level is the physical world of everyday experience. This includes the concrete world of empirical science — what we can see and prove is what we know.

Level 2. The Symbolic

The second level is the symbolic level, and includes both left-hemisphere and right-hemisphere brain functioning with the capacity for critical thinking and imagination, respectively. It is the territory of dreams, metaphors, images, and fantasy, including the playful and creative capacity and world of children. It is also the mathematician's world of complex theory and abstract reasoning, language, and verbal communication.

Level 3. The Mythic/Archetypal

The third level pertains to the mythic or archetypal level of the collective unconscious described by Carl Jung. It includes the archetypes of wholeness as the Self, as well as the trickster, crone, mother, father, and magician that emerge in myths and fairytales. This is the level where synchronistic events connect and where déjà vu exists. In the collective psyche of Peruvian cosmology, mythical beings appear in the animal forms of the snake, jaguar, and condor. These mythic beings are the guiding principles that manifest as emanations of the spirit world and correspond respectively to the three major energy centers in our bodies — the Belly, the Heart, and the Mind.

In Peruvian cosmology, Amaru is the powerful snake of creation that resides in the energy center of the Belly. Amaru is a manifestation of Pachamama, residing in the lower world of Ukhu Pacha that contains the blueprint of creation. Like the snake moving through direct belly contact with the earth, the physical mechanics of "doing" happen by connecting through the Belly. Being in relation with the earth by sensing through the Belly is the way to link to the source of power.

In snake vision, everything is immediate, black and white, all or none — focused on instinctual survival. Snake-vision experience is useful in situations requiring a gut reaction, or an immediate fight-or-flight response. It may feel like a light tingling sensation, a sense of expansion, or an intense rush of vibrating energy. During shamanic initiations, an intense "download" of energy is often transferred into the luminous body through the

Belly, and contractions and/or temporary paralysis in those parts of the physical body may occur. It can feel like a rippling effect, a strong charge, or a surging electric current. Somatically experiencing energy through our Belly is the way we become aware of being in the moment. In these fluid states, we can enter into a place of no separation — where anything is possible. In the world of Amaru, everything exists in a primary, volatile state between spirit and matter. This is the hub of creation, where physical manifestation can occur. Being in the Belly is what Taoists' describe as "being in the flow," in balance with the energy and world around us.

Exercise 2. Experiencing Connection with Amaru

In this exercise, I will describe one of the ways of experiencing the connection of being held in Amaru.

As in Exercise 1, find a comfortable place to sit cross-legged in a meditation position. If you are seated on a chair, make sure your feet are placed firmly on the ground. Take a few deep breaths, inhaling and exhaling from your Belly and close your eyes. As you exhale, feel yourself sinking deeper into your body, moving further with each breath into a receptive and peaceful state. As your attention gradually shifts more fully into what you are experiencing in your core, your breathing will become easy and relaxed, falling into a gentle rhythm. As you continue breathing from your Belly, feel your awareness dropping even farther into your interior as you are sensing through your body.

Now, from this relaxed state imagine being deep in the Amazon jungle where everything is alive — growing and decaying at the same time. A few rays of sunlight have penetrated through the tall tropical plants and trees that are everywhere. Other than the sounds of birds in the distance that are muted by the dense vegetation, it is quiet. The air and earth are moist and still.

You find yourself looking into a deep lagoon that is dark and fertile. It has an ageless quality and you can sense that this lagoon has been present deep within the jungle since before the beginning of time.

Next, imagine bringing your awareness into the lagoon, feeling the essence of this deep feminine, ancient energy, an original source of creation on this planet. Continue "feeling into" the nurturing energy of this powerful presence that is both wise and maternal. Allow yourself to be held in the Belly of the Great Mother, Pachamama. Through this connection, begin to "source" by drawing in the strength and protection of this great feminine protector. When you are ready, still maintaining your connection, gradually bring yourself back to your outer awareness and open your eyes.

In Incan cosmology, as the Great Mother, Amaru is the Belly of creation, manifesting as *yanantin*, a union between masculine and feminine, or as feminine. In the jungle during the early phase of an *ayahuasca* ceremony Amaru appears as the giant anaconda that penetrates our body with its powerful, massive jaws and devours us, enabling us to shed our identification with our persona and physical form, providing the momentum to transcend into the celestial realms.

At times this energy may be experienced as masculine because of the powerful movement and capacity for penetration, Adolfo has assured me that in Incan cosmology, Amaru is feminine and never a manifestation of masculine energy.

Chocachinchay governs the middle world of Kay Pacha and is the commanding jaguar, the spirit of the Amazon. The jaguar lives in the present moment, and through existing in an open and receptive state taking in the world as it is happening through all of the senses. Chocachinchay senses and feels everything intensely as he moves through the forest and jungle. We experience the fullness and fulfillment of our lives through connection in our Heart center.

In Andean cosmology, Chocachinchay takes on a somewhat broader meaning and symbolizes all animals with the capacity to manifest in any physical form in Kay Pacha, the middle world. Thus this jaguar is magical, and is sometimes symbolized as a rainbow, the symbol of completeness in Andean cosmology — where everything is possible.

Although through our energy bodies we may experience a simultaneous and equally intense feeling of connection in the Belly and the Heart centers with Amaru and Chocachinchay respectively, we usually experience the sensations in each of the two centers differently. From my experience, expansion in the Heart center can be felt energetically as a sense of belonging or coming home that goes beyond words. The Heart is the vehicle of relatedness — where we experience the energy of universal love, of *munay*, connecting us to the earth in a state of union.

The capacity to love unconditionally, beyond personal experience and limitation, takes place in the Heart as an expression of Pachamama. This is different from personal love, which focuses on another person, often with the need for reciprocation. As an expression of the energetic relationship with spirit, in the Heart form of loving there is no need to get something back because everything is automatically linked and available. Expansion in the Heart center can "feel as though one's heart is bursting open."

During my first trip to Peru, when I entered the energetic fields of the *altomesayoq* shamans for the first time, I felt my Heart stretching and opening — before any words were spoken. I noticed that my Heart was actually aching. I felt a fullness just being in the shamans' presence and had an overwhelming sense of finally coming home. It brought me to tears. I noticed myself crying regularly over the course of my initial journey. The process of expanding the Heart center frequently involves shedding tears.

Exercise 3. Connecting with Chocachinchay

As in Exercise 1, find a comfortable place to sit. Take a few deep breaths. As you exhale, feel yourself sinking deeper into your body, moving further with each breath into a receptive and peaceful state. As your attention gradually shifts more fully into what you are experiencing in your core, your breathing will become easy and relaxed, falling into a gentle rhythm.

Now, gently shift your awareness into your Heart center, feeling your Heart opening and expanding, similar to the lens of a camera. From this place of expansion, imagine the presence of a powerful, larger-than-life jaguar emerging. Notice the electric-blue aura of energy around him. When you look into the jaguar's penetrating, clear green eyes, you recognize that the jaguar is a guide, an ally, and a protector. The sheen of its thick, jet-black coat is soft to the touch. You see the strength of its massive paws that can agilely spring forward in an instant and feel its massive chest surrounding you. You know that you are safe and are not afraid. Allow yourself to move more fully into your connection with this magnificent mythic being as it grows stronger in your Heart and become more aware of the bond of trust that is forming between you.

You understand that the jaguar is asking you to merge your awareness with his — he has something for you to experience. The jaguar is offering you the opportunity to see through his eyes, and to feel through his senses. If you agree, you feel the power of the jaguar moving into you and you become one in his electric aura of energy. You are the jaguar and the jaguar is you. Suddenly discover that you are rapidly running through a forest, over soft pine needles. Covering miles of ground, you feel the wind racing by. As the jaguar, you come to a summit that looks over a vast valley that stretches for on miles. Surveying the landscape, you now have the ability to detect subtle scents and sounds from far away and can sense everything that is happening in your environment. Your vision and hearing have become intensely acute.

You can hear the voice of the wind. You see particles of sparkling life force emanating from the valley and dancing between the trees. This energetic field connects all that is around you. Merged with the consciousness of the jaguar, you are part of everything that is living.

Now, taking as much time as you need, gradually bring yourself back to your outer awareness, feeling invigorated and alive. When you are ready, slowly open your eyes.

The Mind is the third energy center, located in the third eye or forehead. It is the energy center associated with the condor, Apuchin. The Mind holds the capacity for spiritual wisdom and global vision. Our perception shifts from subjective experience into an objective and inclusive perspective. As the condor flying overhead, perceiving from a "bird's eye" view gives us a vantage point from which we can see the big picture and avoid becoming bogged down in unimportant details.

Dreamers and visionaries use their Minds to enter the realms of non-ordinary reality, outside of time and space. They straddle the boundaries of non-ordinary and ordinary reality and at times are able to maintain a foot in each of the realities simultaneously. Through this process of dreaming while asleep or purposefully imagining with intention while awake, the Mind can craft a vision, using metaphors to interpret what is being seen in a vision.

My husband, Perry, is a visionary. Perry is an extroverted intuitive and sees things through narratives with imagery, while as an introverted intuitive I tend to experience visionary states energetically, usually through my body. The following passage is Perry's description of what having a vision is like for him:

Gathering a vision is rather easy once you learn how to do it. The hard part is knowing what you are looking at. It is important to draw it on a piece of paper when you come back so that you don't lose it. Sometimes my drawing interpretations of the vision has become twisted around, going backwards, in the opposite direction, or upside down. I think this may have something to do with the absence of gravity in non-ordinary reality.

The other problem is that at times I have come back from a vision and have been so excited about what I saw that I would forget that I knew what it was. If I do not draw them immediately, they can rapidly fade.

Weeks before my first trip to Peru, Apuchin began appearing in my dreams in the form of Birdman figures. After arriving in Peru, I was walking through a market with the *altomesayoq* Adolfo. Suddenly, he stopped me. Pointing to a painting of a Birdman being displayed by one of the local vendors, Adolfo said, using a combination of motion-gestures and Spanish words, "There is the figure that appears in your visions."

Level 4. The Energetic/Essential

The fourth level of perception in Peruvian shamanism is the energetic or essential level. This level is pure energy where form, time, and space no longer exist. This is the level where transformation and healing occurs.

Shamanism is focused on feeling. The focus is feeling connection with the collective — not an individual journey. It is an intersubjective rather than an intrasubjective experience. The medicine people say it takes Heart. Shamans begin with the collective and through the collective heal the personal. In the West, our approach is healing yourself first and then healing others. Shamanism focuses on giving back to the community and to the collective, as Doña Alejandrina says:

Figure 2. Adolfo (photo by Frances Marron)

The collective does not necessarily mean people or community. Collective means living a life in which you are no longer your own person but you are collective. You are the land; you are the people. Sourcing from this other, entirely different, way, you do not have to deal with the shortcomings of the personal, which is your ego framework with the persona and shadow — your sense of misfortune, or love, or money, or work. Collective means the makeup of light, life, and fertility that supports you so that, as shamans say, you can grow corn.

Right Relationship (Ayni)

The Q'ero shamans approach to healing always occurs in right relationship — in *ayni* — to the collective. Everything in the universe has a memory of a healed state. Shamans access these memories by sensing the state of the individual they are helping and bringing it into alignment by moving energy using *mesa* stones (the shaman's medicine body) to remember and hold that healed state. Once the body recognizes the healed state, aligns itself with it, the healing is complete. Healing is a non-personal state, and a good healer understands what is personal and what is non-personal. Shamans do not see personal circumstances — they only see energy.

A *paqo's* job is to transport the energy from the collective state of numinous experience into consciousness in ordinary reality. By honoring the connection between all living things, shamans maintain the harmonic balance required to be stewards of wellness. It is always about awareness of the relationship — serving the relation, involving your whole being — it is not only mental. As a practice in daily living, shamanism is a process of following what feels right in your Heart and sourcing from the energetic collective. It is cultivating an energetic connection with the world that leads to feeling alive with *kausay*.

Exercise 4. Building *Kausay* through Celestial Connection

Find a quiet and comfortable place to sit, preferably in nature. Locate a spot that feels right to you, underneath a large tree, on a boulder, near a stream, in a field — or even a place in your backyard or in a park. Sit for a moment taking time to tune into everything around you — the smells, temperature, lighting, sounds, and perhaps the breeze if you are outside.

Close your eyes and relax. Take in a few deep breaths and exhale slowly so that you are breathing deeply from both your Heart and your Belly. Bring your attention into your forebrain and center yourself, so that you are shifting from focusing on other things and are becoming fully and instantly present.

When you feel yourself being present, drop your attention into your body. Begin to sense and feel in your Belly. Imagine a white star located deep in your interior. Using your intent, feel it expanding to a size about three feet in diameter. Experience being surrounded by this pure, vibrant light, knowing that you are perfectly safe and protected.

Now, imagine that the ball of light enclosing you expands even further, growing into a column of light that reaches high up into the celestial realm, farther than you can imagine. Feel the energy of the star continuing to grow and expand, becoming brighter and brighter. You may begin to notice a sense of expansion and start to feel heat or a tingling vibration.

Begin to feel this pure light energy flowing down through the column, bathing you in light, moving through each of your cells.

Again, using your intention, imagine reaching your awareness up the column, reaching higher and higher in the pure white energy. Begin to tune into the energy's vibrational frequency, the way you might stretch to hear a faint but pleasing melody. Ask that your whole being begins to harmonize with this pure white vibration.

Stay in this pure energetic exchange for as long as you are comfortable and can hold a focus, reaching up the column from the nucleus of the star centered in your Belly into the celestial realm and then receiving the abundant energy as it flows down the column into you. This is a process of being in right relationship — in *ayni*.

2. Inca Shamans

Taripay Pacha is the time to meet ourselves through our new evolving medicine bodies.

—Jose Luis

In the training I have received, there are two types of Peruvian mountain shamans: the *altomesayoqs* and the *pampamesayoqs*. The *altomesayoqs* are the most powerful group of shamans, with the greatest capacity to hold *kausay* (life force). Many *altomesayoqs* are cross-eyed, the result of being struck by lightning during their initiation. (Oddly enough, during my last plane trip to Peru I watched a documentary about people who had been struck by lightning and survived.)

Altomesayoqs are the doorways between ordinary reality (Kay Pacha) and the spirit world (Kausay Pacha). Through their capacity to contain energy or hold space, they serve as a gateway for the *apus* or mountain spirits to emerge. *Altomesayoqs* each have a membership with a particular mountain who becomes their benefactor and they speak directly to the spirits of that location. The *altomesayoqs'* capacity to hold power is a function of their accessibility and capacity to connect using their Heart.

Many *altomesayoqs* begin their shamanic path by first becoming *pampamesayoqs*, who primarily focus on healing. The duties of *pampamesayoqs* generally involve tracking the future or the root of a client's or client's family member's illness. *Pampamesayoqs* often use herbs in healings and soul retrieval.

Both types of shamans use *mesas* as part of their practice. A *mesa* is a group of stones (*khuyas*) that carries the life force energy of *kausay*. A *paqo's mesa* anchors the *mesayoq* energetically to the earth, and provides an intermediary space that serves as the gateway into the spirit world with the *apus*. In addition, the *mesa* functions as a doorway into the celestial realm of Hanaq Pacha and the lower world of Ukhu Pacha.

Initiations

Paqos undergo a series of initiations to become *pampamesayoqs* and *altomesayoqs* as the lineage of their teacher is downloaded into the medicine body of their *mesa* and subtle body. Initiations are usually accompanied by a transmission of energy, frequently involving entering into altered or vision states at the essential level of perception. During initiations, altered states are often experienced as a feeling of well-being or being energized. There is often a sense of expanding beyond one's physical body, feeling a vibration or tingling, accompanied by a buzzing sound, with everything appearing more vivid. *Paqos* often describe this state as a process of "rewiring of the energy body." At the energetic level, everything is connected as a web or matrix of light — beyond form and mental imagery.

Reentry

The actual energetic experience takes place at a preverbal and pre-image level. Physically, the sensory experience of *kausay* often "registers" as a surge of energy or vibration that can range from ripples to tremors to spasms. The quality of experience is individual and a function of the particular initiation.

The way the event is registered is influenced by multiple factors that depend upon the transmission itself, as well as how the initiate receives what has been transmitted. A *paqo's* power is a direct reflection of his or her capacity to hold energy, in both an energy body and in the medicine body of a *mesa*. The initiate's receptivity and capacity to contain the energy in the energetic fields, along with the actual intensity of the energy transmission, both in vibrational frequency and volume of what is being downloaded, determines the experience and the initiates perception of the experience.

The intense energy shift that accompanies *paqo* initiation requires major readjustments in perceiving the interior and exterior world. Dealing with linear space and time after returning from shamanic experience is challenging because experience often becomes distorted when translated into ordinary reality. Attempting to bend experiences of non-ordinary reality into the space-time way we organize our experience of ordinary reality does not work because experiences occurring outside of consensual reality are impossible to describe or measure in those terms.

The operation of transferring energetic experience into a cognitive framework is not an intellectual exercise because our intellect lacks the capacity to process energy in a raw, undifferentiated state. Once something is named, it has already occurred and we are no longer actually experiencing it. The length of time we carry the charge of the afterglow of numinous experience in our luminous body depends on our willingness to engage with our vision of the experience and to keep it alive by attending to it. Once an energetic experience can be felt, it can be recapitulated and processed. Writing down the experience immediately after it happens can help in remembering it.

In the reentry process, movement is made through the various levels of psychic engagement — starting from ecstatic energetic experience, moving into mythic and symbolic levels of the imaginal realm, and finally arriving at the literal level of the concrete world. A gradual perceptual shift happens when moving from experiencing an energetic state back to awareness of having discreet physical form. The realm of the energetic collective can only be accessed through intuitive and sensory experience, beyond the boundaries of ordinary ego functioning. Because of this, making sense of an intense energetic experience is individually "felt" as direct experience — it is not possible to keep the integrity of an experience of the non-ordinary reality intact by using linear thinking and verbal language. There is no logical progression. No accurately descriptive words exist.

The process of reentry after shamanic initiation is similar to early stages of infant development. The infant is born into a *pacha* of space and time saturated with feeling-tones, pre-images. The relationship with the world begins through active engagement and creative expression with the physical body in the context of time.

According to Adolfo, humans possess three different bodies: spiritual, energetic, and physical.

Similar to the early stages of development, the energetic transfer of *kausay* that happens during a spiritual shamanic initiation is first taken in through the luminous field of the spiritual body and then into the energy body that surrounds the physical body. The *kausay* that has been downloaded then "blends" into the physical body. The transfer of energy that occurs during initiation permeates the entire energy body and does not remain stationary in one area of the physical body. Each of the energy centers, the Belly, Heart, and Mind, play a different role in the assimilation and integration of the *kausay* transfer during the process of reentry.

Adolfo has explained to me that in addition to the three energy centers — the Mind, Heart, and Belly, which in Quechua are called respectively *yachay*, *munay*, and *llank'ay*, there are four other levels or energy centers in the celestial realm of Andean cosmology that bring completion, symbolized by the rainbow. Only *altomesayoqs* experience the fourth level — also called *kausay*, located deeper in the lower torso — because at the higher levels energy is very difficult to hold and integrate. As *kausay* energy layers into our energy centers, in order to hold on to it — the shaman's definition of power — it must be integrated. I refer to this process as *reentry*.

Hindu spiritual practice speaks of a similar process of energetic transformation. The serpent goddess Kundalini lies asleep in three coils at the base of the spine until she is awakened and life energy rises through the body. The movement of energy that is described in awakening Kundalini energy in the body is similar to the process of reintegration that occurs after shamanic initiation.

Three Phases of Reentry

1. Somatic Perception

For Westerners who are on the spiritual path of Andean medicine, three phases occur during the reentry process after initiation. The first stage of reentry is the phase of somatic perception, experienced as a state of "no separation" in the Belly. The energy center of the Belly functions as the primary vessel that contains the energy, and is the "staging area" for processing somatic memories in the here and now, as the energetic experience begins to be assimilated into conscious awareness.

2. Imaginative Engagement

The second stage of reentry after a shamanic initiation is the phase of imaginative engagement. In the imaginative engagement phase, the energetic experience shifts from physical sensation into a state where words and symbolic mental images related to the experience begin to emerge. In the creative act of shifting from the energetic realm to discreet form in ordinary reality, symbolic imagery forms a transitional bridge that is useful in describing an approximation of the experience. Images and words are symbols that represent experience but are not the experience itself. Describing the energetic experience in images and or words is never exact. This is because the essence of the actual energetic experience can only be accessed as a present state. Descriptions are about what was remembered from the past.

The imaginative engagement phase involves all three of the energy centers, particularly the Heart and the Mind. Symbols arising from our own psyches through the Mind generally have the greatest capacity for holding numinous energy. The feeling connections that we develop about the experience occur in the Heart center. As Jung suggested, numinous archetypal experience often takes place through working with collective religious symbols that have become imbued with meaning through personal associations. Shamans would refer to this as the practice of rituals expressing service and devotion in the exterior world. For *paqos*, ritual becomes the sacred space that holds the Heart connection experience in conscious awareness.

Spontaneous acts of creative expression, e.g. making art without thinking about it, are another way to bring the energetic experience into conscious awareness through physical manifestation. Creative activities such as writing or painting are ways of continuing a dialogue with numinous experience and deepening the capacity to hold *kausay*. The process of creative expression can contain the heat of the energy and acts as both a catalyst and a vehicle for self-reflection and collective service.

Exercise 5. Creative Intention Using Watercolors

Before beginning this exercise, gather the following art supplies needed for watercolor painting:

Watercolor paper with enough texture to hold water and watercolor pigment

A thick brush (Japanese ink brushes are inexpensive and work well)

A palette of cold-pressed watercolor paints

A cup of water

Paper towels

A sturdy surface, such as a table, board, or pad, to place underneath the paper

Find a quiet and comfortable place to sit, in your home or in nature. Close your eyes and take a few deep breaths. With each exhale, feel yourself sinking deeper into your body, becoming more fully aware of any sensations you may be experiencing. Take a few moments sitting and breathing through your Belly, centering yourself by experiencing the sensation of inhaling and exhaling.

As you feel yourself becoming more fully centered, begin to attune to any sensations you are experiencing. As you sit with these sensations, notice if they are tied to any emotions such as emptiness, expansion, tightness, fullness, numbness — whatever comes into your awareness without any preconceived notions. Sit with the feelings for a moment, observing and giving your body an opportunity to "voice" what it is currently holding. Lean into the feelings, magnifying and intensifying whatever it is that you are experiencing so that it becomes more pronounced in your outer awareness.

When you feel that a channel of communication has opened up so that you are holding your body-experience in your conscious awareness, open your eyes.

Now, begin expressing this body experience with the watercolors. First, dip your brush in the water and saturate the paper with the water. After removing excess water from your brush, using your intuition and without any preconceived notion, allow the sensations to direct you to the colors of the palette that best convey the feeling. Allow yourself to paint automatically without thinking. Use colors that you are drawn to. As you begin to apply the paint to the paper, let the sensation that you are experiencing in your body direct the paint strokes. Paint what you are feeling, focusing on the process of expressing what you are feeling, without concern for the outcome. This painting is a record of your current experience.

If you are feeling constrained, work with multiple sheets of paper simultaneously or shift to painting on something larger that allows you to expand your gestures and movements. You may find yourself being drawn to making sweeping movements, or layering color, or making staccato movements, or focusing in a concentrated area. Whatever feels right to you in the moment is what you are expressing. If you feel "stuck" or tentative, paint with your opposite hand, i.e. if you are right-handed, paint with your left hand, and vice versa.

Keep painting until it feels complete. After you have finished and the paper has dried, write today's date on the back and keep the paper in the pad or folder. You might want to begin a series of paintings. This is an alternative to journaling and is a way of expressing and tracking feeling states that you may be unable to put into words.

Working consciously with dream imagery is another means for processing and assimilating *kausay* in the interior world. After returning home after one of my trips to Peru, I repeatedly dreamt of snakes. I had dreams of snakes lying by my feet as I wrote and dreams of carrying them around in my pockets. Snakes became my shadow companions in my inner world. In one of my dreams, I was taking energy from a large snake in the otherworld and giving it to baby snakes that lived in caves in this world. It occurred to me that perhaps this dream image was a metaphor for a *paqo's* job service, bringing the *kausay* of Pachamama, who was manifesting as Amaru in the dream, to feed the expressions of Pachamama in this world.

During the reentry process, the snake dreams provided me with a symbol for working with and assimilating the powerful energy of Amaru associated with the initiation experience. Although on a personal level, the snake dreams helped me in my own reentry process, I believe that they also provided me with a way of understanding the experience of serving the collective at the mythic level, through intention.

Exercise 6. Working with Dream Images through an Automatic Process of Active Imagination

This exercise is one way of developing further connection with mythic beings and landscapes that appear in dream states. It is usually easiest to work with imagery from recent dreams since this is when we are the most connected to the emotional and physical experience of the imagery.

Get a notepad and pen to record your experience, find a comfortable place to sit, either indoors or in nature, and close your eyes. Using your intention, ask that what transpires be for the highest good and imagine yourself in a field of protective white light.

When you are ready, put yourself back into your dream. Imagine the dream figure that appeared in your dream standing directly in front of you. Take a moment to observe the figure, paying attention to any details associated with the image. Ask the figure why it has appeared in your dreams and what it is here to show you. As you wait for the response, go with the information that immediately enters your Mind. The information may come as a verbal or visual message or a body sensation. It is okay to ask for specific information or for further clarification. When you feel that your questions have been answered, or the figure informs you that it has given you the information that it is there to give you, thank the being for the assistance. If it feels appropriate, ask the being if you may visit again in the future. After you feel complete, gradually bring yourself back to your outer awareness and open your eyes.

Immediately write down everything you remember from the experience.

In shamanism, this practice is only done with beings you have encountered in dreams that you do not know in your current outer world, always with the intention for the highest good. These beings may be animals, mythic figures, deceased relatives from your past, or other spiritual beings, that you feel safe or comfortable with.

3. Narrative Integration

The third phase of reentry is narrative integration. Over time, the words and images that have emerged in the imaginative engagement phase are woven into a verbal narrative. In this process, the transfer of *kausay* is made from remembering the energetic experience implicitly through the body into explicit memory using the Mind. In the later phases of reentry, it becomes possible to conceptualize aspects of the process using the Mind — as I am doing now. However, during the initial phase this is not possible because much of the experience occurring in the initial phase is non-verbal, body-centered experience.

Shifting between states of ordinary and non-ordinary reality requires constructing a permeable personal narrative that can adjust to the ongoing changes of the living experience. Shamans are aware that recapitulating past experience into our personal narratives determines who we are at any given moment in consensual reality. Although what I am describing involves mental processing, the energetic experience and the feeling connection to the experience is what informs the experience by "feeding" it *kausay*, similar to feeding the baby snakes in my dream.

Through conscious intention, shamans maintain a fluid state of energetic connection that involves a form of "shape-shifting." Although *paqos* have the ability to communicate about the experience of *kausay* verbally, they continue to "source" from the experience itself. When the actual energetic "encoding" that has taken place during an initiatory experience becomes well-integrated, a *paqo's* connection with the experience becomes "multilayered," and accessible in each of the energy centers.

The cognitive process of recapitulation during reentry enables us to reorganize past experience to fill in the existing gaps in the current state of awareness. Creatively imagining, or feeling into possibilities with new narratives, changes our understanding of what has transpired. Similar to crafting a vision of the future, recapitulation involves altering the perception of the past.

The *paqo's* capacity to hold power is a direct function of their accessibility and fluidity in relation to the energetic experience. A *paqo's* power increases in proportion to the ease and proficiency with which they can simultaneously shift between states of awareness — from somatic Belly experience, to feeling connection in the Heart, to exercising condor vision with clarity. This process is not easy and requires dedicated intention, focus, clarity — as well a maintaining an open Heart. As this capacity develops, the capability to perceive both inside and outside of the time-space continuum develops as well. All interactions — regardless of whether they are occurring in the interior or exterior world — involve multiple layer of information that can be accessed and experienced. The mythic beings of Amaru, Chocachinchay, and Apuchin that are alive in the collective Incan psyche are expressions of these states of awareness, making these ways of perceiving more easily available through the inherent properties associated with the imagery — in the translation of *kausay* energy.

3. My Fourth Trip to Peru — with Perry for the First Time

Entering this sacred place, it is not easy. We enter slowly, little by little, not going rapidly. That is the laws of the cosmos. We need to change to enter more and more, deeper and deeper.

—Adolfo Ttito Condori

June 30, 2011

It was June 30, 2011, and I was sitting on an airplane with my husband Perry, writing, on our 6 AM flight from Denver to Atlanta. Perry was sleeping in the cramped airplane seat next to me with his head pushed up against the window, snoring lightly. The first leg of the journey that we were making from our home in Denver to Cusco had begun and Perry was with me! I was returning to Peru for the fourth time in five years to work with the Inca medicine people in the sacred mountains of the Andes. This was Perry's first visit. He always calls first visits, "adventures."

Last year, because of last-minute problems with his passport, Perry was unable to board the plane and I was forced to go alone. While sitting on a mountaintop during my visit, one of the shamans told me in a coca reading that Perry was not ready and had been delayed. However, this year was different — he was finally with me! I was happy.

The light pressure of our blue-jeaned legs touching in our confined quarters felt pleasantly reassuring to me. I could feel little electric bursts of energy coming from him as he snored away. I settled into a reasonably comfortable position, in preparation for the two-and-a-half-hour flight and closed my eyes.

As soon as I closed my eyes, I became aware of my internal body state as I entered the inner world — entering into a more receptive state in preparation for what was to come. I felt myself moving into energetic connection with the *apu* spirit, Ausangate. Drifting into a deeper state of awareness in my body, I focused my intention, asking for the connection to grow stronger and flow. In the past, I have noticed that flying seems to make shifting into these states of awareness easier. I have found this to be especially true during flights to Peru. I wondered if the *apus* know when we are coming, and I became more open to initiating a deeper connection. Perry has said that he believes that this is because the pull of earth's magnetic field decreases when we are above the earth.

As I focused more intently in my Mind's eye, Ausangate began to appear in the mythic form of a bird with magnificent wings. I could not see his face but intuitively recognized his powerful presence. The colors of his glistening feathers were rich iridescent shades of blue, black, and purple, reminding me of the experience of the depth of night. As he enclosed me in his massive wings in preparation for flight, I noticed that they felt velvety soft. I felt safely held as he gently carried me — as we soared higher into what now appeared to be a bright midday sky.

We began flying high, circling above the earth together in the sunlight and wind. I dropped off — into the borderland between sleep and consciousness — weaving between them as we continued gliding. The work with Ausangate was beginning again, starting with the familiar process of recapitulation. I

Figure 3. Perry Edwards (photo by Deborah Bryon)

allowed my Mind to be carried by this presence that I have implicitly come to know and trust with my life.

After time had passed, I experienced myself returning to a more conscious state. The thought emerged into my awareness that it was important to set my intention for the upcoming journey. Back in the state of alertness that I associate with ordinary reality, the switch of my rational mind had been flipped on and I began reflecting on the encounter with Ausangate.

The psychologist and Jungian analyst in me was curious as to how this would all come together and what it would all mean. My shamanic Mind knew that it didn't matter. The *paqo* part of me had grown stronger, and I realized that it was more important to "feel" the energy of the connection than understand it. Still, I indulged myself. My brain was in full operation and I became focused on thinking. I will try to describe what the experience was like for me.

At various times I have recognized Ausangate in the familiar form of a mythical bird. This manifestation in the inner world was a merger of Ausangate and my spirit ally that I call Birdman. It has been my experience that in ordinary reality we identify others through their physical appearance. In non-ordinary reality, the presence of the spirit can be known and felt without a physical description defining it. One thing I noticed was that I could always feel a tremendous sense of love when such spirits were present.

Over time I have discovered that the spirits encountered in deep states of energetic connections seem to blend into the background but their energy can always be felt. I do not believe that they actually lose their essential identity in a state of fusion — as they would if this was happening in ordinary reality. I believe humans tend to define them in a manner that humans are most familiar with. This is a natural thing to do when we encounter something that is beyond our comprehension. In non-ordinary reality, spirits exist in fluid energy states, without discreet boundaries, and often they appear to be "merging" with other natural elements. However, I am aware that this ethereal manifestation is due to a lack of perception on my part. I am human, and lack the ability to maintain long-term connection with the subtle energetic levels that accompany them. The world they exist in does not have the same connections as the ones I need to live in this world.

The familiarity of Birdman in my vision state was comforting and grounded me in the actual feeling of the energetic connection. I shifted more fully into the experience of this non-ordinary reality and sensed an energetic expansion happening in my body. As I continued to "feel" my way back into the energetic state, I began to perceive an odd but not unpleasant tingling, physical sensation.

It felt as if my body or *poq'po* — the energy field surrounding my body — had grown about ten feet or so in every direction. I had the curious impression of being two places at once as my sense of myself shifted beyond the boundaries of my actual physical body. I redirected my attention back to Ausangate as the focal point of this connection.

In these experiences I do not actually lose a sense of my own identity although I am less attentive to it. My sense of self seems to recede into the background. As this happens, I gain greater awareness of Ausangate's presence through acclimating to a powerful light vibration. The best way I can describe it is feeling like I am opening, sensing, and reaching out energetically through my temples. This is accompanied with the sensation that the top of my head is opening up and developing into a column of light, resembling the shape of the headdresses worn by ancient Egyptians. These descriptions come to mind as I am thinking about trying to communicate the feeling of what is happening now. While it is happening, I experience it more as procedural memory, similar to riding a bike or tying a tie.

Different people always have different sensations, but the sensations will become familiar to each individual as they learn how to gain a connection. The best way to start is by asking the sensations to come to you within a ritual. Like everything, the first time is the hardest, but knowing in your Heart that everyone is capable of doing this makes it easier. There are many ways of achieving connection.

As the connection with Ausangate continued to grow stronger, I felt my Heart center opening and expanding in my physical body. I noticed physical pangs in my Heart that I relate to the experience of falling in love. Usually this emotion comes with an intense wave of gratitude that washes over me. It grew into a powerful wave. I felt blessed to be in Ausangate's presence. I asked Ausangate to take me further into his realm, to show me my purpose in returning to Peru this time.

Immersed in the vision state, I found myself suddenly standing in clouds next to Ausangate on top of a great mountainous ridge high above the earth. From the massive summit, we looked down into an enormous container that lay deep in the interior of the otherworld landscape. I recognized that my existence was only a speck of sand in comparison to the massive energetic presence surrounding me.

As I strained to see more with my inner eye, I could faintly make out a circle of light occupied by spiritual beings. They were all joined together. Their presence surrounded the outer perimeter of the peak, each representing different aspects of the great collective mountain spirit. Something deep inside of me remembered experiencing these beings during initiation ceremonies, yet it was rare for me to see them in a different context. The extremely high-energy vibration emanating from these beings as white light was barely perceptible. Everything was white and there were no distinct forms. What I was experiencing lay at the edge of my range of perception. While seeing this vibration as pure white light, I also felt myself stretching and straining to hear musical tones that were barely audible, and yet there.

In my Mind's eye, I was reaching as high as I could, farther up into the sky, in order to connect more fully with their presence. These beings seemed to exist spatially in a place almost beyond my scope of vision. I felt myself continuing to stretch, trying to gain a better sense of who they were, trying to connect.

In this visionary state, and with Ausangate's assistance, everything felt connected. I became aware that I was surrounded by an energetic community of light beings that were all facets of the mountain collective — a thousand voices together as one. From this heightened perspective, I looked down and could see my physical body contained within my *poq'po*. I recognized that my luminous body was serving as an intermediary, an energy channel between the mountain collective and the outer world of physical reality where my physical body was located.

Ausangate began showing me that if I were able to maintain a receptive inner state, it would be easier to function as an energetic conduit, and the capacity in our power between realms would grow. During various times in my life when I had become preoccupied with events in my outer world, my ability to bridge between realities and experience the light grew weaker. I was suddenly struck with the realization that it was possible to exist in ordinary physical reality while at the same time holding my awareness and existing on the periphery of this energetic realm.

My perspective had shifted. I was observing from the vantage point of non-ordinary reality, looking back into physical reality. Usually I was in ordinary reality looking toward the non-ordinary. My perspective view had turned inside out. I could clearly see how others and I could serve the energetic collective. Ausangate explained to me that in these times of change there is a need for more connection between the energetic realms and the physical world. More channels would serve as more grounding rods or anchors between realities, and this would help to stabilize the pressure that was building in our ordinary reality. This was one of the roles of *paqos*, to teach others how to make a connection.

I could see in the current *pacha*, the time and space of our physical reality, that the collective consciousness of our world was disconnected from nature. Ausangate repeated the words that he had said in the past — this was a time of great opportunity, but also great risk, as humanity was now facing planetary destruction because of actions we had taken over a very short time period. We had tipped the scales of earth's natural balance so much that an adjustment already in motion was gaining momentum and intensity. It would become increasingly difficult to stop the destructive force as it accelerated towards us. Only a sharp gain in our awareness could bring us the ability to cope with the impending changes and heal the wounds we had inflicted on our planet. Suddenly I began to lose focus, and my connection with Ausangate began to fade.

I could feel myself coming back into my outer awareness and was happy when I remembered that Perry was sitting next to me. He was rustling about, making abrupt breathing sounds as he began to wake up. Last year, it had been a very painful departure for both of us, when he had stayed behind. It appeared that this year he was breaking through whatever had been holding him back — he had broken through, because he was on the plane! I sensed that there was a greater purpose for both of us being together on this trip than climbing mountains together. I hoped that together we would continue to develop the capacity of holding space for the energetic connection between the worlds. Perry's eyes snapped open and he said "Wow." I squeezed his arm with my hands, saying "Wow what?" right back at him, knowing he liked that.

I was now fully awake. In the past, I have noticed that what can feel like a significant period in the inner world frequently takes place as minutes in the physical world. Linear time in ordinary reality does not correspond to the experience in the other realms. It simply is what it is. I had closed my eyes for about forty-five minutes.

Perry sat up and eagerly told me that he had received a vision. I said "Surprise, surprise."

Smiling, he said "Yeah," and continued, "It's all about the glacier ice and the glacier water. The glacier ice and water are pure. This is rare because of what we have done to the planet. There's just not much pure water around anymore. High glaciers are more protected because they are above the altitude of most of the damaging air pollution. The only other pure water available is

Figure 4. Incan corn (photo by Tom Blaschko)

deep down in the earth because it is protected there, too. Glaciers are more accessible to a guy like me, who doesn't have a big expensive drill rig."

I asked, "What about the glacier water in the grocery store?"

Perry gave me a weird questioning look and said, "Do you really believe that? Water in the grocery store? I'm going back in."

As quickly as Perry's eyes had opened, they snapped shut and his head fell back on the reclined seat. In his Mind, he went somewhere else.

A couple of hours later we deplaned in Atlanta and boarded another flight to Mexico City. I had continued to reflect upon what Ausangate had shown me in the vision. So if the purpose is to function as a bridge — how does that translate into the day world? As I have heard the *paqos* ask, I wondered how I would "grow corn with it." I noticed that my Western mind was again in full swing and firing off questions. I suddenly felt the need to connect to something sustainable and sensed Ausangate's patient, loving energy surrounding me.

The word "forbearance" came into my Mind. I heard Ausangate's gentle voice in my Mind saying, "Mijo, you grow corn by holding a vision for the people you work with, energetically, by bringing energy into the shared experience to help them discover the patterns they are repeating that limit them. This helps them to remember who they are. Serving is about becoming an energy channel, an open conduit. Writing the next book [this one] is another way to bring this energy through, by providing information that helps others remember their own experience."

In the midst of my earlier airplane vision, while seeing my luminous body as a conduit between realities — I had seen Perry's as well. Ausangate said that our upcoming engagement with the *paqos* was an opportunity for Perry to heal. I could "see" that his energy had been leaking as the result of a rupture he experienced several years ago, when a lucid dream exposed memories of trauma that he had endured as a child. The floodgates opened with a deluge of painful memories rushing into his awareness. Perry had feared for his life during most of his childhood. He had nowhere to turn for help, except for Pachamama. Perry called on Pachamama to survive at a very early age and Pachamama came. He got the help he needed so desperately.

Now, healing from these experiences was bringing back parts of his soul, the parts that had fled the horror he had faced at a very early age. The returning memories had propelled him into a process involving an intense vision state for several years, which had initiated both dismemberment and a rebirth of his soul into his physical body. Perry had been shocked by the realization that for close to fifty years he did not know who he was. I didn't know either, so as pieces of his lost soul returned we both got to find out, bit by bit. I had been sucked into the spinning vortex of chaos with him as the framework of our lives quickly became dismantled, and I realized that the man I married contained parts that neither of us had imagined.

While this was happening several years ago, colleagues in the medical field diagnosed Perry as being in a state of mania. However, Jeffrey Raff, Perry's analyst and a mystic himself, disagreed. Jeff identified that Perry was in the midst of an archetypal transformation, a psychic death and rebirth. As I look back on it now, I believe both were true. Perry had struggled to assimilate the tremendous influx of energy that flooded his psyche, leading to a vision state that looked like mania in the outside world.

As Perry re-assimilated himself in the "day world," he went through a powerful psychic transformation that resulted in a greater capacity for other-world journeying. Perry became able to retrieve information from non-ordinary reality, often with prophetic vision. Perry said that he had forgotten that he had known how to do this when he was younger. I started this book by setting the scene in Peru. Let me continue the description of the players by sketching the relationship between Perry and me.

In the days immediately before leaving for Peru I found myself pulling away from Perry in reaction to the sudden bursts of energy he started running on. They seemed to come out of nowhere. The psychologist in me was well aware that we were both reacting to the anxiety associated with leaving for Peru and that this was most likely throwing Perry into a manic state.

Before leaving for Peru, Perry was up two nights in a row, trying to finish his month's long project of installing an enormous sprinkler system. Last night, he carried huge loads of mulch, hooked up sprinkler heads, watered, and zipped around frenetically — running on what appeared to be an unlimited source of energy. I reminded myself that Perry had a deep commitment to tending our newly planted trees — especially the year-old willow trees that he started from clippings. Even so, I was on full alert.

Whether it was a vision state or mania, the behavior looked the same. I felt myself becoming increasingly uneasy, hoping that another archetypal tidal wave was not on the horizon. When Perry is in an energized phase, I worry about the toll this may be taking on his body and psyche — as well as my psyche.

The last two nights I attempted to retire at a reasonable hour in preparation for the upcoming thirty-six hours of travel on planes and in airports. When I awoke at 2:30 AM in order to leave for the airport way ahead of time and make sure we made our flight, Perry was still packing. I felt my level of anxiety ratcheting up in response.

I heard myself beginning to issue commands and realized that I was being "snarky." I recognized that I was tired and afraid, and I needed to curb it. Knowing that trying to control Perry was about as easy as twisting a tornado in the opposite direction, I asked Ausangate for help. As Perry got closer to zipping up his duffle bag, my son Devin arrived and began helping us load our bags of luggage into the car. After we finished loading the car and were driving away — this time with the bags and passports — I realized that we would actually make it to the airport with time to spare. All was not lost. When we had driven two blocks away from our house, Perry began to snore loudly in the back seat — fatigue had finally settled in and he was out. Devin looked over at me and smiled.

I left the memory of yesterday's activities and shifted back to what was taking place in the present in the inner world. Ausangate showed me that if Perry and I created a bridge together, our ability to hold power (transfer energy) would increase substantially. I reflected on my fear of Perry veering off again and I realized that trying to help him, rather than trying to

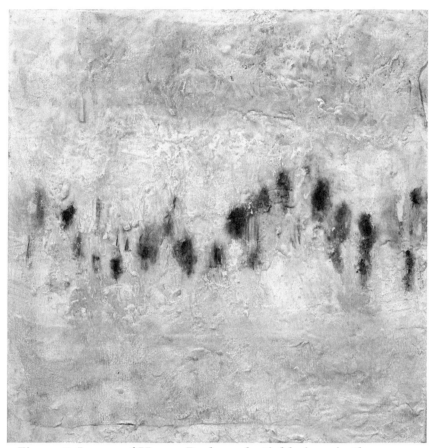

Figure 5. Image of Hanaq Pacha, celestial beings in the upper world (painting by Deborah Bryon)

manage him, was a better course of action. I hoped that the next chapter of our lives together would be gentler and noticed that I had become reluctant to consider what else could be burned away. I had already discovered that there could always be more.

I asked Ausangate what was needed to bring this vision into fruition. He replied, "Things must be simplified."

I probed further. "What does this mean really?" Everyone talks about simplifying. I needed a metaphor.

Ausangate responded by saying, "Mijo, you *are* the metaphor."

I stopped and thought for a moment. He was right. Our lives were more complicated than they needed to be — preparing for this trip had been a perfect example…I drifted off to sleep.

A couple of hours have passed since my last journal entry. We have been traveling on planes and moving through airports for twenty-two hours. It appears that we will have another fourteen or so hours to go before we reach Cusco. Weeks earlier, when I found cheap airline tickets online, I neglected to read the routing schedule. Yesterday morning, after arriving at Denver International Airport and studying our flight itinerary again in more detail, we discovered that we would be flying from Denver to Atlanta, and then to Mexico City. In Mexico City we would be required to get off the plane, go through customs and get back on another plane to Lima with little time between flights. I already knew that in Lima we would have the customary overnight layover in the airport before boarding the early morning flight to Cusco, but adding a stop in the Mexico airport and going through customs made the trip seem much longer and more complicated. (This was before we knew that all of the morning flights from Lima to Cusco would be cancelled due to weather conditions.) I now understood why the airfare had been so reasonable.

One of the things that I have always appreciated about Perry is that he does not become upset with me when I make these kinds of mistakes. I usually tend to become more upset with myself then he does. Even though I can accept that this is a downside of being an intuitive, I still hate the fact that it can be so inconvenient — and expensive — especially when I try to interact with the logistics of airports.

Perry and I had both slept, but it had been sporadic "combat" sleep. We had grabbed a few hours here and there in a variety of contorted positions, in tiny airplane seats and vinyl airport chairs under fluorescent lighting. Goodwill and grace had worn off.

As Perry and I raced between terminals to make connecting flights with little leeway, we both had our snappy moments. The tables had turned. Since leaving our house this morning at 3 AM, I had become the one gunning it to make our connections — checking baggage multiple times while tripping over it as we scrambled between airline counters for tickets and seat assignments.

As we continued to scuttle on and off airplanes, Perry had shifted into meandering at a leisurely pace. Seemingly Perry needed to use every bathroom we passed in long stretches of endless airport terminal. I attempted to feign patiently waiting — with limited success. Each time Perry reappeared from another bathroom in the terminal, I fought the compulsive urge to race on ahead, in an attempt to get him to pick up the pace. Even when we usually had a reasonably amount of time, I tried telling myself that my reaction was justifiable — after all last year he did miss the flight. I wondered if I was developing a mild phobia…

In our sleepless stupor, we became mildly annoyed with each other. From years of experience together, we both knew that when we are this tired it is better for us not to talk. Talking at these times just starts a war. Perry has the ability in these kinds of situations to switch off and zone out. I don't.

Yet, in the midst of my airport twirl, underneath my Amazon-woman persona, I was glad Perry was with me — even though I was not interested in demonstrating it outwardly. We occasionally remembered to say that we liked each other. I appreciated that Perry had been mostly tolerating my emotional state.

When we arrived at the gate for the flight with time to spare I finally began to relax. I interpreted the fact that I still enjoyed the way Perry smells — even after 22 hours — as a good sign. I was glad that the pheromones still seemed to be working in our relationship — even when we were exhausted and did not have the energy to carry on a conversation.

4. Lima to Cusco

The seat of faith...is not consciousness but spontaneous religious experience, which brings the individual's faith into immediate relation with God.

—Carl Jung

July 1, 2011

After landing in Lima, Peru, an hour or so ago, Perry and I grabbed our oversized luggage — with two weeks of camping gear — and wheeled our carts up to the second floor, to my favorite Lima coffee shop. Looking for a place to sit that was close enough to reach an electrical outlet for my computer, while at the same time staying as far away as possible from the foggy smoking lounge next door, we had settled into a red vinyl booth.

It was now 1 AM and for some reason I felt happier. I considered that Perry and I were now "wedging" — a term my younger son used when he was a teenager to describe the experience of entering into a mental zone after not sleeping.

Last year at about this time, I had sat at this same table, facing the same direction, drinking my first cup of coca tea, and typing. I was beginning to enjoy the idea that this had become an annual tradition.

However, this year — unlike last year — I began to notice strange chemical odors were emanating from somewhere. As I

51

tried to pinpoint exactly where the scent was coming from, Perry informed me that it smelled like a combination of Mr. Clean and herbal ginseng tea. My association with the aroma that I had nostalgically associated with coca leaves was quickly becoming contaminated with the unpleasantly harsh invasion of ammonia. I noticed that the cookie I was eating had begun to taste more like Mr. Clean than a cookie.

I tried telling myself that it smelled this way because of the high standards of cleanliness — yet I wondered why I was eating it, as I do not normally eat Mr. Clean that has solidified. A few bites later I stopped. My survival instincts had kicked in. Perry quipped that he hoped that our plane would take off, before somebody dumped a half drum of bleach into the ammonia-cookie batter and the whole airport passed out.

After I had been sitting in front of my laptop at the Formica table for almost an hour, my olfactory senses had shut down enough for me to no longer notice the odor. I closed my eyes, stepping back into my earlier vision and reflected on what Ausangate had shown me during our first flight. I remembered standing on the edge of the large summit with the light beings. Seeing my energetic body from this visionary vantage point had given me a bird's eye view of myself.

Now, sitting in the coffee shop, I remembered the encounter from my current perspective in linear time. My body looked like liquid energy contained within a permeable boundary. I suddenly became aware of being in three places simultaneously. There was the aspect of me watching from a bird's eye vantage point while the encounter with Ausangate was taking place, the energetic expression of me in the other realm, and the me sitting in the Lima coffee shop with my eyes closed. I was aware of *kausay* moving into my energetic body in the other realm and at the same time moving into my physical form sitting in the coffee shop. We were all connected.

From the bird's perspective, I could see that the part of me attached to personal distractions, such as the logistics of travel, appeared as a solid form. The mass was developing within the fluid energetic interior of me and taking up space. That part was stationary and had no light moving through it. It was functioning as an energy block. I realized that holding on to these thoughts prohibited energy movement in this area of my luminous body, decreasing my capacity to hold energy.

The metaphor of a clogged artery came into my Mind, and I thought of my supervisor in analytic training, Joe McNair, asking the alchemical question, "What's the matter?" I could see how investing energy in being irritated was decreasing my availability to function as an energetic conduit. When there is no "personal matter" stuck in the body's energetic structure, the liquid interior of the luminous body is stronger because there is more room available to hold the energy. I experienced a burst of energy with this realization.

As I shifted back into my awareness, I saw that Perry was also absorbed in his own process of reverie, sitting at the next table drawing and writing. Not wanting to be intrusive, I reached over and touched Perry's arm, asking if it was okay for me to talk to him. He looked up and nodded.

I informed Perry that I was exploring the capacity to hold power in service of the energetic collective through intention and simplification. I told him excitedly that living with less mental and emotional distraction created more room for energetic connection! As I listened to my words, I recognized that I was stating the obvious. Yet at a deeper feeling level, this is profound. I wondered if I would be able to effectively communicate what I was trying to say with words.

Perry then showed his notebook to me. I read, "*Apus* of light fly in like birds and form spinning flower shapes that shift and change over Deborah's head. They are a very bright white light that spins, changes shape, and vibrates." Perry had drawn a picture of me sitting and typing and on the same page next to it he had drawn a diagram with forms that resembled symmetrical flower petals that he explained represented the energy of the *apus*. After he had finished explaining what he had been drawing, Perry informed me that he was going to walk around the terminal. I nodded, acknowledging that I had heard him.

When Perry returned, fatigue set in again for both of us. Dead tired, we curled up in neighboring red vinyl booths, under bright fluorescent lights. My head was crunched up against a glass window overlooking the ticket counters in the terminal. I tucked my knees in as tightly as possible, to avoid extending myself too far beyond the physical perimeters of the booth. I drifted in and out of sleep for the next couple of hours. Perry did the same.

I had covered my face with my straw hat to shield my eyes from the overhead fluorescent lighting. In my drowsy, sleep-deprived state, I heard a family in a booth behind me chattering amongst themselves in Spanish. The sounds became the background of my semi-dream state. Some part of me noted that it was easier to block out conversation when I did not understand what was being said. As I slept, I sensed the Birdman's presence hovering somewhere nearby, but when I awoke I could not remember more.

Several hours passed. It was 9 AM. Perry and I were both awake, sitting on the clean tile floor in front of the LAN Peru airlines gate for our flight to Cusco. A loud, muffled voice started blasting out of the overhead speaker saying something I could not understand, but it sounded important. The person behind the ticket counter informed the small group of people in front of her that fog had caused all of the flights to be delayed. We were asked to wait patiently.

Perry complained that his joints and swollen hands were hurting. His mad, last-minute push to finish the sprinkler system had taken its toll. Perry began coating his hands with another layer of thick white hand cream that was immediately absorbed into his dry, cracked skin. Although his hands were still noticeably puffed up, the swelling appeared to be going down. Ten or so applications of hand cream since yesterday had helped. Perry commented that he would most likely use the entire tube of cream before we left the airport.

Over the loudspeaker, we heard another announcement stating that a flight to Cusco had been cancelled due to unfavorable weather conditions. Once again, I was not sure exactly what was being said. Several of us approached the woman behind the counter to inquire about our status. I apologized to the woman that I could not understand the message being broadcasted over the loudspeaker. I realized that she was probably tired of sleep-deprived foreigners asking her the same questions repeatedly. She glared at all of us and impatiently told us to wait for further notice. The flight at the next counter had been cancelled — not ours. She explained that another announcement would be made shortly. She apparently did not know any more than we did.

I tried to muster up a genuine smile, thanking her as politely as possible with my limited Spanish skills, and returned to my designated spot on the floor where Perry and I had set up provisional camp. Our journey to Peru continued — on the airport floor. I hoped that I might be getting a second wind.

Perry leaned over to me and quietly whispered that minutes earlier, while he was brushing his teeth in the public restroom, the mirror in front of him suddenly got foggy for no apparent reason, and now we were being stopped by foggy weather. He also informed me that the large crystal he had been carrying had broken in half. He said that something was going on and he did not like it. As I listened to what he was saying, I did not know exactly what to make of it. I decided not to try to draw any conclusions, while nervously glancing at the ticket counter, hoping that they would soon tell us what we wanted to hear. I had decided to try to think positively.

Perry looked over at me and smiled, saying, "I bet they're taking the bleach off the truck at the loading dock right now!"

The area around our provisional camp became more congested as what felt like hordes of people began moving in. In general, the people surrounding us looked tired, worried, and confused. I wondered if I looked the same way. A foreboding sense of doom associated with bad weather conditions was hovering in the air like a thick blanket. The tempo in the room was becoming chaotic as the noise level increased substantially.

Multiple flight-change announcements that were hard to make out were rapidly coming over the loudspeaker. Although it seemed clear that important information was being given, it looked as if very few people could actually understand what was being said.

As the noise level reached new peaks, continuing to escalate as the crowd around our gate became more unsettled, everything became more surreal. In my sleep-deprived stupor, I felt like I had entered some sort of twilight zone. People were now racing around in many different directions, in response to the recently announced gate changes.

Meanwhile, Perry was focused on laying another thick layer of cream on his hands. I hoped that he was gaining physical relief through this process. I tried to move closer to the wall, out of the path of the pairs of feet that had started racing by. I looked at faces full of anger, frustration, and confusion and wondered if it was time to move. I was beginning to feel claustrophobic.

Another announcement suddenly blasted from the speakers overhead: all flights to Cusco had cancelled due to Cusco airport conditions. In an attempt to self-soothe, I told myself that at least this time we have made it to Peru before any significant flight issues began. This was the last leg of the trip and there was no question as to whether we would eventually arrive in Cusco — the question was when. I worked to stay calm.

The barrage of sounds happening all around me was becoming increasingly more difficult to block out. I considered looking for the earplugs that were buried somewhere in my daypack to muffle the sound but decided that it was a bad idea because I needed to try to stay tuned in so that I could hear the announcements.

Perry told me that we were being blocked and suggested that we drive instead. I said that I thought that was a bad idea and suggested asking Ausangate for help. As I heard more announcements and more noise, my heart began racing in response to the frenetic energy buzzing around me. Suddenly, Perry told me not to look to my left. I complied. I was trying to shrink away from the crowd as I continued typing — writing what you are now reading.

My laptop had become my shield. I intentionally visualized encapsulating myself in an energetic bubble to buffer myself. It was partially working. Perry said that it was okay — we will eventually be able to leave. He reiterated, "Just don't look to the left."

I continued to work on detaching myself from the immediate surroundings with marginal success. Soon we would need to gather our bags and move again. Another jarring announcement that I could not understand was made in Spanish. I remembered Ausangate's words about needing to simplify and preserve energy. I wondered, if this was yet another test.

I asked Ausangate and Birdman for help. I called on Cainan, the powerful black jaguar that had psychically protected me during an uncontained *ayahuasca* ceremony a couple of years earlier in the Amazon jungle. I felt Cainan's energy surrounding me, and imagined him raising his mammoth head and bellowing a sound between a growl and a roar, drowning out the sounds of the crowd. I could picture him baring his teeth and extending his enormous claws out directly in front of us. The visual image of seeing the chaos happening around me as wind came into my Mind and brought comfort. In my Mind I watched the chaos separating in front of me before touching my luminous body.

When the official announcement was made that our flight had been cancelled, we stood up and took a position in the line that was rapidly forming in front of the ticket counter. While all of this was going on, Perry suddenly leaned over and whispered in my ear that I had just been under psychic attack. He said that several minutes ago, a powerful woman with long dark hair — a *bruja* (female witch) — had appeared out of nowhere and had taken her stance just three feet to the left of me. Perry said that she had maliciously fixed her gaze upon me for several minutes. Perry said that when he discovered what was happening, he quickly surrounded me with a protective wall of energy. With the intensity of her piercing stare focused at me, the woman somehow had not noticed that Perry had locked in to the danger she was wielding. Perry said that he called out to Birdman for help when the woman would not let go. After a long, cold, hard standoff that seemed to never end, Perry said the woman abruptly jerked her head away in disgust and disappeared back into the crowd she came from, as if she had suddenly vaporized.

I have learned in situations like these not to attempt to draw any conclusions about what was or was not happening. Oddly enough, I realized the incident that Perry was describing had occurred at the same time I had started feeling anxious and had called on Cainan's energy. I reminded Perry that the woman was no match for Cainan.

Perry smiled at me and said, "Yeah, we blew her out of the water."

We continued standing in line for about an hour before reaching our turn at the counter. Good news! We had been reassigned to the flight leaving for Cusco at 1 PM. The thick fog had lifted and there was now adequate visibility for the pilots to navigate the planes.

Perry and I started looking around for another coffee shop close to our departure gate. Several yards away I discovered an open table strategically situated directly next to an electrical outlet. I swiftly sat down and plugged my laptop into the outlet stand beside me. After drinking a couple cups of strong Peruvian coffee, Perry and I found seats in the terminal to sit and wait for our flight.

I automatically dropped into a detached hypnotic state, feeling as if I were seeing everything out of the corner of my eye. Sinking into the current uncomfortable vinyl chair, I looked over at Perry who already had his eyes closed and was lying on his side in the section of chairs next to me. He had wadded his jacket into a ball, using it as a pillow to shield himself against the discomfort of the narrow metal arm of the chair. I became aware that my current state of fatigue had a mild edge to it, brought on by the caffeine I had recently ingested.

A while later, we heard the announcement that our plane to Cusco had arrived. We gathered up our gear again and joined the other passengers that were forming two lines in queue, depending on their respective seat assignments. Standing in front of us were a couple of families with children, businessmen carrying leather briefcases, as well as a few short grandmothers who were carrying brightly colored shopping bags. A couple of well-groomed men and women in their late twenties or early thirties were also in line, speaking amongst themselves. It has struck me before how well groomed many Peruvian women are, with clear, smooth skin and neatly combed, shiny black hair, wearing gold jewelry and

Figure 6. The Holy Mountain of Ausangate (photo by Frances Marron)

skillfully applied makeup. I idly wondered how long they had been traveling and how they could look so fresh.

About twenty minutes later, we boarded the plane and found our seats. After the plane took off and we had been in the air for a little while, the fog completely cleared and I could see the sacred mountains ahead in the distance.

I leaned over to nudge Perry to show him the landscape and discovered that he had dropped off to sleep again and was starting to snore. I knew that he would not appreciate being awakened, so I left him undisturbed and returned to looking out the window. Viewing the rugged snowy peaks in the distance, I began to focus on establishing an energetic connection with the mountains. In closer proximity, I was now aware of their powerful collective presence. I focused on sensing this energy in my body for the remainder of the flight, and at some point drifted off to sleep.

I woke to the flight attendant's voice announcing over the loudspeaker that we would be landing in ten minutes. I looked out and saw the city of Cusco beneath us, tucked between the mountains. I could feel Perry stirring next to me.

Once we deplaned in Cusco, the remainder of the trip was smooth and uneventful. After gathering all of our bags off the circulating belt in the small airport terminal, we climbed into one of the many cabs stationed in front of the airport and headed for where we were staying in the quaint, old part of the city. A fifteen-minute cab ride carried us up the narrow cobblestone streets bordered by tall, whitewashed stucco buildings with bright blue shutters. After unloading our bags and paying the cab driver, we stumbled into the lobby.

5. In Cusco

Physical objects are not in space, but these objects are spatially extended as fields. In this way, the concept "empty space" loses its meaning.

—Albert Einstein

July 2, 2011

The next morning, entering the lobby, I glanced toward the reception area decorated in wood that had developed a pleasing shiny patina from years of wear and recognized Don Sebastian's short, stocky frame. Don Sebastian has always reminded me of a big bear. He was dressed, as usual, in traditional Q'ero attire, wearing a beaded cap that was pointed on top with flaps over his ears, black wool shorts, sandals, and a poncho over a long-sleeved sweater.

We greeted each other affectionately with big hugs and kisses. Don Sebastian had been sitting on one of the wooden benches that bordered the small, picturesque courtyard of pathways and flowers with the mountains in the background. I poured each of us a cup of hot water from the pot sitting on a table nearby and added coca leaves from the bowl next to the pot. Sitting together on the bench, drinking coca tea, we conversed in broken Spanish. I informed Don Sebastian that my husband Perry was here with me this year. Don Sebastian nodded his head and smiled, as he

Figure 7. Don Sebastian (photo by Brad VonWagenen)

studied the patch of tile floor lying three feet in front of us on the walkway. When I asked about the other *paqos* that would be joining us this year, Don Sebastian explained to me that Don Francisco was teaching in Holland and would not be joining us.

I was disappointed. I have fond memories of walking up and down sides of mountains with Don Francisco, watching him grinning cheerfully as he has patiently held my hand when we were crossing more difficult stretches of terrain.

We sat for a while in silence — occasionally nodding at each other. Words have never been my main form of communication with Don Sebastian. There is a lot that can be shared without chatter.

Approximately ten minutes later, Perry emerged from our room into the courtyard where we were sitting. As soon as I saw

Perry, I yelled enthusiastically, "Perry! This is Don Sebastian! Come over and meet him!"

In response, Don Sebastian stood up and reached out to greet Perry with a bear hug. I watched them smiling at each other like long-time friends. Don Sebastian motioned for Perry to sit down next to him. In broken Spanish, I asked Don Sebastian if he would help us prepare a *despacho* offering for an upcoming fire ceremony. Don Sebastian nodded his head as we spoke and replied in Spanish that we would meet tomorrow night at 7 PM to create a *despacho*. Perry listened to us but did not understand what I was trying to say in Spanish. Out of the corner of my eye, I noticed a tear rolling down Perry's cheek as Don Sebastian and I continued discussing the arrangements. Perry later told me that meeting Don Sebastian was like meeting a brother that he never had but somehow knew for the first time.

After giving Don Sebastian the money to buy the necessary *despacho* ingredients, we all nodded again in final agreement. Perry and I then headed off toward the plazas in the center of town for Perry to find additional clothing in preparation for the upcoming mountain journey. Perry continued to cry without knowing why.

July 3, 2011

It was 8 AM and I was sitting at a table in the breakfast room drinking coca tea, typing on my laptop. I tend to forget that the elevation of Cusco exceeds 11,200 feet (3,390 meters) and that it is necessary to adjust to the changes in altitude. I started drinking tea by the cupfuls to offset dehydration and fatigue. Drinking coca tea does make a difference.

After sleeping for twelve hours last night, I woke from a "death" sleep about an hour ago. I noticed that I was starting to feel "human" and in my body again. Yesterday, Perry realized after arriving in Cusco that he had underpacked, as I had years before. Perhaps you need to experience this for yourself to realize that you really do need to bring more than you think you will need. I suppose packing heavy garments seems unnecessary in 100-degree Denver summer heat— when you are hot, it is hard to imagine being cold.

Last night Perry and I walked around the city of Cusco. As we were searching for warmer gear for Perry, we visited several small, street-front shops managed by Peruvian woman dressed in bright wool sweaters and skirts. We wandered up and down narrow cobblestone streets, ready to jump quickly up onto the steep sidewalks that are approximately 18 inches in width to avoid being hit by the small honking cars zipping by at rapid speeds. In Cusco, cars have the right of way and the drivers are very clear about that.

After an hour or two of shopping, we both lost our second wind and stopped for an early dinner at Jack's Café before retiring and catching up on our sleep. My dreams last night were about movement, change, and encounters with people from my past. This morning, Perry was still sleeping — and I was glad. I knew that his body needed it. While I was teaching Introduction to Psychology years ago, I had read that the human body has approximately two weeks to make up lost hours to replenish itself. Given that Perry had been up the last two nights before we had left, I estimated that he probably needed to sleep all day. Regardless, I knew that Perry would sleep as long as he felt he needed to and that he did not need me to mother him.

Preparing to venture into the old city, I grabbed my jacket and backpack and quietly left our room. On the balcony outside of our door, overlooking the city of Cusco and the courtyard of flowers, I was surprised to see geraniums blooming in the cool temperature at this higher elevation. The plants were contained in flowerpots sitting along the antique, ornately carved wood railing. Cusco really is a beautiful city.

Anticipating that Perry would be sleeping for at least a couple of hours more, I decided to visit the *paqos'* market, to gather *despacho* supplies. The kits I was looking for were individually wrapped in brown paper and contained the basic ingredients to represent the lower, middle, and upper worlds.

Some travelers from Canada who said they had not been able to find the market the day before were standing in the lobby. I asked if they wanted to join me. I remember feeling slightly intimidated on my first visit to the *paqos'* market and appreciated being chaperoned by my friend Julie Palmer. If you do not know what you are looking for, the *paqos'* market can be difficult to find because it is only three innocuous stalls scattered amongst a sea of busy street vendors. Once you know the turf a little better, it becomes easier to navigate.

When we reached the tiny stall that had housed the best selection of materials in the past, I asked the woman sitting behind the glass counter facing the street if she had Pachamama and *apu despacho* kits. The woman looked like many of the *mamacita* shop-vendors in Cusco. She was less than five feet tall with a stocky stature and intense dark eyes. When she smiled, I could see that her white teeth were bordered with gold fillings. As is customary, her black hair was neatly braided, and she was wearing a dark skirt with a red sweater. She nodded politely when we entered her store area and asked me in Spanish how many kits we needed.

The woman reached behind where she was sitting and took cylinder-shaped bundles wrapped in brown butcher paper down from the neatly stacked shelf. Each of the bundles had been labeled with the word *apu* written across the top in felt pen. The Peruvian woman informed me that they cost twenty soles each (about seven U.S. dollars). Next, she pointed toward the large plastic bins on a neighboring shelf with more bundles wrapped in

Figure 8. Shaman's Market (photo by Frances Marron)

butcher paper. The word Pachamama had been written across each of these packages, also in black pen.

The woman explained that she was selling the more elaborate Pachamama *despacho* kits for 50 soles ($18) each. I told her that those kits were more elaborate than we needed, and passed on this information to the three other women who were with me. In general, *apu despachos* contain the elements that represent the upper world for vision, clarity, and initiation, while Pachamama *despachos* have ingredients symbolizing fertility and healing, honoring the land. [Please see the Appendix for more details.]

The Canadian women accompanying me reminded me of myself the first time I entered one of these stalls. They were silent and fully captivated, looking everywhere. Even though the market stalls are tiny, there is a lot to take in. Every square foot of wall space is covered with shelves, stacked full of a variety of supplies — all having to do with shamanism and sorcery. There are clay figures, buckets of seeds, condor feathers, different types of amulets, llama fetuses hanging from the ceiling, a preserved armadillo, different colored bottles with different types of cleansing water, including lavender, rose, patchouli, and much more. The space to stand was about three feet wide. It is easy to get lost in all of the visual stimuli — especially if you have never seen it before and do not know what you are looking at.

I told the woman in Spanish that we were primarily interested in buying *apu despachos*. She nodded and began pulling packages off the shelf, handing them to me. I organized the transaction by collecting soles from everyone. I then handed the money over to the woman behind the counter, after determining the number of individual *despachos* that each of the women who were with me wanted to buy. The five women I was with wanted a total of ten.

After negotiating the number of kits for each of the women in the group, I asked the shop owner for bottles of Florida water to use for purifying and cleansing during ritual. I added bottles of rose and *naranga* water to the growing pile of items that was accumulating on top of the glass counter.

Out of the corner of my eye, I noticed loadstone and crystals buried under a pile of newspaper in the corner. After sorting through them, I found a couple that felt right to me. Two of the women I was with also began picking through them, trying to decide if they wanted to buy any. Sweet-smelling incense, symbolic tin figures to bring good luck, seeds, and a variety of other miscellaneous items were added to the growing pile. I explained to the others that I had learned that intention is the most important element in any ritual or offering — and that I go

Figure 9. Coca leave in the marketplace (photo by Rana Dewall)

by what feels right when choosing ingredients in addition to what I have been told.

As we were paying the woman for our purchases, I asked whether she had the fresh coca leaves we would need for making *k'intu* offerings. The woman shook her head no. I thanked her, finished paying her, and we left.

As we continued to make our way up the street, we passed a street vender who was selling fresh coca leaves from a large green trash bag. After making eye contact, we smiled and nodded in greeting. He motioned that it was okay to reach into the bag in order to feel the freshness of the coca leaves he was selling. The leaves were as they should be, moist and pliable, bending easily. Satisfied, everyone in the group bought a small bag of coca leaves along with small chunks of *lipka*, the enzyme derived from the linden tree that releases the properties of the coca leaf when it is chewed. (The linden tree is sometimes referred to as a lime tree, but it is not the same as the citrus lime.)

When I finally returned to our room, the sun was setting. Perry informed me that he had slept for most of the day. He said he had experienced a powerful dream.

In the dream, Perry had seen two young pumas standing inside a corral with a gate that was wide open. Suddenly, they both leaped past him, airborne at the height of his waist. The puma on the left turned its head, as it sailed past Perry, snapping the gatepost cleanly in half with its jaws, while Perry was holding on to it. There had been a loud crack when the post had snapped in half. Perry had been left with the stub of the broken post in his hands as the two pumas gracefully circumvented him, escaping the corral enclosure. The mother of the two young pumas had been standing outside of the gate, patiently watching the events unfold. Perry said that as they flew past him, he felt their power and felt helpless, but for some reason, he had not been afraid of them. Then the pumas all trotted away. Perry said that he knew in the dream that they would be back and that when they returned, he would learn from them.

I said that Cusco was full of legends about the mountain puma, and that the layout of the city was actually shaped like a puma. Perry responded by saying, "Oh, let's get something to eat."

Perry and I pulled our jackets on and meandered down the narrow cobblestone street to Jack's — our new favorite place in Cusco for breakfast, lunch, and dinner. After devouring a large plate of nachos and a garden burger, I was full. I have discovered that at higher altitudes my appetite increases — and that for some reason I tend to lose weight.

Although Jose Luis always raves about the food in the Sacred Valley as well as the food prepared at camp, I had begun mentally preparing myself for a bland but nutritious diet of quinoa and chicken soup over the course of the next week. Even though I recognized that the diet was healthy and what we should be eating to combat the onset of altitude sickness, I never looked forward to the food, although it was ideal for battling the fatigue that often comes from intense energy work and strenuous hiking. Thoughts like that made the food at Jack's taste even better.

6. Sacred Valley

Since the theory of general relativity implies the representation of physical reality by a continuous field, the concept of particles or material points cannot play a fundamental part, nor can the concept of motion. The particle can only appear as a limited region in space, in which the field strength or the energy density is particularly high.

—Albert Einstein

July 4, 2011

After a quick breakfast, we left early in the morning for the Sacred Valley. Perry and I were sitting with Don Sebastian in the back seat of the motor bus that was now climbing its way up along the mountainous hills that bordered the Urubamba River. We had begun wearing more layers of clothing underneath our jackets.

I heard Jose Luis say that it had been unusually wet and cold this year, even though July is normally the dry season. Apparently, a cold front had moved in from Antarctica, and recently the mountain roads had been closed due to snow. This weather was unusual for Peru. This seemed to be happening around the world. I have heard *paqos* say that water is the agent of transformation. The year 2012 was approaching, only six months away, and we are currently living in a time of change. [Little did I

Figure 10. Entering the Sacred Valley by bus (photo by Brad VonWagenen)

know about the severe storms that would be happening around the world in the next twelve months.] I wondered if the transformation through water had anything to do with the glacier ice Perry had talked about on the plane.

We dropped into the Sacred Valley from a neighboring mountain and began our descent through the rocky landscape toward the river valley. A panoramic view of terraced mountainsides with plots vibrating in green splendor stretched out into the distance. I could see the village of Urubamba from the window. We passed through the landscape of eucalyptus trees, shrubs, and fields of grass, past the farm patches of green, yellow, and gold as we continued on our descent. It struck me that the village of Urubamba had grown considerably since the first time I visited five years ago.

Sitting in the seat next to me, Perry commented on the deep brown-red color of the dirt. He said he was curious about the construction workers' project of forming the red clay from the earth into bricks. Perry was always interested in discovering new methods of construction.

Jose Luis explained that the Urubamba River was the main water source for the entire valley and one of the four major Peruvian rivers that emptied into the Amazon River and eventually flowed into the Atlantic. As recently as last year, the Urubamba River flooded this village multiple times, wiping out bridges, houses, and hotels. The river continues to be a source of both fertility and destruction for the inhabitants of the valley.

Although the Q'ero people were exposed to the hacienda system left by the Spaniards, because of their isolation and their life style they have remained primarily herders and farmers. Their farming tradition is altitudinal, based upon six or seven different ecological levels. Different places raise corn, chili peppers, sweet potatoes, or small potatoes. Living at the higher elevations offers better grass for the llama and alpaca herds, different from the grasses that grow at lower elevations. Jose Luis said that the Q'ero prefer to live closer to these grasses because the animals thrive on them.

As Jose Luis was finishing his narrative, the bus pulled into the pleasant hacienda where we have stayed in the past. After a short flurry of organizational activity at the front desk, we wandered off to find our individual rooms and drop off the bags that we were dragging down the stone walkway. The courtyard was bordered in colorful flowers.

After gathering again as a group, we headed off for a delicious lunch at a popular restaurant on the Urubamba River. After lunch, we made our way back up to the higher elevation to visit the small village of Maras. Maras is the location where we typically meet with the *altomesayoqs* who conduct ceremonies to speak with the *apus*.

Today, the *altomesayoq* Juanito was waiting for us at the gate when we arrived. As he has in the past, Juanito politely greeted each of us is his quiet, soft-spoken manner. The *apus* that are the benefactors of Juanito's *mesa* are from Bolivia. When he is channeled, the Apu Chupícuaro has described himself as the "mountain in the middle." In Juanito's *mesa*, Chupícuaro serves as the doorway or medium for the other *apus* to come through. Cruz Pata and Nuevo Mundo are two other *apus* that frequently visit his *mesa*.

I noticed that Juanito's hair was a couple of inches longer than last summer. As usual, he was neatly dressed in Western street clothes, wearing corduroy trousers and a wool sweater. It occurred to me later that the majority of the *altomesayoqs* I have met usually wear Western clothing, while the Q'ero *pampamesayoqs* usually wear traditional costumes. I wondered if this was because the *altomesayoqs* I have worked with have been from Bolivia and Vilcabamba.

After exchanging greetings with Juanito, we began preparing for our first session with the *apus*, Jose Luis spoke:

This is the beginning of a new time or *pacha* heralded in the Andes. It marks the incoming crossroads one must envision. The timing could not be more beneficial than now. Inkari is the return of the new Inca, the return of light that has been prophesied. The Q'ero believe in the return of Inkari (the mythic hero) through remembering, reassembling, resetting, and re-envisioning via *apu* medicine. This is our new collective way of being. The *apus* and the *santa tierras* — the midwives and stewards in the Andes — are the means of reawakening our luminous memories. Interfering energies have been removed from the site where we are standing, and are in compliance with the *apus'* requests.

The *apus* have different ways of dialoguing and communication. Human language is our trademark. The *apus* are fully capable of not speaking with words and communicating via thoughts, you know? Some of us are able to do that. Anyway, some of the spirits have learned our language, the ways of our culture, our archeology, the premises of the construct of language — and have developed the consciousness to go there. It is very sophisticated. Of course, some of us will say, well, they have to speak to us so why don't we understand them? Remember that language is our trademark. So, the *altomesayoq* serves as the medium, the channel. The *apu* serving as the benefactor in the *altomesayoq's mesa* holds the "mike" for the other spirits to come through. This is also the construct of that language-based interaction that the main spirit holds.

While we were sitting on the grass in the midday sunshine finishing introductions, a cloth bag was passed amongst us in which to deposit metal and electronic devices. These were not allowed inside the room where Juanito would be leading the ceremony. Besides running the risk of "frying" the circuitry of electronic objects, electronics also interfere with the energetic field, making it difficult for the *apus* to come through.

After the introductions were completed, we left the warm, grassy courtyard and entered into the cold, dark room carrying our *mesas*, and wearing the coats and warm clothing that we had brought with us for the occasion. During these sessions, the temperature usually drops considerably. I have learned that I am more comfortable wearing a couple layers of clothing to preserve body heat while sitting still for hours in the dark on the cold benches.

A wooden table covered with a bright, traditionally woven Peruvian blanket, and with a bench placed in front of it, acted as an altar at the front of the long, rectangular room. On the table were the customary red and white carnations used in ceremonies for Pachamama and the *apus* respectively, as well as a variety of flowers arranged in colorful bouquets. Various bottles of beer and soda pop, offerings for the *apus*, had been positioned carefully on top of the table behind Juanito's open *mesa*. We each walked to the front of the room and placed our *mesas* on the simple wooden

Figure 11. A paqo's *mesa* (photo by Brad VonWagenen)

bench in front of the table altar before sitting huddled close to one another on more wooden benches that had been arranged in a pew-like configuration facing the table altar. We were ready to begin.

Juanito was sitting on a small wooden chair in the upper right corner of the room next to the altar. Jose Luis sat on a bench on the opposite side next to the offerings and lit candles. When the candles were blown out, it became pitch-black and we sat waiting in the silence. Complete darkness is required in order for the *apus* to manifest in the liminal space between realities.

Next, I could hear Juanito softly saying prayers calling the *apus*, followed by three long, slow whistles. The whistles were followed by *stomp, stomp, stomp, stomp* sounds that seemed to be moving across the table, accompanied by sets of flapping wings. The arrival of the *apus* is always announced in this manner. I have felt the gentle brush of wings against my cheek as *apus* are entering and departing the room, even when I have been sitting in a row of benches surrounded by other people. Perry said later that it felt like someone was blowing air on the back of his neck continually. He felt like the two pumas in his dream were sitting right alongside him.

The benefactor of Juanito's *mesa*, Apu Chupícuaro from Bolivia, greeted us in his wise, gentle voice. We responded by saying "Ave Maria Purisima," the customary greeting given to the *apus* upon their arrival. It is a Christian greeting that translates as "the holy pure Mother Mary be with you."

When I asked Adriel about the Christian influences, he explained that when the Spanish arrived in Peru, they had tried to extinguish the traditional sacred Incan practices. Catholicism had seeped into a number of the sacred Andean practices to accommodate and assimilate the changes that were happening in the Incan culture. When I have listened to Adolfo talk about Incan cosmology, I am aware that I have not heard him make any references to the Catholic influences. Adolfo seems to me to be staying more strictly the ancient Incan traditions. He expects his students to learn the correct ceremonial practices. Adolfo believes that the precise implementation of ritual matters because he views it as showing careful attention and respect to the indigenous *apu* spirits. In my own work with him, I have had to learn to do the rituals with more attention to the exact details.

In the beginning, the idea that spirits can actually fly through walls and speak during ceremony with the *altomesayoqs* requires some suspension of doubt. However, over time, as my Mind has developed a greater capacity for entering into and holding a receptive state, I have grown more accustomed to sensing the experience energetically in the luminous field. A massive exchange of energy occurred in the room in the *apus'* presence. Because I sense the energy exchange, belief has turned into certainty. Over the course of the last several years, I have become more familiar with the personalities of the different *apus*.

In addition to the time distortion, I have discovered that the impact of the *apus'* message is contained in the energy behind the words rather than the literal words themselves. I have become more aware that although I often feel profoundly moved by the depth of the experience during their communication, later when I review what I have written, the message that they are giving often seems obvious. My hunch is that, as Jose Luis says, words are a man-made form of communication that the spirit world only uses to accommodate us. Profound truths are, in fact, obvious. Profound energy flow that follows the profound truths is something we seldom experience in the Western world. It is the energy flow that moves me.

Apu Chupícuaro from Bolivia and Apu Ausangate successively said "Greetings!" in the Quechua language. As usual, Jose Luis was serving as the interpreter between Spanish and English. Every year, the *apus* are consulted about our destination before we begin our pilgrimage to the mountains. Jose Luis told the *apus* about our upcoming pilgrimage to Ausangate. There is an understanding that our plans will change depending on the *apus'* directions.

Jose Luis translated the Spanish of his message to the *apus* as "Welcome to all of you. We are bringing in positive energy and release negative energies. I ask you for blessings and healing for all the *mesas* and *khuyas*."

Chupícuaro responded by saying, "First thing — clear the debris of stuff that might not be working in your homes, in your Hearts. This journey of emerging into the *apu*, of bringing order into the home, our sense of home might be uphill, but it's a journey of ascension."

Chupícuaro reminded me of what Ausangate had shown me sitting in the coffee shop in the Lima airport. I was hearing for the second time that we needed to live with less distraction to make room for energetic connection.

The sounds of crystals clicking could be heard as the *apu* blessed each of our *mesa* bundles sitting on the altar table at the front of the room. Little specks of light flashed about with the sounds of the pleasing tinkling vibration. This activity was followed by the voice of the Apu Ausangate who often sounds like a kind old man, "We're here to assist you, just call us. I am waiting for you. Have clear Hearts! Cleanse if necessary. There is no need to talk about it now. I've been saving gifts for your *mesas* and my blessings are in there already."

Chupícuaro spoke again. The following paragraphs are Chupícuaro's words during this afternoon session:

The journey you will be making to Ausangate will be a personal uphill battle but we will be there for you. In the initiation rites, to receive *estrella* (higher vision) you will need pure intent and make yourself available to the gifts of life. This is a reality based upon purity, clarity, and understanding. It requires focus and takes order. It requires pacing yourselves in serving the experience. You need steady pacing — how we pace ourselves in the different places we visit — within and without. Some of you have faster paces while some of you have slower paces. In linear time, you fulfill this by slowing down to grow fast. Revealing ourselves to the land is a process of recognition.

Revelation of truth through evaluating personal themes is a matter of timing and presents opportunity. The rhythm of your pacing is what you bring home with you. Your home is the place of your soul. The Atlanteans became powerful as individuals, and destroyed themselves. The pacing Siberia (sovereignty) is an egotistical way of being that can become a double-edged sword.

The process of observation is a deepening process of awareness through which you develop a clear Heart and become a beacon of your own light. Pure observation leads to pure awareness, through holding

space with the collective and becoming a steward of your own journey.

Preparing for the upcoming initiation of the *Mosoq Karpay* rites on Ausangate is a process of healing, transformation, and embodiment. *Mosoq* is a new rite of passage, by converting back to your lineage and walking hand in hand with creation. You are entering a new stage, a new *pacha*. The weather changes reflect these shifts in celestial alignment and the return of light — the return of Inca. In these rites of passage, you will be given a second set of crystals, a means of piercing the veil. This is an *ayni despacho* — coming together with the land and coming together with the mountain spirits.

Let the energy interact with you, not mentally through language. Sense in different ways. In dreamtime, sensing this change causing the energy level improves. One way to increase physical energy during waking states is through bringing in sound using a bell. Another pointer is that your memory is not of personal experience but of memories of other realms of consciousness, of creation. Your innocence was taken when [you] learned the ways of your culture. Let energy move into [your] Belly and Heart — weave new memories. This is a process of remembering. Although it may seem foreign, memory resides within us. Language takes away magic.

The luminous field has different morphic layers. The outer rings contain information concerning the collective. The layers most accessible are the inner ones. These are the physical and the mental layers having to do with the scientific approach. The outer layers deal with dreamtime. In the luminous field, the outer pertains to the collective — and collectives after us. It is a hub that contains filaments of life that connect with theology — a body of knowledge. Memories of your past lives are located here. Find this place of deep serenity and be your own witness. Try to access filaments of light in your luminous field that have not been turned off. These are the layers concerning the dream body or your vision, besides well-being and fulfillment, of your soul's purpose. Re-ignite your memory. Spirits are timeless and

speak to us in the way we think. Huascaran is the *apu* you will talk to that can go in many directions. Try to access this *apu* through the luminous field by being an open conduit. Do not get distracted.

After Chupícuaro finished speaking, the popping sound of bottle tops flipping off the bottles could be heard. This was followed by the sounds of spilling liquid, as when something is overflowing from a bottle. It is customary to leave bottles of soda on the altar for *apus* to drink after a ceremony. I heard another pop, followed by the sound of the bottle cap hitting the floor. At the end of the ceremony, all of the bottles were empty.

Chupícuaro announced that the *apus* were now ready to answer personal questions. I asked Ausangate about the rites some of us had received previously and about our roles in bringing the energy to others as service.

Ausangate responded to my question by saying:

You are the creator of your own pace. Investing in the collective, the universe, frees you of your own quandaries. It's how you create your own rhythm — no one knows but you. The rhythm is your own. It's how you fulfill and arrive at that objective, at any pace — fast or slow. Sometimes it needs to come to a full stop. I'm waiting for you — we'll do the dialogue out there.

The voice of the Apu Misti chimed in next, speaking to the group as a whole:

Pace yourselves, find your own thing. It is how you embody your journey. When are you coming into my domain?

At the time of this session, I was unaware that two years later I would continue my journey further into engaging the energetic realm. As my own work with the *apus* has progressed, I have become increasingly aware of the multiple levels of potential engagement that become increasingly subtle moving further into the energetic domain. In some ways, it reminds me of becoming accustomed to seeing in the dark and being able to detect what could not be seen before — although when perceiving at higher energetic levels, physical context no longer really applies.

The Apu Nuevo Mundo said:

Your *mesas* and your Heart need to be in right relationship. My blessings to the other *apus*. I had two bottles, now I am done. One more sip.

Apu Nuevo Mundo's words were followed by the sounds of flapping wings, indicating that the *apus* were leaving the room.

When the session ended, one of the *paqos* that had been sitting in the back of the room opened the door to the outside. The sun had set. We gathered our *mesas* from the front of the room and walked out into the courtyard, into the clear evening sky that was filled with stars. Although it had seemed like the session had only lasted for about an hour and a half, after leaving the room I found out that six hours had gone by! — an example of how the experience of time becomes distorted, seeming much shorter during ceremonies with the *apus*. The *paqos* that had been with us during the ceremony took turns speaking.

Don Sebastian was the first to speak:

My greetings to you all. As you know, we are here to work with the mountain spirits. I would like you to speak to them as well. It is very important that you learn the ways of *karpay* — it emanates from the mountains. You must speak the language of the land. We have many concerns at home — this work also entails that we receive the healing for these things or people in our countries and our communities. We should know that the mountains are seeing us, hearing us, and have been healing us for many years.

The Q'ero shaman Don André spoke next:

Here we come to see and recognize each other, to remember ourselves in each other. The land has brought us together. Dialoging clearly is what is important. I have no idea where you come from, but it seems it is very distant. The land will always provide for us. I am here to whisper in your ear to remind you of the land, to provide for all of us. That is all I have to say, little doves of my Heart.

Asunta, the daughter of the great late *altomesayoq* Don Manuel Q'uispe, followed:

I salute and celebrate all of you. All these people are telling you about the mountains and the land. They all hold medicines from different situations we may encounter in life. I honor the great distance you have come, and the effort you have made. The *santa tierras* will help us awaken our creative efforts. We are going to make different *despachos* to invite that energy into us and weave fertility that comes from this feminine principle into any stagnated areas. We need to have *atiynioq* — chi — that comes from the feminine. Up in the skies, we have celestial bodies to tell us the time to do things.

The rites of passage we have been given are channels, medicine coordinates of sorts. They are connection to *Kausay Pacha* — mother energy — the original memory of fulfillment. This place, Maras, is a wonderful locus of energy — the apex of all that we do — the *Mosoq Karpay* rites of passage at Ausangate. Healing, transformation, embodiment are all aspects of the work. This is how we can restructure, see how we should live life, and use as a roadmap or coordinates for our life. That process of transformation, *Mosoq Karpay* also allows us to embody the core energy of our Hearts. We will no longer be limited by a small identity but become unlimited. *Mosoq* means "new rite of passage." These rites connect us back to the lineage. They have key aspects of healing. *Pachas* are huge allocations of space and time.

We are at threshold of huge change and are witnessing unusual weather, environmental change, family makeup, etc. Things are shifting massively. Celestial alignment is now changing as result of this Inkari — return of light, of the Inca — this is a metaphor. Inkari was beheaded in the Conquest for the loss and regaining of the "head" of the state.

This year there will be the gift of a second set of crystals. This is more powerful than any of the past journeys, a massive opportunity, fishing in those chaotic waters. This is an invitation to an ultimate rite of

Figure 12. Dona Bernadina (photo by Flora Meyer)

passage. Be willing to let go of personal theology. We are still struggling with fear, violence, etc. We have to face it. We will have to die soon anyway. This work sets the stage for the next seven generations. The veil between worlds is thinner now — the way is the rites of passage. It is time to return to where we rightfully belong — the land. Like striking a match. Unless we want to have uneventful lives, like sheep. Live like jaguars instead.

Doña Bernadina from the region of Lake Titicaca was the last to speak:

I am sorry for being late. I love working with my brother Jose Luis and am happy to be here. Let us work together, and always keep Pachamama in our Hearts. I ask you urgently to communicate with what gives us life — the land and the mountains. Please pray for our brothers and sisters at home, too.

When the *paqos* had finished speaking, we gathered our belongings and returned by bus to the Sacred Valley for a light dinner of chicken and quinoa. Tired from the long day, Perry and I retired for the evening immediately after dinner. I felt relieved to be climbing into bed — ready for sleep and the dream world. Almost immediately, I heard Perry softly snoring next to me. He had fallen asleep as soon as his head hit the pillow. He was out for the night. Drifting off to sleep I could hear Ausangate's voice, telling me that my connection needs to be a direct channel and that I must focus my intent. I was too tired to ask him exactly what he meant.

7. Doña Alejandrina

Don Juan's assertion, however, that the shamans of ancient Mexico had a different cognitive system, was, for me equivalent to saying that they had a different way of communicating that had nothing to do with language.

—Carlos Castaneda

July 5, 2011

Early in the morning, we headed back to Maras for a session with the Apu Huascaran, the benefactor of *altomesayoq* Doña Alejandrina's *mesa*. Doña Alejandrina is known for calling a multitude of spirits with the aide of Huascaran. Doña Alejandrina has developed the capacity to bring a hundred *apus* through her *mesa*. In ceremony flocks of birds, big and small, as well as very sophisticated deities from tiny spirits to the mighty condor spirits of the winged beings enter the room. There are only two female *altomesayoqs* living in Peru today.

Doña Alejandrina is one of the female *altomesayoqs*. Doña Maria is the other female *altomesayoq* living in Peru. In general, Doña Maria has not worked with Westerners because she is dealing with different issues. In her work, she focuses primarily on immediate community issues pertaining to fertility to heal the land. She also helps members of her village who have limited resources with their daily concerns such as tracking the whereabouts of lost llamas. I met Doña Maria several years ago, during my first trip to Peru. Weeks before arriving in Peru, I had a dream vision of seeing a woman sitting in the middle world, holding a bowl of golden light that had two cords coming from it. One cord reached up into the heavens and the other dropped deep into the earth. When I first saw Doña Maria, I immediately recognized her from my vision and tried to explain the vision to her but lacked the words to express myself. I later realized that Doña Maria had spent her life in a remote village and was unaccustomed to Westerners — especially ones that approached her enthusiastically without any way to communicate with her. I would like to believe that I have developed more capacity to contain myself and to be more respectful of another person's cultural preferences.

Adriel recently explained to me that *altomesayoqs* attract the *apus* that are the most congruent with the personality of the *altomesayoq*. Because Doña Maria has spent most of her life helping members of her community living in a remote village and never learned to read or write, she works with *apus* who focus on helping people living close to the land. In contrast, because Doña Alejandrina received formal Western training and has worked in hospitals in Cusco as a nurse, her *apus* have an easier time understanding and interfacing with people from Western culture.

Upon arriving in Maras that morning, Doña Alejandrina greeted those of us who have been visiting her for several years now with warm smiles and hugs. As usual, she was dressed in Western clothes, wearing a red sweater and black slacks. Her hair was neatly pulled back from her face in a ponytail, revealing gold earrings that matched the other gold jewelry she was wearing. It occurred to me that during our various encounters over the last several years I had never seen Doña Alejandrina dressed in any clothing besides a red sweater and black slacks.

After exchanging warm greetings, we walked along the path through a field of tall grass behind a cluster of adobe two-story buildings that were still under construction. I noticed that the building project was much further along since I had seen it last summer. Jose Luis had explained that the houses would eventually serve as accommodations for students visiting the Andean Research Institute (ARI).

Walking up the steps of the red adobe church, I could feel the pleasing warmth of the rising sun on my back, a pleasant contrast to the brisk morning air. Light was streaming through the large rectangular windows of the chapel meeting hall, forming repeating rectangular patterns on the cement floor in the center of the room. I was glad that the morning light coming in through the tall windows was beginning to raise the temperature in the chilly, unheated room. In less than an hour, we would begin shedding coats and outer layers of clothing to adjust to the temperature change.

After walking into the room, Perry and I plopped ourselves down in one of the comfortable upholstered couches that had been arranged in a circle. After taking her seat at the front of the room, Doña Alejandrina took a moment to silently inspect each of us carefully with her dark, penetrating gaze. I imagined that very little slipped past her.

Once again, I was aware of a familiar sense of peaceful well-being, coupled with an undertone of pulsing and energizing electric current running through the room. Doña Alejandrina's presence was nurturing and commanding at the same time. She began speaking in her deep, strong, feminine voice.

I am not very good with names but do remember about half of you. For those who I do not know, I work with angels. That is the role, I guess, that I have been assigned during this lifetime. I generally do not leave home. I do now because there are people wanting to spread the sacred knowledge — so it is a useful proposition.

I salute you for your effort to learn the lineage of the ancestors. However, you must steward your own lineage; be the beacon of light for your own *ayllus*. This is the greatest act of love — finding, through symbolism, that medicine name, medicine coordinate that is the name of your soul, your visionary name. This takes great responsibility. With lineages, the collective, as one event, has to have subgroups, like the blood lineage of the Inca. In order to acquire power, there are doorways, initiations, rites of passage. Different ones are your identity, career, and your profession. This entails a shift in your own creative awareness. For life, there needs to be this process of reciprocation. The spiritual search is parallel to this — both are examples of growth. Inca girls went through rites in order to become a *collya* (queen), moon, or spouse of the sun king. Men went through *ayllu*-based rites of passage to become rulers. When the gift of power is given, one needs to embody this gift.

Finding a medicine coordinate gives us medicine names — not personal identity names — that have to do with vision. Through this process, we become stewards, feeders, proposing a new, happening, collective order to belong to. In the material world, they are linked to career and profession. In Inca times, a blood lineage connected brothers and grandchildren. Outside the "doing" identities, historical identities of fear, etc., we are history-makers, story makers. There is no power in re-enacting old stories. Stories of creativity and love can be given to our grandchildren, to propel them into a healed state. New stories must be made, such that our grandchildren will tell them as their legacy of returning to the land. In this journey we are on, we all have the responsibility to leave behind a legacy, big or small. If it is going to be a big legacy, we must go through big rites of passage. Power is a big responsibility. Power has to do with what we leave behind.

We all belong to different lineages, genealogical trees, and a distant past. We often wonder where we came from. It is easier to speak of the collective we all belong to. The basis of our Andean matrix is awareness — awareness of the inside and of the outside. Historically, here in Peru, the understanding of the *ayllu* village is very important. This is the type of gathering that brings meaning — here now and in the villages. *Ayllus* that are dedicated to the mysteries, Inti *paqos* — like wizards — are still here. There are *ayllus* for anything — *ayllus* of vision. This vision awareness enables us to be open and observant of what happens. *Karpay* is the way we feed each other. It is the collective identity of how we are known and remember.

I am very happy to talk to you about our traditions, about our past, which we carry in our bodies. Clearly, the civilizations that once flourished here have a rich knowledge. We, as humans, carry our past realities. Mountains also have such knowledge of the past.

My hope is to create an *ayllu* — Amaruina, Serpent of Fire. The lineage is from eons ago, belonging to wizards like the Incas, who had special visions. Theirs is an ancient lineage, a spiritual lineage. This is the tradition of vision — the serpent of fire. Pachakuti Amaruina is the name of my child. Rather than giving him the name of his father, I wanted to give him something great to live into. What I have done with my son has made it difficult for him to travel. There is no passport available with this name, but medicine people are paradigm anchors — and we need to push the outside of the envelope.

We have forgotten our roots and do not know who we are becoming. The moment is who you are. It is what we are right now that matters. Even if beliefs are forgotten, the primordial identity is remembered. We have forgotten our primeval identity. We have the tendency to hoard. Every ten years we go into massive warfare, to deal with the inflamed hoarding we tend toward. In that process of metaphorically hoarding life, sometimes we wake up and feel empty, not knowing who we are, beyond the hoarding. We need to re-find the primordial identity. Who are we? This has to do with the primordial identity we have forgotten. The bottom line is that everyone should have the authority, power, and responsibility to create pathways to joy. However, our cultural paradigm isolates us. We do not know what fulfillment — the healed state — means for us. Our identity resides in reawakening our lineage.

In our new socioeconomic milieu, we are removed from our true nature, the land, our ancestry, and our descendants. Power has to do with finding that medicine identity. Therefore, when we die in the modern paradigm — it's a legacy based on suffering. As far as medicine goes, our fighting to gain balance is passed on to our children, because we do not have a lineage. Our epitaph might also be what we have conquered — leaving nothing behind. Work hard and die... The journey continues. We also must create customs to leave behind. Linage enables us to gain balance... As we serve lineage, we need to be creators of tradition, re-enacting presences before and after. Bodies of custom and knowledge. As we undergo our journey, although the person is important, collective identity occurs through the lineage of our becoming — and the ones after us — our children. Here in Peru there are tremendous power places, royal roads, and luminous markers. Collective identity we are summoning ourselves to is more important for our descendants and ourselves. Our legacy — that is personal identity.

My job description, calling spirits, makes me a hermit. I am envious of where you will visit. You are going on a transcendent spiritual journey — sacred pilgrimage — that transcends any consensual reality that informs you. In order for the sacred journey to Ausangate to unfold, you must transcend the personal, meet Ausangate at a higher level. You have to peel off other identities to be embraced by the *apus*. People used to prepare for three months, finding the royal *cekes* to get to the mountain. Before the coming of roads, people prepared to meet Ausangate by finding royal *cekes*.

When the Spanish established themselves in Peru and set up governments, it was a time when no one was in the streets or villages. People would go to the lineage of the land, Snow Star. The local Spanish authority tried to find the Incan people, but they left no tracks. The Incas were actually kneeling or lying by the sacred mountain, Snow Star.

The Spanish then created a legend of the apparition of Christ there at Snow Star and painted a crude image on the rock. However, the bishop of Cusco realized what was happening and painted the rock white. Now, a huge basilica is there. Thirty days before the solstice, for three days this ritual was taken care of by the Indians, the bear people — *ukukos pablitos* —half bear and half man.

The people who served Snow Star had to use masks and change their voices to falsetto because this kind of idolatry was forbidden to them. Today, the bear people have to be selected, appointed. Someone in the lineage must invite you. It takes four years of training to prepare for this. It is a strong lineage. One of the tests of the bear people is to be naked at the glacier. Either you make it or you die. If you die, you are not fit for the job. The suffering of spending a night alone on the glacier, naked, is only entry into the journey.

These bear people represent a whole group of people — they are the embodiment of their village. Once one is part of the bear lineage, the journey begins. *Pablitos* represent the whole dynasty, lineage. For instance, the crones of the village put together the outfits. The whole village owns the bear person, starting with weaving the yarn, with tremendous tears, love, and breath. A big act of collective love supports this process. The tears and suffering, the breath of the whole village, goes into the vision journey of the *pablito*. He becomes the representative of this village that takes the village peoples' suffering up to the mountain, in service of healing.

One of the aspects of the outfits was leaving behind the trusting word "fortitude" or strength. The fortitude is gifted to him, for this arduous journey. On his journey to the mountain, the bear person no longer speaks in any other than a falsetto voice. When he completes the pilgrimage in service of the village, clears the dense energy of his people, and returns home his voice is given back.

How does the bear person release all the dense *hucha* energy of the village? After carrying the *hucha* of his village up the mountain, he stands in front of Snow Star, wearing a whistle around his neck. After metaphorically carrying all the *hucha*, they take the whistle from their chest and exert a collective whistle-breath, in a trance-state at the *hucha*. Once they have released the *hucha*, the *pablitos* move their legs in trance state for half an hour, to regain balance. The music of wind instruments accompanies them. The *pablito* representative is responsible for taking the *hucha* back to the collective of the mountain. The *pablitos'* act of carrying the *hucha* is an act of love.

Next, the *pablitos* make a circle, bringing in the sun. The *pablitos* go inside of the circle and invite the others to whip them to release the *hucha* for their village. Inside the circle of light, sun, the *pablitos* dance in groups to release the pain, dense energies, also whipping each other and drawing blood. Everyone in turn is whipped in the center of the circle, to release the *hucha*. In this state, the *pablitos* are in a trance, beyond pain, serving as conduits for healing. This is their sole identity. The *pablitos* must be clear conduits to reject the *hucha* that the *apu* will take. The *apu* then absorbs and transforms the *hucha* energy.

After the *hucha* has been released, the *pablito* must take a chip of ice from the glacier. He returns home with the chunk of ice so that the holy water can be distributed among members of the village. It is the water of blood — *agua de sangre*. At home, the *pablito* finds everyone waiting for this holy water to be distributed. Raw, primeval energy of the *pablito* is the energy of the *apu* — the *pablitos* are intermediaries.

Nowadays, the *pablitos* serve as the living embodiment, in service to the *apu*. They are the keepers of the space and the dancers. They are the intermediary between the humans and the sacred, which is why they are half bear and half human. This is a metaphor of what we need to become. When they get older and can no longer carry the *hucha* up to the mountain, other *pablitos* will need to be appointed. This whole region has only 10,000 *pablitos* for more than a million people. When one is aging and no longer able to walk at night and make the journey across mountain ranges — the three days to arrive at dawn at Sinaq'ara Glacier — he must appoint a successor. This is the journey in service to their clan they have chosen.

Our question is what is the legacy we are leaving to our people? What is our service to parallel that of the *pablito*? The reason that I bring up the bear people is that they have to be selected. This story has to do with the journey one chooses for the well-being of the clan. Someone must invite you into a trial process for four years. We, likewise, must blend *apu* and human energy.

The other lineage having to do with the Q'ollorit'i pilgrimage, is called Pocatan — Polcatambo is the nation. Their service is to clean after the Q'ollorit'i pilgrimage. Their role in the weeklong festival is to provide service in a different way, to clean up after the pilgrimage and pick up other people's garbage. The cleansing of the others' garbage is also their cleansing. These are examples of traditions. What is, or should be, ours? We need to formulate what is the legacy of service we need to give to others. What is the journey you are undertaking for? Think about legacy — it is a journey of service. Discipline, order, service. What is your tradition? Tradition is very important. Create traditions we can give to our children, as legacies. Come with gifts and love; the doors will open.

The understanding of one's *ayllu* is necessary. We are the living embodiment of our *ayllu*, and must understand and embody this fully. You are a living embodiment of ancestral memory. It is necessary to explore that primordial identity. What is that core energy that fuels us? To find out where core energy resides that feeds the soul. Blood, culture, and karma are the three ingredients that make up lineage. We need to identify the history of our lineage. We need to create a new paradigm of fulfillment, joy. This is when we clear the energies of war and suffering in our lineage — that we can expiate, like the *pablitos* — and release them at the mountain. As history-makers, we need to create for fulfillment, joy, and clairvoyance. We must bring the *hucha* from our families, for a new lineage. Now it lives in you and in your families. We must find how it misemploys power. Bring the collective past that allows us to create new lineage for our families. Then bring back the healing to our village.

Fear — we have been gifted with that in our culture. We want to experience life, but we are afraid. As adults, there can be the fear of not experiencing enough, not leaving enough behind. Get rid of your fear. As we walk into the next stage, we explore our fears. When you merge with the mountains, merge with the *apus*, our fears are challenged. Collective *apu* energy in the Andes — all together maybe like the law of karma — right here in Andes where the *apus* are speaking. Elsewhere, the mountains are not speaking. The collective *apu* energy that comes up through the atmosphere is a dynamic flow that may go elsewhere. The law of karma may be the need to express at this level. The mountains in the United States and Canada are going through change until the voices are back.

When Doña Alejandrina finished speaking, she looked around the circle, making direct eye contact with each of us. I felt a sense of urgency behind her words, realizing that it was crucial that we grasped the magnitude of what she was saying. Silently, we gathered our *mesas* and headed outdoors into the sunlight. Overcome by the power behind Doña Alejandrina's words — and the need not to speak — I moved quietly into the small room to meet with the *apus* of Doña Alejandrina's *mesa*.

As usual, we placed our *mesa* bundles on the bench slightly underneath the altar table that held her open *mesa* along with cut flowers in vases and bottles of beer and soda pop. Once I sat down, I noticed that the temperature in the dark room suddenly felt about twenty degrees cooler. I started adding layers of clothing.

Doña Alejandrina took her place in the front right corner of the room. I became more acutely aware of my body as I settled in to where I was situated, between Perry and the wall. I leaned into Perry's body for warmth and again felt content that he was in Peru and was sitting beside me. The room became dark and silent. We waited.

I have heard that Doña Alejandrina uses a plastic whistle to call the *apus* because she cannot whistle on her own. In the dark, I could hear Doña Alejandrina softly blowing the whistle three consecutive times as she called the *apus*. After the sound of the third whistle, there came the familiar sound of wings flapping, followed by stomping sounds across the table. I heard the resonance of Apu Huascaran's deep voice greeting us in Quechua. We politely greeted him in return with "Ave Maria Purisima," and the session began. In this session, Huascaran spoke to us for an extended period of time.

The following passage was taken from my notes of the conversation with Apu Huascaran that were written in the dark:

When the session began, I heard laughter, which I assumed was from some of the people who were less experienced with proper protocol in ceremony. *Apus* do not understand laughter and it is considered a gesture of disrespect.

Almost immediately, I heard Jose Luis say, "Be respectful! No laughter!"

Next, in Spanish, Jose Luis began describing the plans for our upcoming journey to Huascaran.

Huascaran responded to Jose Luis by saying:

I am at your disposition. I can call anyone, even dance for you. Wait, wait.

I could hear the faint clicking noise of crystals contacting each other and saw sparks of light at the front of the pitch-black room. Huascaran continued:

As you reach Qariwanaku during the upcoming initiation ritual, you will encounter an underground spring of water. The water is so cold, it is jellied, and so pure we must drink it. Locals come here for healing. Good for cataracts — but for you, do not put directly onto eyes. You can also find *choquetacarpo* in this region. It is a plant that is good for lung ailments. It grows at same level as the short grasses.

Qariwanaku is the place where you set the record straight — the record of cumulative effects of reenactments and emancipation. Setting the record straight is like a confession. Through this process look into your own history, follow your own footsteps, look at the reenactments that have tormented you or not brought enough light. Qariwanaku is seven million years old — yet he still calls himself a young mountain. Qariwanaku is the fifth level of the sixth mountain range. In the family relationship of mountains, it is equal to the sixth brother of Ausangate. Its core energy is primordial. It is the place where locals would bring thieves. They would bathe them in the water, and then the *apus* would either clarify the situation or kill them.

The six brothers of Ausangate are the ancestors of the silver doorway, the doorway of initiation. At Qullqi Cruz, there was a doorway of high-quality silver. To get very fine silver, the initiation must be carried out during nighttime, during deep sleep. *Qullqi* is the quality of silver presence at nighttime, a place of mystery that allows you to delve into the nighttime, in dreamtime, in sleep. The night and moon are feminine and silver, while the day and the sun are gold and masculine. Silver is feminine, and nurtures when it shows up. If you can gift silver, you can give the gift of healing. The sweetness of silver — it is the gift of silver to nurture. If you give a tiny silver offering to the *apu* during your journey, you will receive healing. If you carry a family form or tradition of negativity or black magic that you have not been able to release, Qariwanaku is the place to heal this.

Since you are my children and I love you so much, I will give you a recipe for a purification ritual on your journey to Qariwanaku.

Exercise 7. Finding a Stone to Extract Old Memories, as Given by Huascaran

In your Mind's eye, take a picture of a stone that you will pick up later along your path seen in your vision. Form a very clear mental picture of a stone, with all its particular characteristics. Notice the certain peculiarities of the stone.

Visualize its exact location, with its protuberances. You will find this stone.

To potentialize the energy of the stone, a woman should pick it up with her left hand, a man with his right hand.

Once the stone has been found, ask someone to help you to work with the stone energetically for healing, by making circular motions with the stone down your spine.

Move the hand holding the stone in circles from the back of your neck; draw the energy of the stone down three times toward the base of your spine and pull the energy from there. Very old energy is located in the spine. The stone sees that and can extract it. Our eyes look ahead — they do not see what is behind us, but the stone sees.

Simple prayers should be offered to Apu Qariwanaku asking for help in releasing: "Apu Qariwanaku, anything that's resided in my life, my family, my clan — take it out of my spine."

After you have finished, put the stone back exactly where you found it.

The ancient name of Qullqi Cruz was Punko, which means "silver doorway." Then Spanish culture intervened and it became known as Silver Cross. Qullqi Cruz has to do with abundance. It is a highly regarded mountain that physically resides in the third dimension. Underneath the doorway is another door that opens to another dimension. The silver doorway is at the base of the mountain; in the physical dimension, it is about three meters below. Under that, three meters down, there is a golden doorway where anything necessary in the material domain is satisfied. In the past, silver and gold were used to make up the horoscopes in the old *despachos*. Back then, gold and silver were not used as currency; instead, the metals supported the *apus*. Gold metal has to do with purity — tears of the sun, of light — liquid love and light.

Cayangate represents the two types of energy that are masculine and feminine — but even more than that, *yanantin* and *masintin*.

Cayangate represents complementary energies of opposing dualities — fertility, fecundity, and multiplicity. Offer yellow and white corn to this mountain. It is a wonderful place for meditation. This is a place of abundant gifts that have to do with availability. The veils are very thin there — it is a different vortex of energy. Parallel universes come together. You may think I am a crazy old man, but you can see flying objects, extraterrestrials. The place has many gifts especially pertinent to us at this time. But, you must be serene and clear in Heart and Mind to engage these gifts. You must tap into inner knowing that remembers. A joyful state of serenity and tranquility is necessary. You must tap into and shape-shift into the aspect in you that knows other states and other universes.

The mountain Santa Catalina has to do with abundance, and is the keeper of all the herds, the mountain of the shepherds. Santa Catalina is keeper of all the *salka* things — wild and domestic animals. This mountain is dear to animals — mountain lions, pumas — as well as small domestic animals to watch over you. The water cleanses. It is a positive welcoming place. Santa Catalina has the *phururunas* — the sentient beings who watch over the furred and feathered ones. Substitute *phururunas* are available to take over when the old ones die. These watchers are looking for the next evolution of the life forms they are watching over. My solemn promise to you is that I am going to call seven mountain angels to watch over you while you are on the mountain.

Sigrena Cocha is the lagoon with welcoming, cleansing energy. It is a positive place. Once you are done with the bathing purification ritual that you will be doing on your journey, remember to give an offering of white carnations to the lagoon. Alca Cocha, which means "rainbow lagoon," is below Sigrena Cocha. The *apu* will be downloading information by rubbing crystals together. This will reset the sacred lagoon at the higher levels in these other realms of consciousness.

The *paqo* Mariano Turpo has transcended this place, but his spirit has chosen to return on June 24, 2014. He will be born into the village of Q'uispe Conchi. He will be the child born with all the memories. In these realms of consciousness, the spirits such as Mariano Turpo's are bound by love. He wants to come back and assume stewardship of another place — mountain or lagoon. Sometimes power limits transcendence. Power must be for service and fuel for one's transcendence. Sometimes, our power implodes. Power should be a way to transcend and grow, through offering service. There is a state where power implodes — *anamisma*. Mariano Turpo is an enlightened being, who will be there in a different body but with more power.

We are going to work with Ausangate, the second king, the king of *mesas* through the *Mosoq Karpay*. Salcantay is the First King, then all the rest of the *apus* follow after them. We are constructing the *Mosoq Karpay*.

Jose Luis added:

We've been creating vision; new rites of passage. The first ones were given last year.

Huascaran continued:

We are creating the memory of the new time, the new story into which the new group of us will evolve. Perhaps because of the conquest, the *paqos* of the West need to bring about the new *pacha*. New *paqos* merge into new outfits, to create a new story. The old lineage needs to shift. We have always carried seeds; earth seeds, star seeds — different states of blooming ahead of us. We are the keepers of our own essence. It is everything and nothing at the same time. The body you are emerging into, in the fifth essence has to do with both. Fifty percent white and fifty percent dark — one must embody both.

Practice rituals for connecting to internal fire. Retrieve the passion of humanity so it can be expressed. This internal fire can propel as much as it can burn. High vision has to do with being a catalyzing agent to bring opposing forces into balance, but accelerating growth is the key effect. We need to be clear conduits that come from other opportunities. Love of Christ, Love of Land — not just personal love.

Pampamesayoqs all have *mesas*, carrying stones that elicit memories and techniques. How you use them has to do with igniting fire within, and how your fire catalyzes and becomes Kausay Pacha to propel and feed you and fuel dreams. You need to rediscover passion, if passion has been dormant. Moving from extreme to extreme, the rite of passage will be begin by working with earth energetics moving into fire and water and breath. Some will be burned. High and low passions, what lives there in the person, weaving between fire and lack of fire.

Paqos of the West need medicine of the Heart and old technologies to be spoken again. The first set of keys, through initiation rites, was given last year — bringing memory of a new time, creating a new story, a new tradition. The *paqos* from the West will propel and the ancient technology of ritual will be spoken again.

You were given the first key last year, but ninety-nine percent of this involves visionary skills that you must learn. Through this process of enfoldment, you must learn visionary skills that can inform you today, that must be used and may take part with that which is 100,000 years old. Power needs to be for service. The power we embrace implodes. Power is a way of transcending, a way to grow.

Mosoq means "keystone." You must understand what a keystone is, that which you are emerging into — the *insuflar*. The *apus* will blow into the new luminous body made of vision, which will be the keystone. Blow the energy of vision into the spaces. This journey is about transcending. The keystone will be the anchor stone. We need to understand the lead keystone — it is our job together. Energetically, the keystone is underneath what the *mesa* is emerging into energetically.

One day we will die and transcend and propel this medicine. One day we will die in a way that propels the sacred knowledge and vision to other dimensions. Knowledge is part of the living entity passed on. The knowledge will leave this reality. It fuels us. It is our legacy, our passion. It becomes a living entity in your *mesa* that is passed on, a *ch'aska*.

The first key was given last year, having to do with returning to the land, *saminchasqa*, the medicine coordinates. Returning to where we have always returned, anchoring our self where life has always emerged, in the Belly of the physical and celestial mother. The current theology of Western culture is opposed to the presence of land in the body. The first code is anchoring into the land, in the life on this planet — and in the body. Like the benefactor opening within, there is an anchoring of the physical body into the land by reawakening timeless memory. The actual responsibility that is taken on in the *Mosoq Karpay* rites is one of co-creation — sourcing from the mother through the reactivation of memory and creating maps through culture.

This is the responsibility you embrace, as you become a *mesayoq* and co-creator. The metaphor of mother awakens within you. Pivotal energy of the mother that anchors from the Belly into the land. It is a reactivation of the memory of returning to where we always return. Remembrance of timeless memory of this planet. We are floating around with ideas, the belief system that life has to do with the presence of land in our Bellies.

The first luminous code is the reactivation. In this way of life on this planet, our theologies and systems of mind and knowledge are opposed to the presence of the land in our bodies. The first code is reawakening to the memory of this in our body.

The second code requires the capacity to ask the question encoded in the body. Here, we need our own capacity to create in our bodies. You have to craft the question and in the question is the answer. If you do not question, you miss an opportunity to create. The *apus* are here to help us to remember that we know. We are those keystones.

Do you know about the hero that lost his head? We must remember, we know we have to re-ignite with fire. The second key, *inkari* memory, reignites our visionary qualities at the expense of fire.

In the process of re-igniting, we are rooted back to the land like a eucalyptus tree. Dispassionately exercising a way of being through fire like the eucalyptus tree, passionately exercise *saminchasqa* which re-roots us as a tree.

The second key re-ignites the star seeds in the Belly, in the medicine body. The star seeds are the keepers of essence in the luminous body — being everything and nothing at the same time. The fifth essence, in color, has to do with the memory of relationship between darkness and light. This second stage is to retrieve the passion of life, so that it can express itself through you. This eternal fire can propel you as well as burn you — not only to bring opposition into dialogue. Can we do the same in half the time — understanding the eternal fire? You cannot burn yourself in fire if you are clear. There is a need to be clear conduits of the fire. Collective love can propel the experience. How you activate the stove has to do with lighting the fire — by burning away or bringing light. Fire is the Kausay Pacha.

You need to discover passion for a way of being. Last year's ritual had to do with the earth. We are moving from extreme to extreme, from anchoring in the earth to moving into fire. Some of you will be burned by what lives in the basement.

Weaving fire can be a conduit. You can change or postpone karma. Both time and space are required to work it out. Service has to do with a way of being and discerning in the world. The metaphor forms you and transforms into gold. Questioning is good but you need to summon your potential. Revelation has the most accurate response, which is found in the question. Shedding requires momentum.

Energy of dead flesh, catastrophic death happens by fire. Green trace memory — not copper. There is a sacred ritual to connect with fire. Specificity cannot be told. It has to do with the key — passion will be given to you. Fire is the living expression of love and hate — about understanding opposition of passion. Victory is the precursor reconnecting opposites. The more power grows the more fully you experience. May your walk be embraced with ritual that is not literal or symbolic. *Anima* **is the life force of all spirits. This is a reenactment of primordial language through relationship — not theology. This is the journey of your soul. Make it happen.**

The *despacho* **represents the cyclical nature of time, the birth of the headwaters of consciousness, the** *despacho* **must be seen at the primordial level, the potential qualities to source from.**

[Even though Jung borrowed the word *anima*, it is a word I have heard other *altomesayoqs*. We could use *kausay* but I am reluctant because I believe it deals specifically with soul/spirit/energy — not life force in general.]

The session with the *apus* finished with us singing — per the *apus'* request — the song Amazing Grace. (Spirits are drawn to songs being sung.) When the song was finished, there was the familiar sound of bottle tops popping off the beer and sodas that had been left as an offering on the altar at the front of the room. This was followed by the sound of flapping wings and a cool gust of air. Then they were gone. It was quiet and we were alone. Doña Alejandrina made stirring sounds as she woke from the trance state of deep sleep that she enters when she is in ceremony with the *apus*.

When the session had ended, we moved out into the exterior courtyard. A couple of hours had passed and it was now midday. After eating lunch with Doña Alejandrina at a nearby restaurant, we boarded the bus and slowly made our way along the single-lane mountain highway. Our adept driver navigated through the boulder-strewn detour, a result of a landslide that had occurred during the rainy season. As the drive continued, directly in front of the base of the mountain of Waquay Wilka we spotted a sacred ancient Inca site, a stone doorway consisting of two gates. Climbing up the hills on the narrow cobblestone streets, arranged on the sides of old buildings, we saw beautiful stonework carvings of four-petaled flowers, representing levels of the world.

After stuffing ourselves with salads, chicken, ceviche, and pound cake, we drove along the Rio Vilconata to the Sanctuary of the Lord of Huanca which is about twenty minutes south of Pisac on the sacred slopes of the mountain Pachatusan, a Quechua word meaning "one that sustains the Earth."

8. Visiting Pachatusan

A feeling is as indisputable a reality as the existence of an idea.

—Carl Jung

July 5, 2011

Upon our arrival at the church of Señor de Huanca, I felt the power of the *waka* (holy energy spot) at the entrance to the sacred mountain, Pachatusan. The natural pathway of stepped stones led toward the mountain on the right and the church on the left. Unexpectedly, I felt my attention being pulled to the path toward the mountain. There was an energy drawing me, something I knew but did not know — like an old familiar smell, imprinted deep within my memory that had not yet surfaced in my conscious mind. I followed the scent of what was resonating with me.

On the trail leading toward the sacred mountain of Pachatusan, two stones that I immediately felt a strong affinity for were sitting in the middle of the path. It felt as if they had been calling me toward them. I stopped, picked them up, and held them in my hand. I sensed that these stones were holding a tension between masculine and feminine energy — together. The group had marched around and over them without any apparent recognition of their existence. Ostensibly, they had not felt the strong pull to these particular stones that I had. These stones would become *khuyas*, and part of my *mesa*.

Don Sebastian approached me and looked at the two rocks that I was holding — one in each hand. I said, "Masculine y feminine." Don Sebastian nodded and added, "Pachamama y Pachapapa." We continued walking along the path together, in silence. The comfortable understanding from Don Sebastian and the warm presence of the stones that I was now holding in my hands brought a wave of well-being and an ease washed over me. I felt myself acclimating and attuning to the powerful energy of Pachatusan.

Exercise 8. Adopting a *Khuya* (*Mesa* Stone)

Paqos serve Pachamama by feeling Pachamama. This connection happens in relationship with the *mesa*. The *mesa* anchors the *paqo* to the earth, and as an intermediary, serves as the gateway to the spirit world through connection with Kausay Pacha. A *mesa's* capacity to hold energy is a function of the strength of the *paqo's* relationship with Pachamama.

Finding a *khuya* or *mesa* stone is something that happens when you are in a receptive state and paying attention. It is not something that can be forced. When a stone becomes a *khuya*, it becomes a sacred object. Sometimes a *khuya* chooses us. *Khuyas* can appear suddenly in our path. They can also disappear from our *mesas* when our work together is complete and it is time for us to say goodbye.

Building a *mesa* is an act of love, and *khuyas* — like mates — should be chosen very carefully. A *khuya* stone is a living being that becomes a member of our medicine body. Like the human form, it helps if the shape or aesthetic form of a *mesa* stone is unified and complete. It is important that the stone is not missing limbs; that is not chipped or with pieces missing. *Mesa* stones must be capable of holding energy as well as information.

Bringing a new *khuya* into a *mesa* is similar to bringing a new member into a family. Everyone must get along and work together. Each *khuya* has its own location, similar to each member of a family having a seat at the dinner table. Using intention, the sacred stones are woven together to form a rich tapestry connecting our energy body to Pachamama and the spirit world. To let our capacity to hold energy through the medicine body of our *mesa* grow, we need to be in *ayni* with our *khuyas* — and the *khuyas* must be in relationship with each other. This dynamic relationship between *khuya* stones develops either as a union of opposites balancing masculine and feminine energy (*yanantin*), or through an alignment of similar energy (*masintin*).

Mesas can provide us with deep wisdom if we take the time to listen. A *khuya* stone can become an important teacher. Each stone is imprinted with information and energy that we discover as our knowledge and understanding of the *khuya* deepens. A *paqo's* relationship with a *mesa* is a love affair, and as in any significant intimate relationship, it requires attention in order to grow and thrive. Caring for a *mesa* is similar to tending to a young child — or any living being for that matter — it needs to be fed, purified, listened to, and treated with respect. We feed our *mesas* with love and intention, sitting with them and giving them our full attention. I have found it is easiest to connect with my *mesa* when I am in nature, the place where it is easiest for me to shift into communicating with the spirit world.

The popular version of the history of this site at the house of Pachatusan is that the chapel of the Lord of Huanca, referred to as "Señor de Huanca," was built in 1676 and is the holy shrine for both Christ and Señor de Huanca. For centuries, pilgrims have traveled to the location carrying *khuyas* that they have blown their prayers into, as gifts to the Lord of Huanca in asking to be healed. In the middle of the Sanctuary, three holy fountains are believed to hold special healing waters. There are four additional fountains behind the buildings of the sanctuary. Each is at the foot of boulders at the base of the steep slope of Pachatusan. The water emerging from the earth forms the springs of Mamacha Virgin Mary, whose water is said to purify and heal.

According to the *paqos*, Señor de Huanca is a Christian embodiment of Pachatusan that had been honored at this *waka* before the Spanish conquest. When the Spaniards arrived, they built a church on the site and now *paqos* and Christians pray here together to ask for blessings. The *paqos* pray to Pachatusan while the Christians pray to Christ and the Madonna figure that is positioned at the front of the church.

Before entering the church, Jose Luis offered more of the *paqos'* version of the history of the sacred site of Pachatusan:

In Peru, our version of Christianity is a conglomeration of ideas, the result of Christianity being assimilated into Peruvian culture. A lot of the stiff Christian traditions survived by shape-shifting into the existing tradition of Peruvian cultures. Nowadays, festivals and ceremonies have become a collective event. Everyone is out there dancing. There are little boys, dogs, cats, and elders in the street, carrying their respective patron saint.

The patron saint is the ancestor of the land itself. What is the job description of ancestors? To maintain the well-being of all of the cycles of life in the village. So when somebody dies, the immediate thing to do in a family, even if that person has not been a good individual, is what will be beneficial to the village and the family. So, they call the ancestors and there are cleansing rituals. The deceased individual — not like in the Christian traditions — is condemned, walking around trying to belong someplace. The ancestors come and hold that individual. There is a process for the family that usually continues for three years until the soul becomes purified.

The presence of the ancestors is such that each village has a patron saint. During a festival, everyone comes out to carry the saint. They have this big collective powwow of sorts. The powwow that happens here is for the whole city of Cusco because this is their holy mountain. Many legends, myths, and apparitions are connected to this place — and to me particularly. This is my birth mountain, and in my own journey as well, I had gravitated towards all of the mountains, bigger, taller, with more whistles and bells, etc. — right, but then things had to shift. I had to recognize my own lineage. In one of the initiations, this mountain Pachatusan came to one of these *apu* sessions and appeared as a tall mountain with this deep voice. It was an amazing revelation for me. An incredible opportunity to remember stuff that we normally would not be able to remember around lineage — and then there was the ensuing conversations and dialogues of discovery. I was like, wow, not a bad mountain to have!

This mountain nowadays, because of the presence of the Christ now inscribed on the holy rock at the church, gets even more attention. One of the expressions of power of this particular Christ on the rock is healing. Even the locals call the Christ, the doctor Señor de Huanca that heals anything.

Many local people come here every weekend to sit in front of this mountain. My mom comes here, too, every Sunday and all she does is sit — and then she goes home happy. In September, the local people of Cusco come in massive numbers to walk over the mountain pass. The mountain pass is in the shady area, right here in this opening. It takes about eight hours to walk from the other side to here.

So, they walk with a candle to honor the energy, the *apu* benefactor of this mountain — and nowadays, the Christ. They arrive here at dawn so they can sit in mass with the priest for communion. Then they go for a little picnic, and then go to the back side to collect holy water that they bring back to their houses. They sprinkle the holy water on their plants. Then they do a little bit of washing with everything and anything.

In the rainy season, there are waterfalls all over the place here. The energy of this place is quite extraordinary. It really is. It is very serene and peaceful, yet raw energy comes up. After I go home, it brings a certain level of clarity for me, a great sleep and my hearing improves. I hear well. I see well. So, there are a number of physiological things that happen here. My mom says it is good for aging. She says, "See my wrinkles? Look at me now!" She says that coming here is anti-aging.

So, everyone has their own personal experiences. In the journey of initiation, today in this modern era, many of the initiatory steps for the old tradition merged with the Christian traditions. Now, for the new *paqos* that are born in the city of Cusco, the first station that they visit in their initiatory journey is in the center of Cusco. There is a Christ, Taytacha Temblores, the Lord of the Quakes. The second station is this. The third station they visit is the Temple of Viracocha. The fourth station they go to is Machu Picchu. The fifth station takes them to Ausangate. The sixth station takes them to Salcantay. In addition, the actual getting of the *mesa*, the seventh station, occurs at Waquay Wilka. It has the seven Stations of the Cross type of a deal, so it carries a lot of Christian symbolism.

This is the most important place here. As the pilgrims come, they begin their journey on a Sunday, preferably with the Bishop of Cusco, not just any priest. They wait for the bishop who is going to provide the mass. There are a couple of egg-like stones at the church. Once they have communion they embrace those stone eggs and come here. Here they are tested. There is no Mass — rather it is whether the calling to become a *paqo* can be heard, can be known to them here, can be revealed to them. As much as you want to choose a career for instance, you need to know: can you go through with it? Can you graduate per se? Do you have the body of knowledge? Do you have the body of techniques — skills? Does your soul, your energy field have the fitness to be connected, wired to this high wattage of energy? Many people are fried in this process. This is where they are fried, in this second station.

So now, we are going to the church. There are a couple of rooms here where you can light candles. You have candles and this is your ceremony. This is your love, your presence, your identity, your availability to choose whether this is for you. Introduce yourselves to this holy mountain. It is my mountain. I love being here.

Pachatusan means "anchor." Put your respects in that candle. Perhaps if there is healing that is needed, this is a good place. This place, in terms of healing, in terms of release, in terms of resetting, is called forth. We might have to come back here if we do not get the work right. That is serious. So, let us go inside of these two rooms. Let us light our candles. Bring your prayers — whatever they are. Prayers are to the spirit of this mountain, or to the spirit of the Christ that lives in this church.

When Jose Luis had finished speaking, I looked to the right of the stairway leading to the old church. I saw an enclosed area containing rows of metal candleholders. They were mounted in the center and bordered each of the cement walls. In the room, many burning candles had been lit as prayer offerings by other visitors before entering the church.

We went to offer our candles and our prayers to Pachatusan. Walking in, I saw a couple of older Peruvian women quietly saying prayers as they lit candles to place in the open spots of the candleholders.

After lighting candles for my sons, Devin and Colin, and for Perry, I proceeded with Don Sebastian into the church. We took a seat in one of the empty pews facing the massive altar that appeared to be a couple of stories tall. The altar was a combination of ornate gold baroque woodcarvings in a Spanish colonial style, surrounded by a series of nine paintings of Christ and the saints. There was also an image of the Black Madonna. Although I had sat in this church before, on each of my four previous visits, I was amazed to discover that the nine paintings in the front of me were arranged in the same format as the *sephiroths* on the tree of light in the Kabbalah, which was my first introduction into piercing the veil. I just had not noticed that before.

After sitting in the chapel, taking in its energy, we left the church and followed the *paqos* up a stone pathway bordered by eucalyptus trees. It ran along the base of the mountain and at the end of the path there was a grass clearing. When we sat down facing the peak of Pachatusan, I instantly felt a power emanating from the mountain.

I remembered when I had first encountered this powerful energy of Pachatusan, a couple of years prior during an *ayahuasca* ceremony in the Amazon jungle. In that ceremony, the presence of Pachatusan had appeared as a magnificent column of white light extending out from my Belly as I lay on my back, gazing upward. That was when I first learned that Apu Pachatusan was considered the architect of the holy Andean mountains, forming the spine that connected heaven and earth. As is the case with most archetypal mythic figures, Pachatusan appears in various forms and has many faces with different meanings.

Outside in a grassy clearing, the *paqos* began preparing for a four-step cleansing ritual with four different kinds of herbs that they had collected during the last couple of days. The *paqos* all knew how to find plants from the earth and use them for many different purposes. The group gathered in a circle on the grass as Jose Luis began to tell us about the ritual.

Meanwhile, Perry had found a stick from one of the trees behind the church and had proceeded to sit down on the grass and whittle away on the stick with his pocketknife. A large dog walked over and sat down in the grass right beside him, as if they had known each other for many years. They both seemed content and comfortable as Perry whittled away, mumbling little things to the dog at his side, while wood chips fell in his lap.

When the ceremony began, Don André and the other *paqos* took turns calling sacred space and asking for assistance from the *apus*. A couple of minutes later, Don André came over to where I was sitting and began vigorously patting me and my *mesa* which I was holding in my lap, using an 18-inch branch of mint that he held in his hand. Mint is often used by *pampamesayoqs* as an agent of clearing, and is used at the beginning of the cleansing ritual as the energy field is being opened. The smell of the mint was wonderful.

As Don André continued his pattern of rapid movement, lightly hitting the branch of mint against my body, I remembered Don Sebastian had rubbed mint on my stomach a couple of years ago after I had become intensely nauseous and overheated while climbing a steep slope on the mountain Waquay Wilka. The mint had quickly helped to relieve my symptoms so that I was able to resume the ascent up the path on the side of the mountain.

After Don André had finished the cleansing process using the mint, the same process was repeated using the herb *mona* to facilitate vision and clarity. The third plant that was used in the same procedure was *romero* (rosemary) to clear away any unwanted psychic entities. The fourth step involved using *ruda* to change luck.

After Don André had finished administering the ceremonial cleansing, I sat in front of my *mesa*, looking up at the peak of Pachatusan that lay directly ahead. I gradually became aware of feeling a curious expanding sensation in my head and noticed that my forehead had begun to feel heavier.

Maintaining my gaze directly toward the top of the snowcapped mountain, Pachatusan suddenly began to appear brighter. An intense halo of light slowly outlined the mountain ridge in the sky. The sensation of expansion that I had been experiencing in my head started to drop lower in my body. I became aware of a stream of energy being downloaded into my body. It seemed to be coming directly through the connection channel that had been opened between the mountain and me. I focused on maintaining an erect spine and continued to sit cross-legged on the grass. As the process continued, I began to feel light spasms in my Heart growing more intense.

This experience reminded me of a similar experience I had undergone a few years back while sitting on a mountain ridge at the top of Waquay Wilka, gazing across a deep valley to the mountain range of Alankoma. In that experience, what had begun as a subtle tingling vibration eventually registered in my body as a forceful flow of incoming power. The powerful energetic influx had led to a series of painless yet forceful spasms in my stomach which, while they were less intense, reminded me of sensations I experienced while giving birth. A less extreme but comparable process seemed to be happening now. The conscious part of me focused on maintaining an erect posture, in order to maintain the energy flow being transmitted into my body from the mountain. I was in the midst of an intense somatic experience, where no words, images, or time existed. There was only energy.

Waves of spasms occurred between my shoulder blades. Odd cracking sounds came from unusual places in my spine as the spasms continued to run through me. They would cease for a moment, and then a new set of waves would surge into my body. I guessed that this entire process continued for half an hour. Gradually, the spasms of energy rippling through my body subsided.

Over the years, similar kinds of experiences have continued to happen and I now recognize that this is the process that takes place when I am in spiritual union with a mountain. Adolfo explains that as the capacity to hold power increases when one moves further along the medicine path, we move to deeper *nivelas*, or levels, in our ability to feel and receive energy. It seems that this is what happens when our awareness shifts from our physical bodies into sensing from our energetic or spiritual bodies.

As dusk approached, we said goodbye to Pachatusan and climbed back on the bus headed for Urubamba. As I followed the *paqos* to what had become our regular seats in the back of the bus, Don André, Doña Bernadina, and Asunta all smiled at me and nodded. They seemed pleased with the current state of my luminous body.

After a light dinner of chicken stew, I finished my notes and returned to our room exhausted. Perry was already in bed and quickly drifting off to sleep. Unfortunately, that would not be my fate that night. As soon as my head hit the pillow, painful contractions and intense waves of nausea wracked my body. These lasted throughout the night, eventually developing into what felt like a case of the stomach flu.

Now, a couple of years later and looking back with the new understanding that I would gain through further work with Adolfo, I recognize that at the time I was going through a rather intense energetic clearing process as dense *hucha* energy was being moved out of my Belly. In working with other people involved in their own process of energy clearing, I have seen that people often become physically sick when *hucha* is being moved. As energy blockage is gradually released from our physical bodies, the movement of the energy — although equally intense — becomes less jerky and forceful, and flows more easily. It feels more like a wave and less like a contraction. As Adolfo explains it, this is when we begin connecting and experiencing through our energy and spiritual bodies.

9. Asunta and Doña Bernadina

*The Sufis speak of jinn, or angels, who are created beings,
like ourselves, who require our deep imaginal experience to be
brought into our consciousness.*

—Jeffrey Raff

July 6, 2011

Driving upriver to the sacred Inca site of Pisac, the Temple of
the Visionary, I sat at the back of the bus, lodged between Asunta
and Doña Bernadina, whom some affectionately call Doña B It
was as if I was sitting between two nurturing mothers who were
wise old women, yet at the same time were two girlfriends from
junior high school. Asunta was actively showing me the colorful
plastic flower and animal ties on the ends of her long black braids.
As I playfully pulled on one of her braids, she began giving me
the Quechua names of each of the plastic figures I pointed to.

As usual, I struggled to hold on to a few of these Quechua
words, as I would forget them within the hour. Doña Bernadina
laughed at my difficulty retaining even the simplest phrases in
Quechua while Asunta patiently repeated them to me, over and
over. If she was frustrated with me, she did not show it. If only I
had the same patience as Asunta. I felt a warm glow sitting
between them that reminded me of being home. It was nice and
comforting to be in their presence.

121

While I was attempting to retain the words, I was much more interested in playfully interacting together than in actually learning the language. Although my lack of ability to recall previously learned phrases frustrated me, at the time I had come to enjoy the creative process of finding new ways of communicating without words. For the most part, forming relationships without a common verbal language is less of a problem than one would think. Perhaps this is because the Q'ero *paqos* have the ability to keep life simple — and do not consider talking less to be a bad thing. The Q'ero *paqos* live in their immediate experience through their bodies and pay less attention to thoughts using their heads.

It wouldn't be until a couple of years later, when I would begin bringing groups of people to Peru independently and my own individual work with Adolfo deepened, that the need to communicate directly in a common language became essential to me. It was then that I dedicated myself to the daily practice of learning and speaking Spanish with the intention of becoming fluent. Although I had gotten by in the past, once I became focused on mastering the language so that I could understand their words on my own, I believe my efforts were interpreted as a serious commitment to the Andean medicine path.

Meanwhile, Doña Bernadina was quietly gazing out the bus window at the mountain landscape that stretched in every direction. The mountains surrounded the valley we were in. I could see the great mountain Alankoma standing in the distance, in front of the great holy mountain Waquay Wilka, which means "tear of the sacred."

Apu Alankoma has held a special place in my Heart since my original pilgrimage to the sacred mountains. On the first journey, when I was invited to work with the *altomesayoqs*, I underwent a major initiatory experience in communion with this mountain. The energetic download I experienced had drastically altered my perception of reality, and changed my life significantly. It is hard to describe what had actually happened using day-world language, yet it was clear that it was something real. The encounter with Alankoma was my first major experience of piercing the veil, which became part of the title of my first book, *Lessons of the Inca Shamans: Piercing the Veil*.

After this encounter, I no longer questioned whether non-ordinary reality actually existed. There is no point questioning something you know in your soul. I also decided that searching for proof to justify the experience — to answer the critical voice of the inner scientific community that still occasionally emerged on the hamster wheel inside of my head — was a waste of time.

I again looked over at Doña B, who was apparently looking at something that I could not see. As we continued to stare out the window, she suddenly pointed to a condor that she spotted flying overhead. It was as if the condor had heard her calling and flew over to investigate. In her friendly manner, she nudged me with her shoulder and excitedly exclaimed, "Apuchin!" Looking up into the sky in front of us, I watched the condor gliding gracefully through the air and decided that this was a positive omen. Apparently Doña Bernadina thought so, too.

When it seemed that we might be approaching our destination, I took my *mesa* bundle from my backpack and removed the two new precious *khuyas* that I had found near Pachatusan yesterday. I wanted to carry them with me on the upcoming hike. For several minutes, I attempted to reassemble my *mesa* bundle on my lap as the bumpy ride down the unpaved road continued.

Asunta reached over and gently took my *mesa* from me. It had become sloppily wrapped in the *mastana* cloth. Matter-of-factly, she reopened the *mesa* and began to skillfully fold it in the traditional way a *mesa* bundle is carried. I was enjoying the caring attention she was offering me, another opportunity to connect with her in this simple activity. It occurred to me that any activity could become a game when approached with a playful attitude.

As I read this now, two years later, I am aware that my perception of the event has changed. Maybe this is because my attitude toward the work has matured. Besides the fact that I have become more adept in my ability to fold a *mastana* cloth, keeping my *mesa* in a disorderly way now seems disrespectful to the sacred energy of the *khuyas*. Having my *mesa* enclosed in a careless fashion — now — would feel unacceptable to me because I am aware that it is not a game.

As I looked over, Asunta's beautiful, intense, dark brown eyes sparkled through long dark lashes as she smiled at me. Her petite frame, less than five feet tall, seemed particularly tiny at this moment. I reflected on what a contrast this was to my other memories of Asunta. Asunta might have a small frame, but she was no pushover. Although at times Asunta can appear docile as she has in this most recent series of interactions, I am fully aware that this is an illusion. I felt the spirit of Apuchin bursting forth from the interactions with these two wonderful shaman women.

The day before, I had watched her authoritative presence calling the mountain spirits to our fire ceremony. During the invocation, I could actually see a column of white light opening above her head as her fierce voice belted out the names of the *apus* she was calling with vibrational intensity.

She was a force to be reckoned with, regardless of her seemingly benign appearance today. I knew that her gentle and caring demeanor could shift into ground-shaking thunder at will.

Asunta makes it known to everyone she meets that she is the daughter of the late *paqo* Don Manuel Q'uispe, and proudly carries his lineage. Don Manuel is considered by many to be one of the greatest — if not the greatest — *altomesayoq* that has lived in this century. After more moments had passed, Asunta closed her eyes and began nodding off. Our bus ride through rolling hills

Figure 13. Asunta (photo by Perry Edwards)

continued. It would be a while longer before we reached the place where we were going.

I reached in my backpack for my bag of coca leaves and offered it to the other *paqos* sitting with us in the back seat. Don Hilario, Don André, and Don Sebastian each took a small handful and politely thanked me, nodding and smiling. Another hour later, we finally arrived at our destination in Pisac, at the base of the Temple of the Sun and the Moon that lies on the outskirts of the village.

I climbed off the bus after adding attire for hiking. I was wearing a wide-brimmed straw hat for protection against the intense rays of sunlight that were now beaming down directly overhead and a *ch'uspa* across my body (a small woven bag with a strap used for carrying coca leaves). I carried my backpack that held a water bottle, sunscreen, my notepad, a small tape recorder, and the two *khuyas* from my *mesa.*

I noticed that Doña Bernadina and Asunta had thrown the *mantas,* or *unkunas* (blankets), which held their medicine bundles and other personal belongings, over their shoulders. The wide-brimmed hats (*monteras*) that they were wearing are part of the traditional Peruvian highlands outfit, made of plain-weave woolen fabric and decorated with colorful ornamentation.

The prominent landscape surrounding the sacred site of Pisac consists of layers of terraces, stair-stepping up a series of steep slopes. The layers of earth were retained by masterfully constructed stone walls, configured in precise geometric patterns that locked together. Perry was becoming very excited about the precise joinery, and he kept chatting about how hard it would be to do this with cranes, diamond blades, and air hammers. At one point, he started becoming flushed, exclaiming, "And they didn't even use mortar! OSHA would have just shut them down!"

We began to ascend the ancient royal trail up toward the top of the mountain crest called the Hitching Post of the Sun. There we would work with our *mesas* in connection with the land.

I opened my *ch'uspa* bag and carefully dug around, searching for three whole coca leaves that were in good condition to make a *k'intu* offering for the land, in preparation for the strenuous hike ahead. Climbing the mountain path to the Temple of the Sun is a difficult hike, up what I estimated to be over 1,000 steps. Most of us were breathing heavily, and we stopped several times to catch our breath. I could see Perry calculating the altitude gain in his head, but I did not ask.

Asunta and I walked together. Her sturdy brown legs moved rapidly, even up the stone steps that were each over 18 inches tall. As usual, she was wearing black sandals — with no support — and seemed to be doing just fine. In contrast, I was trudging up the mountain wearing a pair of decent hiking boots, struggling to maintain the pace that we had set for ourselves. Occasionally Asunta considerately stopped and waited for me to catch my breath. Each time she stopped, she smiled at me and said, "*Tee-os-o*," which I learned meant "restful sitting." Together, we repeated the word as a mantra — enough times that I could actually remember it.

I have discovered through my work with the Andean medicine people that the Quechua spiritual language, with many words to describe energy states and different aspects of love and connection, has no corresponding words in English.

We also said the phrase that sounds something like "*tee-a-so nay-chay*," that translates to "as sisters we walk together." I loved listening to the soothing sounds of Asunta's voice inflections and the phonetic sounds she was making. I pronounced the words aloud and enjoyed saying them back and forth with her.

Repeatedly reciting the phrase "*tee-a-so nay-chay*" created an easy rhythm as we walked. I fell into a meditative state from the song, which seemed to carry me up the steep slope. In cadence with our steps, our breathing joined together. I was pleased to have found another way of connecting with Asunta. Suddenly, I realized we were at the top.

My eyes first focused on several magnificent boulders positioned in the middle of a large clearing. I could see waves of energy coming off them, radiating into an electric blue sky. The beauty was stunning. Quickly I noticed a moving silhouette on top of one of the boulders and realized it was Doña Bernadina, playfully dancing around and twirling her bright skirts up into the air. Perry was in the shadows, at the base of the boulder looking up, snapping shots of her dramatic spontaneous movements with his camera. Seemingly unaffected by our climb, Doña Bernadina was warming up for her performance as the rest of the group started reaching the summit. She is usually a bit of a ham and I could tell that she was enjoying putting on a show for

Figure 14. Doña Bernadina dancing (photo by Perry Edwards)

all of us. Doña Bernadina twirled in circles, lifted her brightly colored skirts, and nimbly kicked her legs into the air as she danced above the boulders.

I watched as she flipped her long shiny braid of hair back and forth behind her back. Similar to a young girl becoming a ballerina, Doña Bernadina appeared to be extremely pleased with herself as we all viewed her performance. She was enjoying the fact that we had all become captivated by her charm and her stamina. Knowing how to work the situation, Doña Bernadina lightheartedly began calling out, "Inka Cola, chocolate," playfully demanding payment for the show. I marveled to myself that this woman was a grandmother several times over! Perry was laughing, as he took shot after shot of her, pretending to be a professional photographer. I think maybe Doña B actually thought that he was.

When things settled down, we found places to sit and began working with our *mesas* in the powerful boulder field. The boulders seemed to send their energy into my stones as I worked with them. I could feel energy waves all around me in that high clearing. Afterwards, we made our way down the mountain and plopped ourselves back on our bus.

We stopped for lunch at another local restaurant that was offering a buffet. Before sitting down, I went over to the cooler of soda pop and returned with a bottle of Inka Cola for Doña Bernadina, in payment for her performance. She smiled happily. I brought back a second bottle for Asunta, who does not like being the center of attention but deserved an Inka Cola too.

10. Hallpay

While our mental link existed, the potential to experience the body-oriented state left. The connection could no longer be sensed, only remembered and talked about.

—Nathan Schwartz-Salant

July 7, 2011

When I woke up in the morning, I discovered that I was running a fever and did not have the energy to pull myself out of bed. I quickly became aware that I was not going anywhere today and was grateful that the trek to Ausangate had not begun. I asked Perry to find Doña Bernadina and ask her to come to the room with the hope that she could treat my condition.

About ten minutes later, Perry came back with her and she had her customary oversized bundle slung over her shoulder. She came over to the bed where I was lying, gave me a hug, kissed my cheek, and then looked at me questioningly. I explained my symptoms to her in a process of charades. I made motions of clutching my stomach, acting as though I would vomit. I then tightened my fingers in the area over my stomach and made sounds to indicate the sharp pains I was feeling, followed by dropping my head and shoulders to give the impression of fatigue. I looked at her and said, "No *kausay*," before slumping back onto the pillow.

Doña Bernadina looked at me, said "Ah," and nodded. She started saying, "Piss, piss." After I looked at her quizzically, she ran into the bathroom ostensibly looking for something. She came back empty-handed. Apparently she had not able to find what she was looking for. Doña Bernadina then began to make the sound of urinating and made a downward gestural motion between her legs.

I realized that "piss" literally meant piss. It then occurred to me that she had been looking for a glass. I got up and retrieved a glass, buried under a pile of towels on top of the bathroom counter. Doña Bernadina nodded enthusiastically. Seemingly this is what she had been looking for. Then Doña Bernadina told me in Spanish that Perry needed to piss in the glass and that I needed to drink a little of it and rub some on my belly as well. I looked at her pleadingly, trying not to make a disgusted gesture, but hoping that she would find some other treatment for my condition.

Using hand motions, I explained to her that I had received a rather intense energy transmission at Pachatusan. She nodded and asked me which *paqo* had performed the cleansing ritual. I told her Don André. Doña Bernadina responded quickly, "Uno momento," and swiftly disappeared out of the room. Minutes later, she came running back in with a small plastic bottle. She poured Perry's urine out of the glass, rinsed it out, and poured a small amount of water from one of the bottles I had purchased the day before. Doña Bernadina then opened the plastic bottle she came in with and poured a small amount of it into the glass with the water.

Other than being orange and smelling like an herbal concoction, I had no idea what I was about to drink. I decided that it was probably better that way. Doña Bernadina motioned for me to drink the contents of the glass, which I did. Anything was better than drinking Perry's urine. Doña Bernadina then poured some of the liquid from the plastic bottle into her hands. She placed her hands in front of my face and ordered me to inhale

Don Sebastian, Jose Luis, Don Francisco (Brad VonWagenen)

Machu Picchu (Rana Dewall)

Beginning of the journey to Ausangate (Frances Marron)

Sigrena Cocha (Devin Arnold)

Ausangate camp (Devin Arnold)

Ardiel and apachetta (Devin Arnold)

Judy Bath, Mari Spiegelman, Deborah Bryon, and Tatiana Jacob
(Perry Edwards)

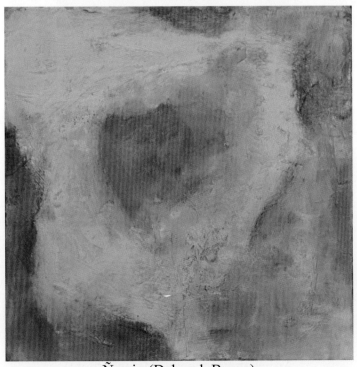

Ñawin (Deborah Bryon)

four times. After following her instructions, Doña Bernadina rubbed the liquid all over my head, including my hair and face. Next, she poured the liquid into my hands and motioned me to rub my hand together and to deeply inhale the odor. After I had done as I had been told, Doña smiled at me and quickly left the room. I fell back to sleep right away and slept soundly for eight hours. Upon awakening, I still felt exhausted but my stomach pain was gone.

Although I did not attend the healing ritual or the *apu* session with Juanito on July 7, my fellow travelers, Carol Dearborn, Marti Speigelman, and Judy Bath, shared their transcriptions. The summary of the session that day is compiled from their notes.

We walked up and stopped in the deep, dried-up riverbed for the Luminous Body Ceremony, which involved anchoring *kausay* to the land.

The ceremony itself is described in the following exercise. While this is not a beginner's ceremony, at some point those who follow the Andean medicine path will most likely have the opportunity to perform this ceremony for others beginning to follow the quest to learn how to honor Pachamama.

Exercise 9. The Luminous Body Ceremony (as recorded by Carol, Marti, and Judy)

Materials used in the ceremony:

White powder (used for church whitewash) symbolizing male *kausay* from the sun

Red soil from the land (symbolizing the feminine)

Red and white carnations and geraniums

Holy water from Señor de Huanca (the church at the base of Pachatusan)

Red yarn and black yarn

Two big clay pots were filled with the soils

Description of the Procedure:

The left foot from the knee down was cleansed by a *paqo* using a red flower with water, while calling on the spirits of the land and *apus*. Next, red dirt was applied to the left leg, calling on *kausay* (life force) and spirits. The left ankle was then tied with red string. Working with the left side of the body was done to stimulate *kausay*. The red soil was used for calling on the "deep Belly" places of the Pachamama in the land to bring forth *kausay*. This process was repeated then with the white clay and black yarn for the right side. After the *paqo* had completed the procedure, feet were dried off and we sat in silent prayer with our feet drying in the sun. The *apus* and Pachamama were called, while we anchored ourselves in our *mesas*. The remaining water and flowers were offered in *ayni* to the riverbed.

After the luminous-body cleansing ceremony was completed, the group left for Chincheros. Chincheros is an archeological complex, filled with sacred shrines, temples, terracing, and breathtaking views. It was the designated date of the next healing ceremony.

At Chincheros, Jose Luis laid the groundwork for the ceremony for connection to Sawasiray:

As a medicine person, you have to have an engine that will create relations. Our ego states and trance states need identities. The ego tries to find new relations with qualities the individual lacks. The driving mythology is scarcity. The relationship with life needs to be open — then life can claim you and you bloom!

How does our knowledge of relationship with Pachamama help us with more qualities of relationship? *Mesas* are made from the events that have gone through healing and now have become tools. The *mesa* is the living embodiment of land. You come here to Peru to retrieve yourself. Don Manuel Q'uispe would say that the mountain has been calling you. So, you are now here to reclaim that piece of you that has already been here. The quality of relationship will unfold later.

Your *khuyas* may have been a dinosaur. The *khuyas* witnessed more, beyond time — quantum timelessness. This knowledge is still latent — it is not held in form. *Yanantin* refers to relationship — a relationship with mountain. How can this relationship assist us?

Then Jose Luis led the ceremony of connection to Sawasiray.

Exercise 10. Ceremony of Connection to Sawasiray

(as recorded by Carol, Marti, and Judy)

The beginner lies down with the *mesa* under his or her head — at the medulla oblongata. This is the space where the beginner's dream body leaves. *Paqos* establish *cekes* between the beginner and Sawasiray so that they can begin to work with relationships. The *cekes* will be between the Belly, Heart, and Mind — then they will blow into the crown. The crown will create a state of *tinquy* relationship with the mountain Sawasiray. The *paqos* will use bells and *mesas* with each energy center in the body, and will then breathe into the students' crown with the *mesa*. Following the ceremony, everyone goes to the various locations of rock formations, sits, and weaves themselves and their *mesa* to Sawasiray with k'*intus*.

While this is a ceremony performed with a particular mountain, similar ceremonies may be used with newly awakened mountains in other parts of the world when the student is ready to start leading.

Adolfo has talked about related rituals of connection. According to Adolfo, there are four kinds of relationships that bring connection through practicing *hallpay*.

The first type of *hallpay* is called *sapan hallpay*, which occurs between an individual and Pachamama. A ritual of *sapan hallpay* is a personal meditation that involves opening the energy centers of the Belly, Heart, and Mind, as a means of connecting with the greater cosmos. The *sapan hallpay* creates the opportunity to become open to receiving messages from the spirits. Engaging in the ritual of *sapan hallpay* at the start of the day is a personal offering and way of connecting with the spirits. Using intention to initiate an energetic connection, an offering is made before asking for information. As information is received through the practice of individual *hallpay*, an internal transformation takes place that brings balance. This is something that you can do daily or every other day, depending on the time that you have available to do this.

The second type of *hallpay* is *yanantin hallpay*, which is a complement of opposites, involving connection between a man and a woman. This is a practice of masculine and feminine energies working together in a state of union, with balance and harmony. *Yanantin* encompasses finding stability in different aspects of daily life. It represents equilibrium and accessing the vitality of *kausay* through maintaining steadiness in thoughts, feelings, and actions. According to Adolfo, this includes matters involving love, health, and work — especially if you are a teacher. In the practice of *yanantin hallpay*, each person opens his or her fountain of energy. The blending of energy brings a connection between masculine and feminine that joins with the energy of the cosmos.

Another form of *hallpay* that occurs between two people is called *masintin hallpay*. The practice of *masintin hallpay* is between two similar energies. *Masintin* demonstrates equality and consistency. The ritual of bringing two energies together enables the spirits to assist us in maintaining balance and working in harmony. Two people working together in the practice support the implementation of the *hallpay* ceremony by complementing what is missing or deficient — whether it is masculine or feminine.

Traditionally, the practice of *hallpay* involves two people feeding one another coca leaves by making a *k'intu* offering that has been fed with energy by the people who are making the

Figure 15. Adolfo performing the ritual of *hallpay* (photo by Rodolfo Ttito Condori)

offering. Whenever an offering is made, it is necessary to hold a clear intention for connection. Incan ancestors performed this ceremony before discussions, as a way of opening dialogue in right relationship, in *ayni*.

The last type of relationship is called *yaqui hallpay* and involves the *ayllu* or community. *Yaqui hallpay* is a way for everyone in a group to support Pachamama. *Yaqui hallpay* is a way of experiencing the energetic union living in community. There is always more power when a community is unified. Adolfo has said that when we work together, we can achieve many things because each person in a community contributes a thought that can serve as a seed of knowledge. The practice of *yaqui hallpay* increases the energy available for everyone to share. The greatest potential for expression of energy happens in a group.

Exercise 11. Practice of *Hallpay* (from Adolfo)

At the start of the day, *hallpay* is performed. *Hallpay* can also be repeated a couple of times in the middle of the day to maintain connection with the cosmos and for balancing energy centers. By doing the work of the *hallpay* and making these offerings on this daily basis, your energy centers will begin to open, enabling you to start to see and learn more things. You will find new knowledge, new thoughts, more understanding of the spiritual cosmology by expanding the Heart with love, with *munay*. You can also perform *hallpay* at the start of ceremonies or to improve the relationship with someone you want to work with.

In the actual ritual of *hallpay*, after calling sacred space and purifying yourself by rubbing your hands with Florida water, you begin by making a *k'intu* using three leaves grouped together. (In Peru coca leaves are used, but bay leaves can be substituted. Adolfo has said that using mint leaves is also fine.) Stems should be down with the leaves facing up, with the smallest leaf on top. The three leaves represent each of the three worlds, the lower world of Ukhu Pacha, the middle world of Kay Pacha, and the upper world of Hanaq Pacha. Next, taking a deep breath, blow your blessings into the *k'intu*, imbuing the leaves with power from each of the three energy centers, the Belly, Heart, and Mind, using clear intention and focus. This is known as *phukuy*.

Then, make the offering of the *k'intu* as a gift. When you feed Pachamama, it is called *sapan*. *Yanantin* is for opposite energies of masculine and feminine. *Masintin* involves similar energies where you wish to support each other by strengthening areas that may be weak. When you make an offering for your brothers and sisters together, you create a stronger union for your community. This is called *yaqui*.

Practicing *hallpay* will strengthen and deepen your connection to Pachamama, the universal feminine energy. The practice of *hallpay* will enable you to connect with the spirits of the plants, the element of water, lightning, the moon, stars, and everything living around you — even some of the stars are celestial angels. Without the practice of *hallpay*, you do not have a ritual to open yourself up and be available. You must feel the energy, the force of this *kausay* in order for transformation to take place and for you to strengthen your spiritual connection. Through *hallpay*, your energy field is automatically restored and balanced. The spirits will support you and help you continue in your work, when you invoke the spirits with the *hallpay*.

You can practice *hallpay* anytime when you feel the need — at the beginning, in the middle, or at the end of any ceremony. It is beneficial to begin your meditation with *hallpay*, and especially at times when you feel the need for extra support. It is good to perform *hallpay* in the middle of a ceremony, as well as when you are finishing the work. *Hallpay* is an act of gratitude and devotion, a way of acknowledging and thanking the spirits and Pachamama for their help and guidance.

I used Carol's notes to write this description of the afternoon session with the *apus* that visit Juanito's *mesa*. Apu Chupícuaro, Apu Cruz Pata, Apu Ausangate, Apu Misti, Apu Sokllacasa, and Apu Potosi each arrived and introduced themselves.

Cruz Pata: **How is everything going?**

Jose Luis: Well, thank you.

Cruz Pata: **Take advantage of good days.**

Someone visiting the *apus* for the first time asked, With young medicine, how do we deepen our ability to hold this experience?

Chupícuaro replied:

First, age or size does not matter — age, training, where you are, none of that. How you carry your medicine is what matters. I mentioned this in our first meeting; you need to be stewards of your own momentum. Be the steward of your own pacing. You have to have gentle understanding for self. You are embarking on a way of life that is far different from what you have experienced in consensual reality. This might be your soul or Heart call. The first stage might deal with elements. To live in a way that life can be full is a good vision. It is energizing. You need to merge with the river of life. Bless the tears that you cry.

What is important is that you need to fly; you cannot walk as you have for eons. You will understand the revelations as you fly. There will be a process of opening of your own inner knowingness that is the mechanics of flight. One small theme to consider is that as you see the horizon, it may seem far. The horizon, the objective, the goal is really a function of your availability. It is up to you.

Cruz Pata continued:

I have something to add. I have to appreciate the Heart and pursuit of steadfast focus in your journeys. Give yourself freedom to craft your own rituals to step away from your normal makeup. Ritual will allow you to connect and exercise presence, and you will feel energy. Maintain the focus through the ritual. Make everything a ritual at all times.

Another person asked:

I understand *apus* reside in other dimensions. When we die, do we go the same or different dimension as the *apus*?

Chupícuaro replied:

You do not have to die to do that. We are in the dreamtime. There are many dimensions within. Here, it is a simple state of deepening your own conscious state. When you are young children, you used to fly — do you remember? As adults, do you? You had the capability, but your energy had to be reallocated into other themes — problems, etc., and the other energy eroded. However, there is a solution. Go back to earlier memory. There is a path to regain your wings.

Jose Luis spoke:

Unfortunately, we live in a cultural paradigm that has models of identity that we submit to. Life is mechanistic, robotic. Our own creativity, our innocence has been taken from us. You can go back into child memory where you were in a state of elevated innocence where everything is possible. There are many ways to go back. Use your *khuyas*. Some of you have already tasted that state of innocence unbeknownst to you. Concentrate — can you feel the energy coming in? Can you perceive the gateways? Use your *mesa* to access the power.

Here's a simple way — open your *mesa*, light a white candle, and place your hand on top of *khuyas*. Bring the energy of the *khuya* that has witnessed expansions of time. There is primordial energy that you can call upon. Do this for 15 minutes.

The next question was asked:

Taripay Pacha is the impediment to achieving this state — a loss of innocence — or is there something else there?

Chupícuaro answered:

It depends on each person, independently and collectively. It begins with the individual. Taripay Pacha has to do with igniting your inner fire, your *fuego sagrado*. Taripay Pacha has been in motion already. It is how you find your trail. You have started — it is visible in your *mesa*. Taripay Pacha implies a new era, time, life, set of tools for creation to shift. A new way of doing life. It has been heralded. You can choose to have Taripay Pacha today. It is up to the individual today. Many cultures — for example, the Mayan, the Incas — they have their own way of collective intelligence. Culture is only culture. This is about a maskless time of change — beyond identity, beyond theology. It is the awakening of your inner knowing. It begins within. You might look at it as a change of name, but it goes deeper.

I have something further to add. The *mesa*, you have to bring it to life. You might be asking, "Why am I not an *altomesayoq*? Why am I not calling the *apus*?" You need to empower stones. First, map the land. Know the geography that deals with the powers in the land. Then, empower your *mesa* with it. A *pampamesayoq* has to be a healer who provides healing energy from the land. You are a conduit of this energy. *Mesas* can look pretty — but — they need power. You have to use them to bring forth healing energy. The power of Ausangate has to go home with you. This is your time. Use it. Your *mesas* need to be ignited individually. Ignite — alive and active — in interaction with you.

Little *mesas*, big *mesas*, beautiful, ugly — you live in a society of comparisons. You have forgotten that you are children of the land.

There is no comparison. Comparisons generate distinction. You have forgotten the ancient memory of collectivity. Individuals of power are collective — in the new time we need to be collective. There is no other way. Whatever you bring forward from an individual position will only be short-lived.

The difference of the *mesa* of the *pampamesayoqs* is that *pampamesayoqs* create *despachos* and do healings. The *altomesayoq* invokes. I will talk about the *pampamesayoq's mesa*. What people forget, it is not the actual *despacho*; it is the love in the creation. It is the emotion, the feeling that brings transformation. If it is commercial with no feeling, no Heart, then no healing will take place. It is about the capacity to generate Heart — *tukuy munayniyoc*. Traditionally, an *altomesayoq* is an individual who has mastered the ways of the *pampamesayoqs*. Working as an *altomesayoq* entails responsibility. You are given power through being in light, in destiny. You will be thrown off if you become seduced by your own power. At the end of the day, the relationship between *altomesayoq* and spirit is a two-way relationship that should always be an open-ended map. If it becomes a closed system, then energy is not flowing. Power has to do with free flow, expansive with the breath of life.

Another question was asked: Communities are failing, what is our role?

Chupícuaro continued:

This is a natural predicament of communities. In order for our societies to change, a new paradigm needs to be created. Nature is in process of deconstructing itself to be reconstructed. It is always a process. This new cultural paradigm is out of personal choice. We need to erase ideas of good or evil — that is a concept that only lives in the Hearts of people. We have polarized our understanding of love. A new alignment is needed with a spiritual paradigm. We then begin again.

For example, language creates our belief systems. It is what separates us from life. You need to be watchful how you use naming. Learn language that is more in tune with the visible and invisible — in tune with our organic nature. All conflict and warfare is a result of differences in belief pertaining to the word. You need to evolve back into your true nature. Look at the education you give to children. You are passing on violence and fear — you are so irresponsible.

A follow-up question was asked:

As we engage in cosmic pursuits, how we can fortify and protect our physical bodies as we are exposed to toxins?

Chupícuaro replied:

You can lock yourself in a dark room, or stand tall and fight. Live life to the fullest — live with such presence and fullness that you generate that type of energy. You will be fine. Create meaning in your life. You are born, live, and die and what have you done? This is life. Be frontal in life. Bring order to your inner self. Alignment, clarity is what is called for. If this is not present, life will ruin you.

Chupícuaro's next comment was directed to Jose Luis:

You know your horse wranglers?

Jose Luis: Yes.

Chupícuaro:

They were a different way in the past, now they are different again. Here is a parable: A mule driver and his assistant had a large group of mules they were driving. They arrived late in the day and set up camp. The animals were feeding, and the boss called to the assistant, "Night is coming, rope up all the mules so they don't run away in the night." Therefore, the assistant went around pounding stakes into the ground, tying each animal to a stake. When he reached the thirtieth animal, there were no more ropes or stakes to be found. "What do we do?" asked the assistant. The boss replied, "Just pretend that you have the materials and pound an invisible stake into the ground, and tie up the animal with an invisible rope." So the assistant proceeded to do as he was directed. The next morning, the assistant loaded the animals with their packs and undid the tied up animals. Well, the first thirty animals began to move with their packs into line along the trail. The remainder of the mules remained in place as if tied to their invisible stakes. Again, the assistant asked the boss, "What do we do?" The boss replied, "Go and untie the imaginary ropes from the imaginary stakes." The assistant did as he was directed, and the remaining mules moved freely into line.

Chupícuaro then asked Jose Luis:

What do you think?

Jose Luis answered:

Customs run deep.

Chupícuaro:

Hmm, yes. And what do your sons and daughters say (referring to the group)?

Various responses included:

Intention...We don't know how easy it is to be tied down...The boss had a bigger vision...We are like a pack horse...What are my guiding mythologies?...Reality and imagination are the same thing.

Chupícuaro responded:

In order to build, we have to overpower nature. We build, take down, and rebuild. We see walls through our own walls. In order to participate, we need to bring down our own inner walls. You cannot see from only one lens of perception, there is more to it. Undo the walls that hold your own inner understanding, only then can you see you are free. The challenge is to think beyond what you perceive. Do not get trapped in the reality of being born, getting married, buying a house, having a mortgage, being in the hospital, and then dying. Liberate yourself — celebrate life! Faith, power, will — you have to use it. This is your time. Stop worrying if you left your cat at home with no milk. This is your time. The journey is what is unfolding out of your deep love. A journey of liberty is what it takes — like Buddha, Christ. If you maintain an open-ended map, it will not be polarized by good or bad.

The *apu* session ended.

11. Machu Picchu

The apus *generally are masculine and Pachamama is feminine. Together they work in harmony and balance. The height of the* apus *is about the relationship to the cosmos, to the celestial, so it is because of their height that they are associated with that connection. It is almost as if they bring that energy down.*

—Adolfo Ttito Condori

July 8, 2011

Bright and early, our guide Hamilton herded several of us to the train station in Ollantaytambo to take the train to Machu Picchu, known as the "light city of the Incas." It was built in the 1400s before the Spanish arrived. After we had boarded the train and found our assigned seats, Hamilton informed us that Machu Picchu would be especially busy this week because it was the peak of the tourist season. Yesterday happened to be the 100-year anniversary of when the site was first discovered by the historian Hiram Bingham. Because Machu Picchu is now considered one of the Seven Wonders of the World, Hamilton warned us that the anniversary celebration was a huge tourist attraction, and that there would be a lot of people.

Riding on the rattling train, winding through the picturesque river valley of Urubamba was like a trip back through time into a

145

primeval river gorge. Enormous boulders, the size of buildings were strewn in the middle of the river that rumbled down the ravine. Many of the monolithic stones appeared as graceful sculptures, masterfully carved into beautiful curved shapes by the pummeling torrents of the river. The water had transported them down the valley, placing them in an orchestrated arrangement. At times, they were piled in clusters, like children playfully competing in a game of King of the Hill.

Perry said that it was hard to imagine the force necessary to have achieved this. He kept his nose glued to the train window most of the time, but occasionally turned around exclaiming, "This is incredible!" or, "I just saw a killer dinosaur bone!" Several nose prints dotted the window, but he did not seem to notice or care as his eyes locked on the river show in his own state of intense observation. He did not even notice when we got off the train at Aguas Calientes that his window had lots of nose prints all over it, and all the other windows were clean. Sometimes Perry leaves a trail behind him when he is comfortably absorbed in things —and the trail can be everywhere.

The train pulled into the busy station of Aguas Calientes, where people were swarming all over the station. In single file, carrying backpacks filled with sunscreen, bug spray, *mesas*, sweaters, sandwiches, and water, we clamored off the train and wove our way through the crowds with Hamilton leading the way.

Hamilton led our entourage of seven or eight people onto one of the shuttle buses heading for Machu Picchu. There were many buses running as shuttles, back and forth between the station and the entrance to the site. Rows of them were efficiently parked at the front of the entrance to Machu Picchu, in a formation like a fleet of ships waiting to take the next load of people back down the hill to the Aguas Calientes train station.

The number of buses was an indication of the multitudes of people that we would soon be encountering. Hamilton ushered us off the bus to the entrance, through hordes of tour groups parked at the front gate. I was pleased that Hamilton was so quick at navigating us through the front entrance. He was a small man who made decisive moves, so our group became like a snake, slithering our way through the crowd.

We rapidly discovered that the steep, narrow path leading up to Inihuatana, the Hitching Post of the Sun entrance, was packed with even more tourists. I noticed that I was beginning to feel uncomfortably hot and slightly claustrophobic, sandwiched in the middle of a pack of wall-to-wall people — at a standstill. Perry said it was like a Grateful Dead concert that he had been to in his early twenties — except he didn't smell any pot.

Standing literally inches in front of me, an attractive, dark-haired woman wearing sweet-smelling floral perfume, sunglasses, and a wide-brimmed straw hat was enthusiastically saying something in Italian to her friend who was squeezed in next to her, making expressive hand gestures, apparently to prove a point. Directly behind me, a large man, who I could tell was not wearing deodorant, kept randomly colliding into me, the result of his being pushed forward by the surging crowd behind him. In a chain reaction, I in turn was pushed into the hat of the woman ahead of me, bumping into it with my nose. Perry cut in front of the non-deodorant man and held my shoulders steady from behind, guiding me like a bumper car though the chaos.

As this was going on, in the periphery of my vision I noticed several young and middle-aged male Peruvian workers, wearing dress shoes with no traction on the soles, trying to make their way down the dirt trail on the hill next to our path. They were carrying oversized loads of musical equipment that were three to four feet in length and width. The men were attempting to walk single-file down the steep pathway, precariously balancing their heavy loads. Presumably, the sound system that they were trying to carry down the hill was left over from the fireworks display and celebration that had happened last night.

Because of the chaos in the crowd, most of the people seemed oblivious to the strain of the men carrying their loads. While continuing to hold the weight of the massive speakers and amplifiers, they patiently waited for breaks in the crowd to cut through. Seeing the men struggling gave me a different perspective, and a sense of gratitude. I remembered that I was visiting this sacred site by choice, not working under extremely challenging conditions to support my family, like they were. Even with the heat and the crowds, the stone ruins were amazing, and the opportunity was there to experience deeper connection with Pachamama.

I looked over at Perry who appeared fascinated by the structures and unaffected by the intensity of the crowd of people. The energy of the masses had become somewhat overwhelming for me. As an extrovert, Perry has an easier time dealing with these situations than I do. Perry looked over at me and, noticing my mild distress, and suggested that I focus on blocking out the noise. He has frequently said to me, "It's easy…it's a switch that you just turn off when you are hearing something you don't want to listen to."

On occasion Perry would tell me, "Your problem is, you actually listen. Stop doing that…it causes cell damage. You get caught in a rip tide pulling you out into the ocean of nothing." Right now, I was just looking for the switch.

After another twenty minutes or so of trudging up the hill as a pack, the crowd began thinning out because people were able to disperse in different directions. The small group of us followed Hamilton further up the path to a grassy overlook. After we found an out-of-the-way place to stand, Hamilton began speaking to us: "Do you see over there? Have a look. That wall all the way up was where the noble people stayed. There were flowers, orchids — all kinds of red flowers over there, called *qantuta*. This is now the flower of Peru. The people mostly farmed corn or maize, and during other times pumpkins and beans."

Hamilton explained that the hilltop that Machu Picchu sits on is at an elevation of approximately 8,000 feet (2,400 meters). He said that the stone structures had been strategically divided into three areas for agriculture, living, and religious ceremonies. Even though Machu Picchu had been a retreat for the Incan nobility, 12,000 people may have lived here at one time!

When Hamilton finished his commentary, we made our way up to the highest grassy spot in the area. This overlooked a magnificent valley with a sea of clouds. In the foreground, green terraces held by smaller stones encased the sides of the mountain beneath us.

With Hamilton's consent, Perry and I wandered off by ourselves, away from the groups of tourists. We found a spot to sit off the path behind one of the large stone formations that looked out over the Urubamba Valley. After some time passed, Perry and I made our way down the bank of the grassy hill into one of the enormous stone configurations that defined the various temples, palaces, and sections of the city. After roaming through the living quarters into the area where the Incas performed sacred rituals centuries ago, the commotion of the crowd seemed to fade further into the background and the energetic presence of site came more alive. We were standing in a powerful living *pacha*, in the veil at an intersection of time and space.

I found a comfortable spot and sat on my opened *manta* (poncho) to protect me from the tiny green, biting bugs that blended into the grass. I opened my *mesa* and dropped into connecting with the land through my Belly. I felt my mood beginning to lift and my spirits rising as I looked out across the breathtaking mountain landscape that lay ahead, stretching on for

Figure 16. Macho Picchu (photo by Tom Blaschko)

miles. As I gazed out at the summits that appeared magically out of the sea of mist, I remembered being about four years old and picturing angels living on a floor of clouds. It occurred to me that this landscape was similar to what I had imagined heaven would look like back then.

In Incan cosmology, the universe is considered vertical, consisting of the three stacked lower, middle, and upper worlds. Initially, I had found it somewhat confusing. It had seemed to me that the mountains should be part of the middle world, Kausay Pacha, since they were part of Pachamama. Later I learned that the *apu* mountain spirits reside in the upper world of Hanaq Pacha because the tops of the mountains are higher than the skyline. From this vantage point, it all made sense. The mountain peaks soaring up through the clouds, created the impression that they were actually emerging from the clouds, not the earth.

As I looked at the closer peaks, one in particular drew my attention because it appeared darker than all the rest. At first glance, it appeared to be a vertical black mountain shaped like a lingam, which is a sacred rock used in altars in Hinduism to honor the god Shiva. I squinted to try to make out why it looked different and surmised that it was because it was covered with dense foliage, with the sun positioned as a backdrop. I am not sure what it was about this peek that sparked my interest. It felt oddly familiar, like having a close relationship with an animal that I instinctively knew very well.

As I looked out across the mountain vista, I permitted the focus of my vision to soften and blur a little. I sank into a more relaxed state. I began to notice bright pinpoints of light particles dancing across my field of vision. These began growing more pronounced and effervescent, gradually gaining in intensity. A sense of being in liminal space between the two worlds of past and present — and between ordinary and non-ordinary reality — unexpectedly grew more acute. After some time passed, I noticed that the sun had drifted down closer to the horizon and was now casting elongated shadows on the stones. Perry and I motioned to each other that it was time to leave. After silently gathering our belongings, we made our way back to the bus to find Hamilton. The size of the crowds had diminished considerably and the temperature was pleasantly cooling off. We made our way back to the Sacred Valley the same way we had come. Another day had passed.

12. In Maras

When we work together, we can achieve many things. Every person in a community contributes a thought that can serve as a seed of knowledge or a practice such as a hug that can bring joy and happiness. These gestures build the power of the energy available to be shared by everyone.

— Adolfo Ttito Condori

July 9, 2011

At dawn, we met the *paqos* for breakfast before returning to Maras to work with Doña Alejandrina and the *apu* benefactors of her *mesa*. At breakfast, I alternated between drinking coca tea and strong dark coffee with milk because I like them both. Perry already had decided that he was not a huge fan of coca tea and was staying with the thick black coffee. In general — like many of us — Perry tends to be a creature of habit and drinking coca tea had not become part of his routine.

Sitting at the breakfast table next to me, Perry was preoccupied. He was busily jotting notes in a race to capture remnants of last night's dreams before they completely faded from memory. I looked across the breakfast room cafeteria at the silhouettes of the *paqos'* stocky figures standing in the morning sunlight that was streaming through the entrance. The brisk morning air was warming with the rising sun.

3

54   *Lessons of the Inca Shamans, Part 2*

I watched Don Sebastian and Don André saying something in Quechua to Don Hilario who kept silently nodding his head. There must have been some humor in what was being said because Don Hilario began to smile and Don Sebastian and Don André started laughing. Except when they are in sacred ceremony, the *paqos* that I have worked with tend to be playful, good-hearted pranksters who are always looking for opportunities to laugh and have fun. Although Don Hilario is usually the quietest and most serious of the three, his face still frequently breaks into a broad grin when he finds something funny. The three of them wandered out into the courtyard to gather up the textiles and traditional items that they had laid out on the grass earlier to sell.

When we arrived in Maras, Doña Alejandrina greeted us at a wooden gate sitting several feet from the street. As usual, she was wearing a red sweater with black slacks. As we walked into the interior courtyard, Doña Alejandrina welcomed each of us with a bear hug, inspecting us closely as we meandered through the door and into the courtyard. We plopped down onto the grass, organizing blankets and digging into backpacks for notepads. When everyone was settled, Doña Alejandrina began speaking:

The vision of the *apus* must have a multiplying effect on people. The church is less strong. It is the time of the return of the children of the land. In the stage where we are, the *apus* are making themselves known. The *apus* have been the keepers of the old ways of living, an evolution of a new collective. It is time for the voices of the ancient ones to return. This new dawn is the time of the collective.

Loneliness occurred when the sky god came and left. The sky gods are our Minds.

Westerners have paid homage to the sky god. Know that this practice does not allow for growing corn. The new messengers, *paqos* and *altomesayoqs* will be people like you. The next *altomesayoqs* chosen will be a man and a woman.

There are currently eleven *altomesayoqs* living in Peru. In Peru, one has to be careful when becoming a shaman. It is not an identity. Children of *paqos* do not want to carry lineage. The *apus* have said that there is a window from 1992 until 2023 to produce a dialogue and open a new doorway. The sacred merges into the mundane, and spirit and body come together. This will change everything when there is a sacrificing of life in service of the sacred.

We are going to have a conversation with the mountain spirits. If you have a question, bring it into the room. Make it a good one that we can all learn from. It is nice to hear the answer from the source. The last time we touched on lineages, clans, who we belonged to. Any questions now? Please ask.

I asked Doña Alejandrina about what I frequently experience in my body during meetings with the *apus*. I explained to her that at times I felt myself shifting into an awareness of an energetic state that seemed to lie underneath words being spoken. I said that I had noticed that while one part of me was attending to the *apus'* words, nonverbal energetic communication that I was experiencing in my body was occurring simultaneously. I asked her to comment on the experience of toggling back and forth between the two states. Doña Alejandrina responded to me by saying:

It is necessary to weave harmony between the Belly, Heart, and Mind. The universe will be more discernible if the Heart and Mind are in a harmonious state — fifty percent matter and fifty percent spirit. This is a technique of equilibrium influenced by the mental makeup of our people determined by our culture. Westerners spend more time in their heads while in Peru people live more in their Hearts.

Doña Alejandrina went on to explain that modern technology keeps our minds busy. There is a reenactment occurring in the daily experience of living in the modern world, and one day we will learn to fill the void through our Bellies.

Perry then asked Doña Alejandrina:

Is the *apu* glacier ice more sacred because of the elevation and no interference from human activity?

Doña Alejandrina responded to Perry by saying:

Glaciers have been sitting there for a while and less of a human imprint is present. If it is a holy mountain and at the summit, the energy is potent there. It can make you dizzy. The energy is different because of that purity.

Another question was asked:

The *apus* are making themselves available — is this by trying to understand the collective, as well as individual purpose of this journey?

Doña Alejandrina answered:

Very simple. The vision of the *apus* is the gift they bring that has a multiplying effect on people. One vision, I do not know it directly, but Hernando [her assistant in *apu* sessions] tells me, that for Huascaran [the *apu* benefactor of her *mesa*], the driving vision is of multiplying the vision blessing that he offers to you. You need to bring the blessing to someone else — walking on the street or wherever.

Vision concerning the collective and individuals such as us involves layers that are not in any specific order. This is a result of the new *pachakuti* [period of cosmic transformation] that we are emerging into. This collective time is ending. The new time holds the return of Inkari — children of the land, children of light.

Gods, spirit benefactors have always been keepers of animals and plants. This is the time for the Sky God that has been invented by man to go away. Sky God is the Mind, the sense of self-searching. It is the time for communal collectivity in this land, in vision together. Loneliness is here because of Sky God's creation — individuals. We are returning to the collective and the hands of the Church are subsiding. It is time for us medicine people to return. The return of the ancient ones is needed now. In this stage of social unrest, it is time for the *apus* to make themselves known once again.

Why they are revealing themselves to us? Because we understand that our Sky God is not growing corn. Locals here in Peru are still in the process of creating a Sky God. People in the West have already gone through this process, so the *apus* are now revealing to Westerners. The reason that the *apus* are revealing so openly is based upon the hope that the new messengers [the new *altomesayoqs*] will be individuals such as you.

The collective of Peru must go through the process of redefining themselves as medicine people. Be careful not to point fingers — is being *paqo* the coolest? Is it economical gain? We are talking about new messengers of medicine.

Peru is going through a process of discernment. Currently there are economical changes affecting us here in Peru. The children do not want to continue the legacy. Again, this window of opportunity is open from 1992 to 2020-ish. The *apus* are open. Perhaps one of you is in their eye to bring this medicine to your community. My personal opinion is that the angel spirits would love to be benefactors. Perhaps you will become a doorway in the process of witnessing, I try to be a regular person, but there is another thing in me that I recognize in ceremony.

Next, Doña Alejandrina described the experience of the *altomesayoq* in ceremony.

In the merging, when the angel comes in, if spirituality is fit and strong it comes through the feet. The spirits of the land come and fill you. This is what calls the other spirits. It is a process of adaptation, of merging of two diametrical conversations. When one can produce the dialogue, it becomes the doorway. Study, have an open Heart, and prepare. I am not able to tell which of you — I am only a doorway. The sacred merging into the sacred body. *Yarrow* means "sacred;" *gamen* means "merging." This changes your outlook in life; it changes everything. Surrendering life in service of the sacred and knowing how the sacred comes into your life.

Doña Alejandrina closed the discussion before we met with the *apus* by saying:

In this session, we will bring a couple of *apus*. When there is energy that comes to you, capture the energy using your breath and blow the energy into a *khuya*. Later, download the information by lighting a white candle and work with stone to download the information. The stone and candle create a *ceke* path to access the information. The information will be flying around — catch it by using your breath.

Still sitting out in the grassy courtyard, we made our preparations to meet with the *apus*. As usual, we removed all of the metal and electronic objects that we had been wearing or carrying in our pockets and placed them inside of our backpacks, which we stored in a nearby storage room. After we had double-checked ourselves to make sure that we were not carrying any metal, we gathered our *mesas* along with the layers of additional clothing we had brought with us and moved into the small room where ceremonies were held. We placed our *mesas* on the table altar at the front of the room and found seats on the wooden benches.

Before the ceremony began, Doña Alejandrina told us to prepare for a healing by consciously bringing forth any negativity that we were ready to release from the basement of our luminous body. Perry and I agreed to hold the intention of asking for the removal of anything that was preventing us from joining as open channels in *yanantin*.

A couple of years ago, I had a vision during a trip to the sacred Anasazi Indian site of Mesa Verde in southwestern Colorado. I was told that energetically joining, by holding together the elements of masculine and feminine energy, magnified power. Since then, we had practiced working together in the sacred space by becoming a joint conduit to hold the numinous energy that was coming through. Perry and I had each developed our own ways of entering into non-ordinary reality, and like two dance partners that are used to leading, attuning to the rhythm of the other's energy pattern was awkward. Part of the motivation for taking this journey together was to learn how to merge together and balance in *yanantin*. Before the session, Perry and I both reaffirmed our intention to the *apus* and Pachamama.

Waiting in the cold, pitch-black room, I could hear Perry breathing softly next to me. As usual, I appreciated the warmth of his body on my right side. I was comforted by holding his rough but gentle hand. I felt a wave of gratefulness wash over me, remembering again that Perry had finally made it to Peru with me.

My mind began to drift back to memories of events that had happened in our lives ten years ago, soon after Perry and I decided to pursue the path of shamanism. In the darkness, I replayed aspects of our journey that were extremely arduous for both of us. It uprooted our lives and belief systems, as well as the initial foundation our relationship was built on. The sequence of life events that happened during that time felt out of control. Perry had entered a manic state and I had felt pulled in the opposite direction — down into the underworld.

The subsequent journey brought me to primal places in my psyche where I was forced to face my own internal demons of darkness. During this period, my father died suddenly from a stroke, my younger son developed a serious drug addiction that frightened all of us, and my oldest son was injured trying to protect him. I consider this period as my encounter with the shadow, the era of the Black Snake.

After the period of dismemberment that led to our temporary separation, Perry and I found a way to come back together and began rebuilding our lives with each other. The ordeal that we experienced together stripped away many of our previous attachments to material comforts. Ultimately, having to let this go brought an unexpected sense of freedom. The illusions of what I had believed I needed to survive emotionally and contextually were forcibly removed. Aspects of my personal shadow that I tried to bury, that lived in my unconscious psyche, emerged —

Figure 17. Birdman (painting by Deborah Bryon)

like a genie being released from a bottle. An overwhelming, deep-seated childhood fear of abandonment became the worthy opponent that I was forced to face in the daylight, that I overcame in the process of learning to source from Pachamama and my inner ally, the Birdman.

Remembering my connection with Pachamama and the Birdman suddenly brought me back into the present.

As we continued to wait for the arrival of the *apus*, I tuned into connecting with Perry through our luminous fields. I concentrated on feeding energy to the psychic channel we were creating, while dropping deeper into an altered state.

From her seat in the right front corner of the room next to the altar, Doña Alejandrina began praying quietly to the *apus*. I heard her speaking softly in Spanish, blowing a long, soft whistle between prayers.

Huascaran, the director of Doña Alejandrina's *mesa*, arrived immediately after Doña Alejandrina finished the last of her invocational prayers to summon the *apus*. The familiar flapping of multiple sets of wings flying into the room through the walls was heard. The sound of the wings was accompanied by our voices repeating the customary greeting, "Ave Maria Purisima."

Apus began entering the room so quickly that Jose Luis' words began running together in an attempt to keep up with all of the introductions.

In addition to the sounds of the deep masculine voices of the *apus*, we could also hear the high-pitched feminine voices of the earth spirits, the *santa tierras*, announcing their presence as they came in the room through the dirt floor. I became aware of a current vibrating through the room. It quickly grew stronger as the influx of the winged beings continued.

Several minutes later, the sound of flapping wings died down and the greeting acknowledgments were completed. The *apus* who would be joining us during this session had arrived. (Apu Huascaran, Santa Tierra Belen, Apu Sinaq'ara, Apu Qariwanaku, Apu Sacsayhuaman Cabildo, Apu Chupícuaro, Apu Wanakauri were a few of the *apus* that had appeared.)

The *apus* took turns speaking. The benefactor of Doña Alejandrina's *mesa*, Huascaran, started:

I am content and happy to be with you once more. I will call two more *apus* to help in the purification process. It is necessary to call Machu Picchu, as there have been rituals for the anniversary, rituals for cameras and people. As far as I know, Machu Picchu is 1500 years old, not 100. Machu Picchu.

Apu Sinaq'ara : **Greetings.**

Apu Sacsayhuaman Cabildo: **Greetings.**

Machu Picchu: **Greetings.**

Apu Qariwanaku : **May your *kausay* be vibrant.**

Apu Huascaran: **This is a plural *mesa*. So that I don't take over with Machu Picchu and Santa Tierra Belen, what would you like to do today?**

Jose Luis replied: What is the lineage of the *apus*, of the different expressions? Would you please give us an understanding of the lineage, of the hierarchies, and of where they live? Also, what is the process of selection?

Huascaran responded by saying:

Nature itself has dual aspects, opposing energies. This duality, this hierarchy is in the Catholic Church. There are archangels, angels, seraphim, etc. We belong to the third level in the hierarchies of angels. There are three orders. Angels and archangels belong to the lowest order, and cherubim are the highest.

As you know, there are three worlds, Hanaq Pacha, Kay Pacha, and then us, the mountain angels in Ukhu Pacha. The Ukhu Pacha is entirely terrestrial in the division of three.

In South America, the king of the mountain angels is Salcantay. Salcantay directs all mountains in South America because of its high purity and majesty. Only in certain extraordinary occasions will he come to a *mesa*. Salcantay holds the power of life and death. He is the one that puts blessing at the birth of a new morning. He has power over the four elements and is the one that has direct contact with the celestial *yanantin*.

The second king is Apu Ausangate. There are virtues with each king. The *apus* are between heaven and earth and have love for humanity. Ausangate is the observer and can multiply everything. He has the power to multiply alpacas, sheep, and all that belongs to the Andean community. He can multiply faith, health, intent, presence, and power. If Apu Salcantay is not available, Apu Ausangate takes over.

Some of the *apus* have the job description of being guardians. For instance, there are seven guardians of all regions of Cusco, and all gravitating to the navel of Cusco. Conversely, each village has local *apus*, and in any location those *apus* are easy to pinpoint, these guardians — they stand taller. Do you want me to list them?

Jose Luis: Yes, please.

Huascaran continued:

Apu Sacsayhuaman Cabildo is the main guardian, the keeper of knowledge and wisdom.

Apu Picol is the herder of people.

Apu Senqa, the shape of a nose, is the keeper of water of Cusco. He rules all rainwater, lagoons, and rivers. When the *apu* is cloudy, it will rain in the city.

Apu Qullqi is like an accountant. He is in charge of records of all births, deaths, and all who come to or leave Cusco. He can tell you who will come or who will never come back to Cusco at all.

Apu Pukeen is in charge of all construction, housing construction, and brings the earth up to build a home. When building a home, make offerings to this *apu* to stay on track with the timing of building.

Apu Momma Simona is related to fecundity and fertility. She gives the power of healing to people. Tradition says she is married to the sun because in the city she is the first peak, to receive the sun's rays in the morning. She has a yellow head in the morning. Sometime, it would be good to do a pilgrimage to visit her. The trailhead will have hawks and eagles as you climb. These guides will take you.

Adolfo later explained to me that Momma Simona is one of the mountains neighboring Ausangate. Although it is less common, and not usually discussed in Andean cosmology, some *apus* are feminine. According to Adolfo — different from our guide Hamilton's explanation — the *apu* spirits of the Andean Mountains reside in the middle world, which is different from the celestial ream of the upper world.

Many think that the *apus* are just sitting there but that is not accurate. Our work requires much energy. We work as much as you do. In each pueblo, there are many *apus*. It is nice to acknowledge and greet them. Other *apus* have different functions. Every location, or collective, has to have seven guardians. This relates to the seven energy levels in our cosmology.

Other *apus* that live in the Hanaq Pacha are closer to creation. They live in another energy state. They do not manifest, and they do not use words. They hold Mind-to-Mind conversation with no words. It is fluid when we take messages there. Some *apus* that come from the other dimension do not belong to this third dimension. For example, Apu Corrichaska is from the fourth level. He is in charge of and registers all of the stars in the sky. Corrichaska knows of the soul's vision. One star belongs to each individual that incarnates in the body. Carry out the vision. Corrichaska reawakens the vision. Many individuals offer *despachos* to Corrichaska in order to come closer to their vision. If you are forty years old, you place forty *k'intus* in the *despacho* with a five-pointed starfish in the middle. The *despacho* is then soaked in honey and covered with golden sugar. Corrichaska's love elevates energy and dreams come to you. There is a return of the vision. This might take place in one day to three weeks. Corrichaska's dominion is in the upper realms. Incas had knowledge that a falling star means that new vision is coming into the world — a child being born. If you see fifteen falling stars, fifteen children are being born in that area.

There are some other *apus*, such as Apu Sinaq'ara , that only speak Quechua. *Almakispichi* means that when a person dies, and the soul is wandering and unable to purify, Apu Sinaq'ara will open the door and redirect the soul, nudging the soul in the process of redirection to nature/creation. *Almakispichi* also means "purification." As far as we know, most individuals do not know when they will die, when death will come ambling by. Apu Sinaq'ara has other angels that will come to direct the soul. Angels under guidance come and heal what happened in the soul's physical life so that it can regain purity to return to creation.

Un parlero is a midwife of the dead to be born into the next *pacha*, through ceremony the midwife moves souls from this to the next. We (*apus*) also follow the same pattern. Our *pachas* are much longer. We are born and we die.

Jose Luis: Where is Pachatusan in the seven guardians?

Apu Huascaran responded:

Figure 18. Jose Luis (photo by Brad VonWagenen)

Pachatusan is not only for Cusco. Pachatusan is a very important *apu*. There are guardians that have specific responsibilities. Pachatusan is a portion of the collective and has a larger scope, as part of the universe. Pachatusan is the axis of all local and collective *pachas*. Pachatusan is the axis for happiness, the energy that moves human lives. *Faramya* (pompous asses) say energy moves from one area to another — but talk to Pachatusan. The breath of Pachatusan gravitates living energy and is the axis of the earth. Some are lucky to have Pachatusan as a *sayak* (benefactor). Pachatusan's bigger expression is a universal expression.

Apu Waquay Wilka is in the middle level and provides *mesas*. Directors of *mesas* are prepared for individuals to become *altomesayoqs*. Salcantay decides this. Waquay Wilka provides physical *mesas* as ordered by Salcantay. Right now, *mesas* given to Waquay Wilka that have not lived up to vision and agreement might be removed. If the *altomesayoq* does not live up to the oath, then the *mesa* is removed — for the first time one year, the second time for three years — then that is it for life.

The next *altomesayoqs* will be a man and woman from the West. This is because they are from a culture that has already been exposed to and dealt with the seduction of materialism.

Apu Sawasiray, ah, my friend. He embodies the power of youth. The youth (not age) has to do with those that dream. Sawasiray is a dreamer. He goes to sleep and brings dreams back into reality. Ones that do not dream are dead in life. Eternal youth equals dreaming.

Do you have any other *apus* you would like to ask about?

I asked Huascaran about the properties of Alankoma, the mountain that I had connected to during my first energetic initiation. That initiation changed my life and was the basis for the book *Lessons of the Inca Shamans: Piercing the Veil*. While in the midst of the initiation process that occurred on top of a mountain with Alankoma, I had physically experienced an infusion of powerful energy that, during the vision, had appeared as light in the energetic form of a bird. Apu Huascaran responded:

The mountain Alankoma is known as the keeper of the eagle's nest, the place where eagles, condors, and falcons reside on its summits. Old time Alankoma — it has been fifty years since he talked. He is still a steward. He is just in a still place. People who are interested in eagle nests gather and gravitate to this mountain. Alankoma is popular because on top of the mountain there are mineral salts the birds love to eat. They choose to nest here because these salts produce heat so their nests are warm.

Other *apu* spirits were asked about.

Apu Patapac hides and finds — hide and seek. Do you know the story of forty thieves? This *apu* is the *apu* benefactor of cattle thieves. The mountain opens up and takes the animals in, and then closes. It has an underground river. There has been much erosion over the years. If you crawl, you can see the interiors, the spaces inside are huge. The mountain is not so famous now.

Apu Kaylash, ah, an *apu* of initiation. Truly a great *apu*. Apu Kaylash helps like a ladder bringing initiates to enlightenment.

Apu Everest is the light of the world, a sacred mountain that keeps the light of the world. Interpretation of light is up to you — whatever that might mean.

Someone asked about Wanakauri. Huascaran answered: **Let's let him answer that question, as he is standing right here.**

Wanakauri spoke:

I am the one that grows a child into a man. My work has to do with instilling morality, discipline. I have to keep seductions away from my children. I bring light within to those who are hunched in fear. I am the Prince of Light, if you want to stand in the world.

Next, is the structure of the hierarchy of the *santa tierras*, the feminine spirits who are collective expressions of Pachamama residing in the earth. At core of the earth, there are three *santa tierras* residing that function as the glue that keeps the earth together. At the next level, the middle layer, having to do with crystals and light, there are seven other *santa tierras* — each with specific job descriptions. One *santa tierra* governs water having to do with karma. Other *santa tierras* oversee plants, trees, animals, minerals, and land formations. On the earth's surface, there are thousands of *santa tierras*.

Santa Tierra Belen said:

We are very beautiful. We are keepers of all seeds and our job is to bring seeds to life. We are expressions of what dwells deep within the planet from the core, inside to out. The first level of *santa tierras* live in the upper crust of the earth. We are responsible for the different jobs that women have — weavers, tailors, raising children, tending the fire in the kitchen. You should know all that live in the upper crust are virtue, entirely for your well-being — to hold you. We have always carried seeds — earth seeds, star seeds — different states of blooming ahead of us.

At the second level, there are seven *santa tierras*. The *santa tierras* that dwell here rarely come up to the surface. They have seven virtues. They came up from the second level to remove *hucha* (karma) from this group of women.

Practical rituals are used for connection to internal fire, to retrieve the passion of humanity so that it can be expressed. This internal fire can propel as much as it can burn. High vision has catalyzing agents to bring opposing forces into balance; accelerating growth is the key effect. We need to be clear conduits that come from other opportunities — the love of Christ, the love of the land, etc. — not just personal love. Some will be burned. The high and low passions that live in the person require weaving between fire and lack of fire.

Pampamesayoqs all have *mesa* stones that elicit memories and techniques. How you use them has to do with how you ignite the fire within, how your idea of fire catalyzes and becomes Kausay Pacha to propel, feed you, and fuel dreams. You need to rediscover passion, if passion has been dormant.

Huascaran then blessed each of our *mesas*. He said, **We are four spirits here. You can ask us questions.**

Perry asked, "Why when you put a cone of ice out on a cold night do some of the cones become invisible?" Perry had discovered in some of his experiments that inverted ice cones he placed outside at night would start to disappear at times in photographs that he was taking. At the same time, some of the photographs revealed small swirling specks of light moving in a vortex over the tops of the frozen ice cones. Perry asked the *apus* about what he was witnessing in the photographs.

Huascaran responded, **There are water spirits in the water that are being released and freed up again.** I could feel Perry's energy vibration as he sat next to me, could sense that he was very excited about the answer. I imagined that he was smiling in the dark.

Huascaran then responded to someone else's question that I could not hear with the following answer:

In Sanskrit, Peru means "mountain of gold." Gold provides the state that one gets propelled into fulfillment. What is that potential within you that you need to decipher? There is the journey itself. We can travel blindfolded and overly trusting. We have awareness of trust. Questioning is good. You need to summon yourself to this process of revelation. You must generate active responses in order to fully understand your questioning. In the question lies the answer. I appreciate your journey. Big and little steps. It has to do with *ch'uyanchasqa* — the shedding of what is. It requires a certain speed, should become your vehicle and make use of what you are to do.

Santa Tierra Belen asked, **How about questions for me?**

The next question was asked, How does fire live within us?

Santa Tierra Belen replied:

Love, hate, anger — it's about understanding passions. Passion is the precursor to potentialize love itself. On its own, it is a universal organizing principle of the opposing force. The bigger qualities as healer/sage start showing up and take keystone.

A woman asked if they would find a vision stone to find connections to past lives here in Peru. Santa Tierra Belen answered:

Why do you want to find past lives you already know? You have many stories here and a story of being a sage-like person. You already have memories of Peru. If you already remember that, maybe you

have already found the stone? How about finding a stone that will help you retrieve new information. The past you already know.

Jose Luis began translating Huascaran's instructions for the purification process that would follow:

Apus will come, so come to the table and place your forehead exactly in the middle of the table resting there. The bell will be in the middle. Come with your *mesa*, we will take turns cleansing and healing for you and your *mesa*.

Huascaran spoke up:

This journey begins as well as it begins now. Open your Mind and Heart. Your Mind is filled with cluttered electronics — emails that keep you disconnected. Clear your Minds to connect with the gifts you are gleaning. May your walk be embraced with the Mind-set and Heart-set of ritual. Make that your everyday walk. This journey is a journey of your soul — master of power and master of deficiencies. Go strong and return triumphant.

After the *apu* finished speaking, I drifted between states of consciousness as I focused on dropping deeper into a sentient energetic state. Throughout the session, Perry and I had continued holding hands. I gradually become aware that the two of us had become energetically encased within an intense vertical column of light that dropped into the earth, while reaching up into the celestial realm.

Sitting in the pitch-black room with my eyes closed, I tried to adjust to the interplay in the energy exchange that was happening between us, while attempting to contain the celestial energy being downloaded through the connection of our luminous bodies. A "hum" of energy pulsed through our bodies and it suddenly began to feel much warmer. Gradually, the flow of energy felt like it was starting to even out as I became more acclimated to it. A consistent current was now moving through me. The sensation was curiously comforting and pleasant, and I felt oddly at peace.

Huascaran began calling pairs of us forward for the energetic clearing. Although we were in complete darkness, the procedure reminded me of participating in communion in the church. We took turns shuffling slowing forward to the altar, with our hands reaching ahead. Although I could not see anything using my eyes, I was surprised to discover that I was able to orient myself through kinesthetic intuition. Sensing with my body, I knelt in front of the altar, placing my forehead against the table as Huascaran had instructed. I could feel Perry kneeling next to me.

As I was kneeling, I started to feel wings gently flapping against my head and down my back and arms. Using my intention, I opened my luminous field for greater connection with the *apu*, while thanking him for his help and assistance in my Mind. Throughout the healing, in my Mind's eye, I directed my concentration on being a clear channel, while asking for any energetic obstructions to be released. My body was still lightly shaking after I returned to the bench and sat down again.

Sitting on the bench, I stayed focused on integrating the influx of information that was still being downloaded into my luminous body, maintaining my spine in an erect position. I tried not to think about what was happening and instead paid attention to tracking the sensations I was feeling in my Belly. I know that the process continued for a while although I am not sure for how long. Then, the session ended and we walked out of the room into the bright sunlight.

As I stepped outdoors, I shielded my eyes with my hand and squinted to get my bearings. I felt like I had just woken up from a long nap. I slowly trudged up the set of stone steps to retrieve my backpack, and then found a comfortable spot to sit on the grass. I quickly began taking notes of what had happened in the session with Huascaran before the details began to fade away.

13. Temple of the Winds

There is no consciousness without discrimination of opposites.

—Carl Jung

July 10, 2011

Today we made the steep hike to visit the Temple of the Winds on Waquay Wilka, which for the Q'ero *paqos* is the seventh mountain that gives the sacred *mesa* to the *altomesayoqs*.

Perry and I stood at the base of the mountain, looking up at the temple. Although the sun was shining, the wind suddenly picked up and began whipping around us. Papers began flying around and hats were lifted off people's heads. It suddenly became very difficult to hear. Q'ero *paqos* have said that there are good winds and winds that make you sick — when *hucha* energy piggybacks on the wind. The bad winds leave one with headaches and take away clarity. Medicine people undo the *hucha* of the bad winds by making *k'intus* with coca leaves.

After the wind had settled down again, our guide Hamilton provided us with some background information about the site:

Here it is windy — not only in the afternoons, but all day. The farmers are still growing maize and growing wheat, using llamas to transport all their crops. Now there is only one of the aqueducts working, the lower part. This place is amazing because these enormous

173

stones are not from here. Actually, the quarry is eight kilometers away. Now you can see a huge rock up there, right? This place was first built by another civilization called Qullqi. These people, this Qullqi civilization, built here in the flat area and their city was destroyed. So the Quechua people learned from them and started to build on the hills. So this is why the Quechua people do not have anything left from the other civilizations.

I am going to talk a little bit about water. They say the water that they use came from the glacier way up there. The people who live here worship water and worship their relationship with water. These fountains are the remnants of the ancient civilization that continue today. Farming is still the main activity in this culture, so it is necessary to have a good relationship with cycles of water. We have all these fountains everywhere. You have been in Machu Picchu and have seen the cascading presence of water.

Water, like fire, is important in the cosmic vision of the shaman. The *altomesayoq* Doña Maria works with a *santa tierra* and an *apu* called Aspo Kenta Rebacha — a very funky name that means "shot gun" That is the name of that spirit. One of the job descriptions of this *apu* is to ensure the proper flow of water. Somehow, this *apu* regulates how water should be allocated to animals and plants and people.

The steps of the Inca cross that you see everywhere, represent the three-layered universe that the *apus* have spoken about. This symbol pertains to our immediate universe, how we relate to the world — to what is above us — the sun, the moon, the stars, and the mystery of night and day. We relate to where we are standing as the place where life emerges from because the soil, the dirt, and the crust of the land hold all the roots as an incubator. Our homes are held in similar foundations. So that is how we relate.

You are going to find the Andean Southern Cross with its three-step symbolism on four regions. The symbolism has to do with our geographical understanding. For a medicine person it is your medicine coordinates and the four regions of the geographical land.

At the same time, the Andean cross is a symbol of ascension. In North America you have the medicine wheel. The medicine wheel has to do with the horizontal reality. Here we do not have a horizontal reality because we cannot see past the horizon. We are blocked by those mountains. So we are forced to see above the geography. The geography molds your identity and character. The environment has a lot to do with the way you perceive the universe. What if you live in the Amazon? What if you live in Harlem, New York, right? That environment has a lot to do with the way you understand reality. So, here this three-step symbol has to do with a vertical reality, not a horizontal reality.

So in order to see, we have to climb mountains — particularly for indigenous people that are not locked in valleys like in Cusco. The people in valleys in Cusco do not see anything else. The cultural effect on their everyday life is stubbornness. People in Cusco never get things done. After much talk and a lot of whipping, then they will finally come up with a result. People from the plains, the Amazon, or the coast agree faster. This is because living in the valley causes them not to see past what is in front of them. So seeing possibilities is not easy for them.

For the Q'ero people living up here, their perception allows them to see that horizontal reality but from above. Perception is deeply engrained in the geography that you are in. The Q'ero are farmers and herders, and when they farm, they have to trade and when they herd they have to go to different places. They have to be able to constantly walk on little mountain passes, go down to ravines. In the case of the Q'ero, they have five ecological levels where they live and farm. They farm corn down at this level and have potatoes up here. They graze the animals a little higher up so they have to cross altitudes.

Moving between levels creates their perception. They have this condor-eye way of seeing. Whenever you ask them where the next village is, they will say around the corner because they are watching from above. It is really around the bend, around the mountain, around the rock. This is pretty much the same as the medicine wheel except that it is not horizontal, it is vertical.

Cycles of water are other elements. Evaporation, rivers, precipitation, and rain are aspects of the whole, full circle of the water journey, the backbone of this range. We run on this gigantic boa constrictor of sorts, and she is the keeper of the cycles of water. We ride on her back — from the underground rivers, into the rivers, into the plants, and into the little seeds that turn into fruits. The fruits are eaten and that begins the seeds. It starts all over again.

Each culture has their own myth of creation, with heroes. This messiah-like individual knows and brings knowledge and ways of wisdom. In different cultures, this demigod, a hero that brings people out of the caves into civilization by teaching them the culture, ways of living in villages, and relationships. This hero goes by the name of Viracocha.

According to the Incan myth, Viracocha emerged out of the island of the sun, now in Bolivia, where the first tears of light that turn into gold and corn landed on the island. The Incas had heard of this place from other civilizations. In order to legitimize their presence and their conquests, they embraced the native myths of origin as well. For instance, they built the house of the chosen women at the island of the moon. This is a wonderful place with ornate doors and gardens.

Tanopa, the child of the sun and the moon, grew to become a king with a vision. He journeyed and came to the city of Cusco. Along the way, he founded cities, taught people how to use instruments, and brought seedlings for new trees. He went into war as well. However, Tanopa did not stop. He kept on walking and he went out to the ocean and in the ocean, he went to oblivion. He went to the deep horizon of the ocean. The prophecy is that his return is awaited. Tanopa will return from the stars.

Different cultures near different bodies of water know Tanopa by different names. Lake Titicaca and the Pacific Ocean are two of the bodies of water. In the Pacific Ocean there are multiple cultures. One of them is the Mocha people, who know him as Nilam. The picture of

Figure 19. Boats docked to a floating island in Lake Titicaca (photo by Tom Blaschko)

Nilam is of the wind beams that we have — two little wings and a huge halo.

Tanopa is depicted with the same outfit as well. A common representation of Tanopa is with wings, holding a scepter. This agrees with the Andean belief that the first people came from the stars. The all came walking across an ocean filled with stars. It is not the ocean that we know but rather the great Milky Way, the other ocean with stars. The latest incarnation of Tanopa includes his female counterpart, the spirit of the waters of Lake Titicaca. Nowadays in modern Spanish cosmology, you have the Madonna of Candelaria in Peru and Madonna of Copacabana in Bolivia. She is sitting or standing on a crescent moon with stars around. That nomenclature is not lost — the expression is different. Now it is the forgotten candelaria, which is one of the many names of the Holy Mother Mary in the Christian tradition. So, Tanopa went back to the stars. Tanopa came, brought creation, and then left. Here is also a myth about Tanopa's return.

There are many books and treatises that have been written, in which they site Asteonoku and some civilizations around that lake — a gazillion years ago — as the place where possibly the first peoples in the Americas started building the first temple cities and pyramids. One of those pyramids, Calas Asiah, is as old as some of the pyramids in Egypt. These people left a legacy behind that is still alive today. When the Incas came, those people were long gone — at least by a thousand years. They had left these huge monoliths, impressive sized statues with wings. They have this writing, like Meso-America among the Aztecs, Toltecs, and Mayans, that nobody has been able to decipher. They also have calendars and certain things of cycles that we know, including cycles of the moon, the sun, and other celestial bodies, that we cannot know who or what they are. The reason is that this is a dynamic place and everything is moving — the horoscope, from house to house. We now know it as the earlier age, the age of Torres, which was 60,000 years ago. Twenty-three thousand years ago must have been the time when these people were there, before the last creation. We are the creation.

There was another creation, perhaps a version of the Atlanteans on Lake Titicaca. There was a massive collapse and people disappeared. This is the fourth creation. They vanished, but they left inscribed in the stone their mythologies of creation. This is similar to this new Q'ero mythology regarding the return that emerged after the conquest of Peru when the Incan culture was beheaded. In a metaphorical way, they lost the head of that culture and they became the sheep of the Spanish and the church, etc.

So, this is about the return of a new head, a new order. They talk about Engady and the return of the head, the head of the Inca. A new Inca emerging. This is no different from Tanopa returning from his voyage in those deep spaces of that starry ocean.

After Hamilton finished speaking, we began to hike up the steep dirt path, following the switchbacks toward the top of the mountain Ollantaytambo — the Temple of the Winds, overlooking the Sacred Valley. The sun was sinking lower in the sky and I could feel the temperature dropping as the winds whipped through our clothing. The physical exertion from the climb counteracted the chill factor, and I was surprised that the combination felt exhilarating. The magnificent view of the valley below continued to become more spectacular as we hiked further along the path to the top.

When we arrived at the peak of the mountain, we encountered a stone monument with four openings. Each opening held a different energetic vibration for clearing. Jose Luis began speaking:

The winds of the east are of renewal. These are winds of discovery and winds of rebirth. The winds of the north are the winds of the animals. These winds are the winds of this massive body, a huge canopy of light. But this energy, because of the canopy, does not reveal itself. It has to do with mystery and not knowing. Dealing with this energy requires shape-shifting for your own innocence. The winds of the west have to do with your own resilience that emanates lights. The south winds are the winds of love. When love comes to you, you create. It is your personal power. Your way of love is your way of articulating that quality. Love itself is carried in those winds.

You will come here with your *mesas*, bringing *k'intus*. You will put a big rock between your legs on the ground where you are standing. Underneath the rock, you will place the coca leaves. Adriel will be calling those winds with his prayers. He will be actively calling the winds by name with his *mesa* and with his veil. As you go to each one of these altars, open your *mesas* and see if there are stones that need to be left behind. Here, you can create an opportunity to empower those stones with the same winds, helping to bring them to a new level, into new plateau. The *khuya* can work in your lives in your medicine.

Figure 20. Adriel (photo by Rana Dewall)

Following Jose Luis's instructions, I began the ceremony in silence, first making twelve *k'intus* for clearing. I considered whether it was time for me to say goodbye to any of the *khuyas* currently living in my *mesa*. Were any carrying past wounds that I was ready to let go of? Sitting with my open *mesa*, I looked over at the smooth, rounded dark brown stone that was about an inch and a half in diameter and about four inches in length. It had originally come to me on the riverbank of the Amazon during my first trip to Peru. For the last several years this *khuya* held the energy of the Black Snake in my *mesa*. I realized that it was time to let it go.

As I began the process of moving through the four openings, representing the four directions, saying goodbye to my relationship with the Black Snake marked the end of a seven-year *pacha* that had started with my first steps along the path into shamanism. As an aspect of my shadow, the Black Snake had been strong medicine for me. It had initiated me into my shamanic journey by facilitating the dismemberment of my old life and way of looking at the world. Although it had been incredibly painful, the Black Snake had been a powerful teacher that had taken me into the underworld where I encountered my deep fear of abandonment that had claimed me most of my life. The Black Snake had shown me that I could survive everything being stripped away by learning how to source from Pachamama.

After our long and painful journey together, I was surprised to discover that saying good-bye to this *khuya* was accompanied by intense feelings of sadness. Although working with the energy of the Black Snake had brought dismemberment to my life, I realized I had grown to love the Black Snake through the wisdom it had given me. I thanked the Black Snake for the valuable lessons as I blew a prayer of appreciation into the stone, preparing to say a final goodbye.

Crying, I placed the stone on the altar facing the direction of the east winds during the ceremony, asking for renewal and rebirth into a new *pacha*. I left my *khuya*, which had held the energy of the Black Snake in the third space, and stepped into the fourth space to embrace the opportunity for new birth. I looked out toward the sacred mountains in the distance beyond the Urubamba Valley, which had become backlit by the orange glow of the setting sun.

We finished the entire ceremony at dusk. The sun had moved into the low point on the horizon and was quickly setting behind the mountains. Realizing that it would be dark soon, we raced

Figure 21. Perry at the Temple of the Winds (photo by Deborah Bryon)

swiftly back down the narrow mountain path before it became too difficult for us to see where we were going.

The descent was not strenuous in terms of physical exertion, but it required agility and demanded my full attention as I maintained my footing with speed. From my time spent hiking in these mountains, I had begun to practice shifting into a body-awareness state of allowing the mountain to hold and pull me in what felt like a cord running from my Belly that connected directly to the mountain in the path ahead. My attention became focused on the cord running from my Belly into the mountain. By the time we reached the bottom of the mountain, the sun had set and the temperature was continuing to drop further.

Figure 22. Judy Bath, Mari Spiegelman, Deborah Bryon, and Tatiana Jacob (left to right) at the Temple of the Winds (photo by Perry Edwards)

After dinner, Don Sebastian met Perry and me in our room to help us create a *yanantin despacho*, to bring masculine and feminine energies into balance. He began by taking a *despacho* kit from the *manta* he used to carry his belongings and placed it next to us on the floor where the three of us, facing, were sitting cross-legged. After placing his *manta* on the floor, he emptied a small bag of coca leaves on top of it and took the wrapping-paper sheet, which would be used to contain the *despacho*, from the *despacho* kit.

Instead of beginning with placing the customary white scallop seashell at the center of the *despacho*, he asked Perry and me to help him create fourteen *k'intus* of two leaves each for Pachamama and twelve *k'intus* with three leaves each for the *apus*, They were then set at the side.

Later, working with Adolfo, I would learn to make *k'intu despachos*, also used for purposes requiring focused intention — such as clearing in a relationship, asking for purification, or establishing a stronger connection with an *apu* spirit. Although simple, I have found that the practice of creating *k'intus* in *k'intu despachos* with a specific intention and focus tend to bring about a deep meditative state with powerful spiritual connection. The *k'intu despachos* that I learned to make with Adolfo are formed with twelve *k'intus* — three rows consisting of four *k'intus* each. On top of each *k'intu* is placed a piece of llama fat, three kernels of corn, and a piece of a red carnation to create an altar offering.

In the *yanantin despacho* that we were building with Don Sebastian, he would continue to add additional elements beyond the basic *k'intus* formation. Don Sebastian built this *yanantin despacho* as described in Exercise 12 below. When it was finished, he wrapped the *despacho* in a *mastana* cloth that he had brought with him to take to Ausangate.

Exercise 12: Procedure for Building a *Yanantin Despacho*

A red flower is placed underneath at the bottom, with white cotton on top to symbolize clouds and to create a division between the lower world of Ukhu Pacha and the middle world of Kay Pacha.

On top of the first layer of clouds, rainbow string and colored cotton are added to represent the upper world of Hanaq Pacha.

On the right side, white flowers are placed as an offering for the *apus* and red flowers are positioned on the left side for Pachamama.

Groups of *k'intus* are then arranged in rows from top to bottom.

Colored paper confetti and gold and silver string and paper are added to represent the sky.

White daisies are added in the right corner for the *apus* and red geraniums are set in the left corner for Pachamama.

Candy and confetti are added as the next layer for Kay Pacha.

Another layer of clouds is added.

Red ribbon is laid toward the bottom for Pachamama, rainbow-colored ribbon in the middle for Kay Pacha, and white ribbon is put at the top for the *apus*.

Additional flowers are added in each of the four directions, white flowers for the *apus* and red for Pachamama.

Different grains and candies are sprinkled on the left for Pachamama and on the right for the *apus*.

Silver-paper rods and candles are dropped on top of the right side for the *apus*.

Gold-paper rods and candles are dropped on top of the left side for Pachamama.

A piece of a dried starfish is included for vision, positioned on the right side for the *apus*.

A candy house is placed on the offering for security and a candy car is added for mobility for Pachamama.

Confetti is scattered over the entire *despacho* representing festivity and high spirits.

Wine is sprinkled over the entire *despacho* next for fertility to find the spirits. (Don Sebastian used cola because we did not have wine in the room. The *apus* and Pachamama understand the intent).

After blessing it, the paper underneath the *despacho* is folded. First, the bottom half is folded upward. Next, the top of the paper is folded down. The right side is folded in first, followed by the left side. After the *despacho* is folded, it is wrapped and tied with a string to hold it. When completed, it is placed in a *mastana* cloth.

After Don Sebastian had finished the *despacho*, the three of us stood up. Don Sebastian then sprayed Florida water into his hands. While Perry and I held our *mesas* close to our bodies, he blew into our Head, Heart, and Belly. Next, he thumped us on the top of our heads with his *mesa* and sprayed Florida water over our heads as well. He especially pounded Perry's head with his *mesa*. Then he hugged and kissed both of us, saying, "Adios."

Before leaving, Don Sebastian took the remaining Zero Cola to pour the rest of the bottle outside into the ground for Pachamama. Don Sebastian told is that he would carry the *despacho* to Ausangate to feed it additional power before the fire ceremony.

14. Ausangate I

So far, I have explained the phenomena by the force of gravity, but I have not yet ascertained the cause of gravity itself...and I do not arbitrarily invent hypotheses.

—Isaac Newton

July 11, 2011

At 4 AM, we boarded the bus, headed for Ausangate. As we made our way through the western valley, we passed through the grasslands of the Andean plateau at sunrise, stopping in the small villages of Ocongate and Tinqui for water. When our bus was close to the base of Ausangate, our road turned. We circled around the foot of the mountain so that we would begin the hike from the north. As we descended into the valley facing the direction of the rising sun, the great mountain of Ausangate was on the horizon, looming large in the distance. At the sight of Ausangate, I saw a tear run down Perry's cheek. I knew that we both felt honored to be in its powerful presence. Even though I had seen this mountain many times before, each time is a renewal like coming home.

As we continued on, Jose Luis told us more about the folklore and history of this region:

Nowadays, we have cars and do not walk on foot as we used to — up until twenty years ago. Everything that you see is very modern. Even this road that we are traveling on was built three or four years ago.

However, years ago, there were different types of sorcerers who lived in this valley. They traveled at night as heads, by leaving and disconnecting from their bodies. The identifying feature of these sorcerers was their long hair. Normal *paqos* would not have long hair. Anyway, the stories and legends have to do with these flying heads getting stuck in certain houses — and sometimes you would find them walking along a trail. Then the priests and the good *paqos* would have to come and help reinsert the wandering heads back on the sorcerers' bodies, using a ritual of prayer and exorcism. Sometimes, the heads were tied up with ropes so they could not move, in order for the priests and *paqos* to bring them to the local church to practice a healing exorcism of sorts.

To me, it seems that it was the materialization of the sorcerer's dream body seen by the people. Many stories about these traditions involve those flying heads. So the proverb that came out of those stories that was heard and transmitted to people was not to cause fear. Well, actually, in a way it was to cause fear so that the people would learn to develop respect and courage, but not to get caught in the panic or fear such an event would happen to them. The teachings of these stories really have to do with standing, standing strong, standing really strong.

So if you are at a mountain pass and one of these flying heads comes to scare you or seduce you, you have to be very, very strong in your command and not let this thing disempower you. You need to curse, you need to spit at it, you need to throw coca leaves, and you need to take your belt out. They recommend that you have the local brand of unfiltered cigarettes that you should smoke to the head, you know, and always carry a little bit of Timolina with you. Timolina is a liquid with a very pungent smell that you rub on your body, particularly when you are panicky or you are in distress, because it changes the energy. It lifts the fear per se. So, have a little bit of Timolina, coca leaves, and tobacco, when you are traveling. They are necessary tools.

So, again, in these situations, people had to stand in an empowered, courageous, serene, uncluttered way. They had to defy with this combative presence and character. You have to be strong. You cannot let anything — flying heads or anything — put you down. And this is analogous to the necessity for mountain people to have strong souls. Souls that are rooted in the land, you know. Their *anima*, their spirit, is rooted and held by the *apus* because this geography is — as you see — very harsh. Back then with no transportation, it was even harsher because you had to walk with your animals from town to town — going up and down the mountains. So it was more challenging. You could not do those journeys if your spirit was panicky or weak or challengeable.

You have to have a strong, strong spirit and a strong, strong soul so when adversity comes to you — and big scares, such as the flying heads, come up — you can stand up to them and come out victorious. Part of the teachings of shamanism, when you begin a healing journey, really has to do with strengthening your psyche, strengthening your *anima*. You need a clear *anima* and clear soul, a soul that is held and anchored that is vital and energizing, and that can reset itself on the go. You are going to have accidents, you are going to face challenging situations, but none of those is going to break you into pieces. And if they break you, you will have the ability to reset yourself.

So, stories such as the flying heads are ways to make people strong. Particularly the farmers and the herders that have to trade. They have to travel and have had to deal with different people and different traditions as well. And even though you may see the Andes as one constant culture with one given language, Quechua, it is very different.

For instance, now that we are going to go into this valley of Ausangate, the traditions are different from the traditions of the Sacred Valley, different from the traditions in Rio Urubamba. For example, the traditional outfits that they wear are diverse. Their outfits display their unique iconography. The iconography is woven in their textiles and tells a story about their cosmology, their traditions. So, every place has different iconography. Yes, there are common denominators such as the mountain spirits, the ancestors, and the different expressions of Pachamama, herself. However, as far as what their land produces — there are different varieties of potatoes and different festivals. Nowadays because of Christianity, the saints that are the patrons and benefactors of the towns are different — so their festivals are different.

In the Q'ero region, the village traditions are even more different since they are not in the middle of roads connecting places. The Q'ero have continued to live in isolated places, so their traditions have remained untouched, unchanged by other traditions. The only time the Q'ero would reveal their craft as far as their ceremonies, etc., was when they would come to Snow Star thirty days before the solstice. Anyway, that was the only time in which the Q'ero were seen in all their regalia, traditions, etc. They would dance, they would march, they would pay their homage to Kujawami, Apu Towianami, and Apu Q'ollorit'i (Snow Star). Q'ero traditions are different in their approaches and in their dances. All their dances are very animistic.

One of the ways the Inca or the Quechua people have been successful is through their mastery in trading. They are masters of trading. You have to be *ayni* with the people you are going to barter and trade your potatoes with. You have to be in *ayni* with the land, in *ayni* with the new people that you meet, and in *ayni* with the road, the trail that you walk on. In order to be in *ayni* with everything, you have to be strong. You have to have a soul that is recognized and held by the land that is fueled by the spirits of whatever place you go. One of the ways to enhance *ayni* is to deepen that relationship with spirit by serving the land with *despachos*, by giving to the unknown stewardship and vision of your future exchanges and engagements as a tradesman. It is all about *ayni*. I need *ayni*, too. You have a way to understand what pertains to the land, what pertains to other villages — and what is yours. When that awareness is your guide, your guiding road, your guiding map, nobody, nothing, or no enemy or event such as a flying head will be able to mess with you or to take anything from you.

In the West, where we are, it is different, you know? In the West, we live in a culture of such fear that our souls are very fragile. Events, car accidents, the wars, being fired from a job, being — I do not know — scared and in the basement of your house can really shatter you. It can really offset the different systems that you have in your body, in your dream body, your vitality, physicality, your vision — and whatever. We tend to leak energy. That can open up unconscious doorways through which our life force leaks as we are in states of confusion. We live in states of longing. We are unable to sleep deep, etc. It is a cultural thing that is happening to our souls. When it comes to healing, we need to have a vessel. Not our bodies — but our souls. Our soul is the vessel that holds our human experience with our physicality, visions, etc. that needs to be anchored and that needs to be held, that needs to be in right relationship. Our *ayni* needs to be strong. It needs to be vital. So, this is why legends and traditions are necessary.

At about 9:30 AM we reached the place where we would start our journey on foot. The cooks, wranglers with their dogs, and horses with packs were already there waiting for us. I had met the crew a couple of times on past visits and was happy to see their smiling faces. After the customary greetings, the wranglers loaded our camping gear on the horses. We prepared for several hours of steep trails. Jose Luis had advised us earlier to bring the appropriate layers of clothing, sunscreen, and our *mesas* in the daypacks that we would carry on our backs.

Perry commented to me that he had never been on a luxurious camping trip like this with wranglers and horses carrying most of the gear. We picked up our packs and slung them over our shoulders as Jose Luis said, "Let's go."

We began the steep climb up toward the snow-capped peak of Ausangate, heading towards the first of two mountain passes that we would cross at elevations of approximately 15,000 feet (4,600

Figure 23. The beginning of the journey to Ausangate (photo by Frances Marron)

meters). The initial leg of the hike was difficult for me because I was not feeling well. In addition to the inherent strenuous physical challenge of the hike itself, my stomach problems had returned at the higher altitude.

As I looked up the incline toward Ausangate, Doña Bernadina patiently waited for me. Step by step — *poco y poco* — I deliberately made my way up the mountain. She and one of the other *paqos* asked me if I would like one of the horses to carry my pack, but I declined. It was important to make this pilgrimage walking on my own. Reaching higher elevations, we stopped frequently to take sips of water from the bottles we were carrying.

At one of the stops we made, Perry began searching for rocks and other mysterious things in the little rivulets of water coming down the slope. I watched him take a stone out of one of the streams and hand it over to Doña Bernadina. Doña Bernadina looked at Perry and quickly tucked the stone somewhere in her skirt, smiling. Perry interpreted this to mean that Doña Bernadina also knew that this stone was a keeper.

As we were approaching the top of the first summit, Doña Bernadina motioned for me to place a heavy rock, weighing approximately fifteen pounds, inside the cloth bundle that she was transporting on her back. I believed that Doña Bernadina might be performing the ritual of carrying *hucha* to the mountain that had been practiced by the bear people as Doña Alejandrina had described to us a couple of days ago. Doña Bernadina explained that she had a somewhat different purpose. She was carrying the rock for the *apachetta* that we would be creating at the top of the summit. An *apachetta* is a pile of rocks built with prayers and intention, to form a structure for healing. The *apachetta* we would create would hold our ceremonial *k'intu* offerings to shed *hucha* for our families, ourselves, and other members of our community.

As we made our way up the pass, I shared coca leaves from my *ch'uspa* bag with the other *paqos*. I broke off a small piece of *lipka* to chew with the leaves. When we crossed over the top of the ridge that we had been climbing toward for the last hour, an expansive green valley with a stream running through it opened up below us. I was happy to discover that the rest of the day's journey would be downhill.

The powerful energetic presence of Ausangate towered ahead of us, as glistening sunlight bounced off the glacier-covered peaks. The thought occurred to me that I did not know where Perry was. I looked around and became slightly concerned. Finally, I spotted him ahead in the distance at the side of the trail holding on to a massive boulder. As I approached him I realized he was sobbing, clinging to a large boulder, as the Ausangate glacier field seemed to loom over him. I walked over to him and stood for a moment

Figure 24. Adriel resting at the base of an apachetta (photo by Devin Arnold)

before gently placing my hand on his back. I knew he was going through a healing, so we just stayed there for a while. When he was ready, we both got up and walked quietly back to the trail.

Don André's smiling face appeared out of nowhere as soon as we crossed the ridge. He motioned for my hand as he walked beside me and I willingly complied. I appreciated his sure-footed patience that enabled me to increase my speed down the dirt pathway that consisted of loose patches of dirt and pebbles. Together, we scrambled down the trail making up and singing songs to Pachamama, Mama Cocha, and Apu Ausangate using words in Quechua. Don André smiled at me as sang the melody that had come to me — and corrected me when I left off "Apu" before singing "Ausangate." As Don André and I continued along singing together, Perry began bolting down the trail ahead of us. I knew that running would help Perry move the emotional experience that he had just had through his body.

Gradually, the steepness of the trail down the mountain diminished as we continued for a couple of hours longer. Perry and I were exhausted as we crossed the green valley grass on the last leg of our hike that day. The sun was going down and it was starting to get cold. As we approached camp, Doña Bernadina was waiting there at the edge of a stream for us with a horse and bridle in her hand. She stood there smiling in the final sunlight — in her bright skirt and open sandals — and motioned to us to come toward her. As we got closer, we noticed that the valley stream was about twelve feet wide and a couple of feet deep, with fast-moving water. The stream separated us from our campsite on the other side.

Initially, we were not exactly sure why Doña Bernadina was standing there with the horse. However, it soon became apparent to both of us that she was planning to take us through the water on horseback. In disbelief, I obediently followed her instructions and got on the horse, watching Doña Bernadina wading through deep, fast rapids in sandals as she led the horse across — with me just sitting there for the ride.

Doña Bernadina then went back for Perry to repeat the process. I saw the same look of disbelief on his face as well. Neither one of us got a drop of water on us as she led the horse back and forth through the cold glacial rapids.

When Perry and I walked into the camp at about 4 PM, the sun was fading and the air temperature was cooling off rapidly as dusk approached. By 6 PM, it would be dark and the temperature would drop significantly lower to freezing temperatures overnight. As we picked the last tent available for the night, Perry struggled with the zipper trying to open up the tent flap. He tried and tried and then finally lay down on the ground in frustration and exhaustion, looking at the sky. Hamilton arrived out of nowhere in what seemed to be a couple of seconds and started laughing. Of course, Hamilton simply pulled the zipper down and we were in.

Perry said, "You saved my life, Hamilton. You saved my life." Hamilton smiled and disappeared.

Peacefully exhausted, after a late lunch of quinoa soup and coca tea, Perry and I climbed into our tent and retired for the night — at 5 PM.

Perry wrote the following journal passage about his experience during the day while I drifted off to sleep:

I'm on a trek in Peru with Jose Luis and the rest of our group. I'm carrying stones and magnets in my many pockets. I am having a great time calling, "Hoo! Hoo!" with Doña B as we cross little water gullies that are running downhill. The things that are suspended in little glistening pools of water seem to be magic and hang at the door of infinity as I jump across them in delight.

In one spot, I see a little waterfall in one of the foot-wide rivulets — and it is only dropping sixteen inches. At the bottom of the waterfall there I can see two vortex swirls of water, one going clockwise and the other counterclockwise, right next to each other in the plunge pool at the base of the waterfall. They are actually almost touching each other as they swirl in opposite directions. Little six-inch vortexes next to each other just churning away. I cannot come up with a good explanation of how this could be possible.

I had meandered a ways off the trail and the group was marching on ahead. So with an unpleasant muscular lurch backwards I rolled away from the magic vortexes and scrambled upwards to catch the group.

Everyone has stopped after a long uphill stretch and is sitting to rest a little.

The sun is very bright and we are now at an altitude over 15,000 feet. Doña B watches me with curious eyes but doesn't say anything like, "What are you doing?" So, I pick up my pace, falling into a swinging rhythm as my boots march down the trail. Silently, I start singing a song. The song picks up power inside of me as I feel it expanding inside my chest.

My boots pound down the trail in a steady rhythm beat. It is like a big drum inside me. The chant gains power and starts to surround me with its energy. I thank Pachamama for showing me her power and I tell her that I am paying attention. I am smiling as I continue in silence down the trail, as my mind belts out the ballad and my feet pound out the beat. I know everything is good. Occasionally Doña B glances at me but says nothing. Doña B is wisdom and power in action.

Everything has changed after crying under the Ausangate glacier field. At the base of Ausangate, I remembered the truth. Ausangate reminded me in silence who I really was and what I really had. The truth. It was okay with Ausangate that I did not even look at what I always knew was the truth. I felt so small there. I was infinitesimal at the base of Ausangate.

I knew more when I was a child. As a child, I made a promise to Mother Nature. A trade that I could not escape from. A contract. I had traded my life, because I knew my father was trying to take away my life. I traded my own life because I thought I would lose it. I made a deal.

I told Mother Nature that I would do something great for humanity. I would do something great for the earth. That was the deal. I traded that for my life. For being able to have my life, that is what I traded. In addition, what had I done? Nothing. I had done nothing. I even forgot I had made the trade. And I knew better.

It was okay with Ausangate. It was just not okay with me. I cried as my essence tore apart inside me. I was worthless. But I was still alive. Incredibly so, it really was not too late. I could still change things.

A couple of hours later, looking down, my mouth suddenly dropped in amazement. In the valley below, I see the packhorses starting to gallop across the valley floor. They know...they always know. It was the camp and they would get food and water. They wanted it now, of course. The vivid green grass they thundered across seemed like a magic carpet of waves they were dancing on. The pure glacial stream gurgling and running its course down the valley was full and alive. This was Mecca, and I sensed great things coming out of this valley below me. No wonder they were running. I should be running, too.

In that moment, I realized I knew of this place. This was the valley where the hundred-year-old shaman spent his lifetime. The keeper of the rainbows had cared for this place. Jose Luis had told me about a shaman who was over 100 years old that could run up hills like a deer. The shaman had embarrassed Jose Luis and a friend one time, when he tried to show them something on one of the peaks overlooking the valley. The shaman had said to them, "Follow me" and then quickly started to run up the mountain showing them the way.

However, the keeper of the rainbows did not look back and did not realize that he had left Jose and his friend behind without any way for them to track him and find where he had gone. Even though the shaman was over 100 years old, there was no way of catching him! Jose Luis and his friend had to turn back and never got to see what the keeper of the rainbows had wanted to show them.

I loved Jose Luis's story and was in awe as I stood over the valley of the keeper of the rainbows. I understood why the keeper of the rainbows called this valley home. It was an easy thing to understand.

Around midnight, after falling into a deep sleep inside the tent, I suddenly woke up to a powerful wave of energy vibrating through my body. I could hear Perry breathing next to me, fast asleep. Becoming more awake, I consciously opened myself to connecting with Ausangate and felt the surge of energy increasing. I began shaking nonstop as I allowed the energy to run through me. I felt it rumbling like the cold rapids in the stream outside our tent.

I had been through a similar process before during my experience on Alankoma and recognized that I was receiving a download of energy. I heard Ausangate telling me that this energy transmission needed to become grounded between Perry and me. I shook Perry lightly to wake him and told him what was happening. I felt an intense love for Perry as I opened myself to channeling the energy that I was receiving from Ausangate.

Ausangate, Perry, and I became one. We were the river, streaming through the valley. I recognized that an initiation had begun and we were in the middle of it. I sensed wings emerging from our backs. Suddenly Perry sat up like a soldier and hit my back sharply with his fist, right between the shoulder blades. The blow reverberated down my backbone. I felt my teeth rattling from the shock of the impact and I had the instant sensation that something was breaking up and releasing inside of me. We were being flooded with waves of energy.

When I opened my eyes, I could see tiny sparkling white light particles dancing everywhere around us inside the dark tent. We had shifted into a state of union, as energy continued to steadily flow through us before gradually diminishing into light waves that eventually faded away. I felt an incredible sense of well-being as we drifted back to sleep inside the tent.

15. Ausangate II

[Einstein] had the revolutionary idea that gravity was not just a force that operated in a fixed background of space-time. Instead, gravity was a distortion of space-time caused by the mass and energy in it.

—Stephen Hawking

July 12, 2011

When we awoke at dawn, at 6 AM the next morning, we both felt well rested. Perry began making some morning jokes, and I knew all was well with him. We eventually peeled back our tent flap to find the smiling faces of Jose Luis and Hamilton peering in. Hamilton laughed and cheerfully began making jokes about Perry's struggle with the zipper the night before.

Jose Luis said. "You were in there for thirteen hours!" I smiled and told him that we had been tired.

Perry said, "I don't even know where I was!"

The morning air smelled moist and clean as Perry and I climbed out of our tent, ready for breakfast. Once outside the tent, after stopping quickly to tie his bootlaces, Perry raced off towards the cook tent in search of food. I saw him enter the tent, before hearing sounds of rumbling and laughter from the wranglers who did not speak any English at all. A couple of minutes later, Perry emerged with a sausage omelet on a tin plate and a smile on his face. The sounds of the fire crackling outside the cook tent and the melodic rhythm of the rushing water in the background was perfect breakfast music as I sat and ate a bowl of porridge and drank a cup of coca tea.

After breakfast, we packed our gear to continue our trek. Before departing, Jose Luis gathered us in a circle and explained about how the ancient Incas worshipped the water. Jose Luis pointed to the stream going past our camp and said, "This is pure glacial water coming down from Ausangate. This is sacred water. Why don't we all take this rare opportunity to get a blessing from the water before leaving this campsite?"

We all began walking up and down the bank, looking for spots to place our *mesas* and receive a water blessing. Some of the shamans took off most of their clothes and waded out into the stream. They splashed around playfully in the rapids as they most likely had done many times before. It was amazing they could do this and not go into hypothermic shock.

As I sat down on the bank to work with my *mesa*, I began making *k'intu* offerings to honor the water and the land. I shifted my focus to weaving the energy of the water into my *mesa*, in connection with Ausangate.

As I looked up, about ten feet upstream from me, I saw Perry pull his tee shirt up over his head before dipping his entire torso above the waist into the water. I watched him dig his boots into the bank to keep himself from sliding into the water. It looked like he was rummaging around in the rocks on the bottom of the streambed. Then, accompanied by a splash of water, Perry suddenly burst back out of the water.

Shaking his head, he whipped tiny, glistening water droplets from his hair. He was clutching an object tightly in his right hand. When his feet were back on the bank and he was standing, he looked over at me and enthusiastically exclaimed, "It's a water

Figure 25. Ausangate (photo by Frances Marron)

flute. It is the keeper of the rainbows' water flute! He left it behind on the bottom of the stream!"

Perry walked over to where I was sitting, leaned over, and kissed my forehead. He held out the reed flute that he had magically found in the water. Then he put it in my hands and said, "You can have it."

As the flute began to dry, I tried to play it. I discovered that it was possible to generate sounds by holding it sideways — the way I had learned to play a flute.

I got up and moved down the bank several yards further from the stream, and I sat down next to Don Sebastian and Don André. I continued my attempt at making a few audible sounds.

Don Sebastian and Don André appeared to be mildly entertained by my musical labors. Don André good-naturedly motioned for me to hand the flute to him, while Don Sebastian pulled another flute out of his bag in exchange. We began a game of trading flutes back and forth. I was pleased that I had been able to settle into playing a repetitive melody consisting of two notes. Every time I was ready to put the flute down, Don Sebastian and Don André would gesture for me to begin playing again. Later I realized that they had been amused by the way I held the flute while attempting to play it. Don Sebastian began creating a pleasing melody on the flute that he had brought with him. After watching him, I realized that the flute should be held directly in front — not sideways.

When the rest of the group had finished working with their *mesas* near the water, we reassembled in a circle. The *pampamesayoqs* sat together and took turns speaking about the preparation for the upcoming initiation ceremony. The demeanor of the *paqos* became more serious as they tried to convey the importance of what they had to say to us.

Don Sebastian was the first to speak:

The mountains, the *apus*, and the *santa tierras* have been watching over our steps, over our breath, and in every exchange, they are guiding you. You are going to receive this life force, this energy. This is a transmission of *kausay*, life force energy. The vitality, which lives in these mountains of Ausangate and all the other sacred mountains, has this power, this quality to give you.

Every step that you have undertaken, up and down the mountain has brought you to this place. Perhaps this journey has removed pain from your Hearts, sadness, etc. The mountains know this. The *santa tierras* have witnessed this and they are going to renew your *kausay*. They are going to give you this fine energy because when you walk in the world like the medicine people, there is no tiredness.

This lake, Sigrena Cocha, is very powerful. It has the ability to release, eject, and clear anything that has been sitting too long in your Hearts — perhaps sadness that will go away in the cleansing ceremonies tomorrow. Tomorrow, we will prepare the big celestial *despacho* and all the mountains and all of the *apus* will come. This is the greatest act of love that we can possibly provide: giving all to this land, to this living entity around us. You will be rewarded tenfold.

Through this exchange, through the celestial *despacho*, anything that dwells in our bodies that has not been healed, come into wholeness, or into right relationship will be fixed, because the powers are so strong. That is what these mountains do. They give us *kausay*, this life force. This *kausay* generates more *kausay* as we walk in the world, as we heal others.

You have come all this way and you have done your work in such sweet ways, you are going to go home rewarded because of the effort that you have paid. Rewarded because of the Heart you have put into the ceremonies. Everyone in their home, in their own corners and neck of the woods has visions. You have things to do and the energy that you are going to take from here will make those things come into fruition.

We are in different levels in our advancement toward power. We are at different levels embracing the power of nature, as *paqos*, as the medicine people that we are becoming — and are already. There are young *paqos* and master *paqos* in this group. Sometimes it is an uphill battle dealing with life, with feelings, with what is behind, with comforts, etc. But this has great rewards. The work that you are doing, what you are giving of yourself, your availability will pay twofold.

Tomorrow you will receive the *Mosoq Karpay* rites of passage of a time to come. Those *karpays* have not been given before in the way that they are beginning to be given now. This is unlike any other *karpay*, any other rite of passage. It will undo the way you live, and generate a new way of being, of vision, for you when you return to your homes.

We are going to give you the big *khuyas* that belong to these *apus*. I have been praying and asking for those *khuyas*. They will then guide you and become the devices with the capacity to multiple any engagements that you are able to grown corn with, by bringing it into fruition.

How big is your Heart? How big is your *tukuy munayniyoc* (all-encompassing love)? How deep can you go? How much can you surrender? The amount of love, the depth of your availability, and the power that you bring forth through your love is what makes the transaction happen. But if you doubt, if you weaken, if you go into your little corners of whatever, it is not going to work.

We are going to wire you to these mountains, through your Heart, your Belly, and your Mind. This is not any simple wiring. There are particular prayers that are only spoken when that wire is done at these rites of passage. I am learning in dreamtime what these new prayers are about. This is a different type of *karpay*.

Tomorrow we are going to call those powers from these power places. We will ask Pachamama and the *apus* to pull, connect, and bring this power into your bodies. This process requires a big Heart. It requires such strength, from all of the *paqos*. In our prayers, we are going to step up to the plate. That is what I am here for.

So, that is pretty much what I know about the ceremonies. There are different layers and hierarchies of power. Deep in your psyches and Hearts, you understand what power is. If you do not understand what sits here in these mountains or in this land, then go to our omnipresent gods of all worlds. He is or she is the one that provides the what-to-dos even to the mountain spirits, which I can bring *karpay* to your evolving medicine bodies.

Thank you so much, little doves of my Heart, for being here to do this work. It is very important for me.

Next, Doña Bernadina began speaking:

Brothers and sisters, we have walked this far together. We have invested a lot of effort in this and are in this wonderful place with the blessings of our god creator Viracocha. What a great journey you have undertaken. You have come from distant places, from where your homes are, to these high places. This might be cold and challenging, but this is where the power of nature resides. The spirits of the land provide us with everything — from the very basics to the information of medicinal plants and the different ways that the land gives us gifts to heal others and help transform people's lives.

This is a time to pray together. Really pray. More than we have prayed. Tomorrow is a big day. We are going to talk to the spirit of this great lagoon, the counterpart of the big tall mountains. She has great medicine for us, great enchantments. The spirit of this body of water will come into your Belly, refresh you, and reenergize you. It will make you remember creation, but we need to pray together.

Tomorrow we have a big encounter, with the big entities above the lake, Ausangate, Salcantay…This is our time to meet nature. It is not only your transformation into becoming individuals of power. It is also about how you become individuals of power as you bring this medicine back to your homes and your families — that is when you will become a person of power. Unlike any other time, this time we have been preparing for so long. We have been carrying the sacred crystals, like a little baby, nurturing them in our Hearts.

Jose Luis, who had been interpreting, interjected:

The greatest act of love that I've witnessed today was by Doña Bernadina. She has carried these two huge stones up the mountain to clear *hucha*, so that we are worthy of the medicine represented in that baby, in the crystals.

Doña Bernadina continued speaking:

Unlike any previous time, you are going to be gifted. I do not know why. I do not have a reason. But you are going to be gifted the most precious *khuyas* ever. Not only the crystals, but also the encoding in your luminous bodies from the sacred crystals. These are keystones. You must nurture these keystones and grow your medicine with them. You must be strong. You cannot let them sit or leave them behind. If that happens, bring it back to us. These sacred gifts should not be neglected.

Here we are not working only with little *apus*. We are working with big *apus*, a more and larger celestial presence, and these *khuyas* have the way to connect to a higher domain of consciousness above those physical *apus*. I asked you, and I am very forceful with this. This is an act of love. This is not a little adventure.

All the *paqos* here each have to do a ceremony of our deeds and misdeeds. If we have not been able to hold the space for you tomorrow, we need to deal with that misdeed of not being able to instill in you the Heart and the love and the seriousness of this interaction. So I ask you to come respectfully, with big Hearts. This is what is needed to make this come to life, when you are given those rites. Otherwise, I will have to explain to the spirits why I was not able to hold the space for you. On August first, as all of us look at what has taken place in our lives in terms of service, there might be little details that we will need to account for with the *apus*. I would not like to do that.

The spirits are hearing me. Spirits come and transform into little flies, or as big birds — or a little animal comes. The spirits are hearing what I am saying, and I have to be truthful to you and to the spirits. I love you so much. That is all I can tell you at this time.

After Doña Bernadina finished, Adriel stood up and began speaking:

Brothers and sisters, I am very happy to be here in this place with you. So, here we are and maybe this place will respond by providing answers to our questions. Life is a constant search. Places like this provide great answers to questions for those who have searched. In life, in this search, in this journey — whatever that is — a little journey or a big, extensive, epic journey, one of the first things we need to ask ourselves is, "How clear have I been? What are my attachments that I bring with me, particularly those attachments that have not been able to allow me to grow?" This is the place to clear that. We need to ask spirit God for forgiveness, for blessing, to remove this from our lives.

This is a *karpay*. *Karpay* is an organizing principle of life. Here we set a new momentum for life, a new way of being in the world, a new way of walking in the world. The doorways of heaven and earth will open, and spirit will come. Their hands will be extended to us tomorrow throughout these rituals. All we have to do is reach out and hold those hands that are inviting us. Tomorrow is the big day in which we set the new pace. We have been talking about this for a while. Tomorrow we will set it into action.

Why am I saying that? Why is it that I am emphasizing removing any pending engagements — or asking for forgiveness, or clearing yourselves? So you will come into this place of right alignment, because in places like this all the powers of the universe show up, all the celestial powers — even Jesus will come here. Tonight we are going to do a *karpay*, the ritual of feeding each other, loving of each other, and then we will have a fire ceremony.

Tomorrow will be the purification ritual, in the waters of this great lake. We are going to do individual *despachos* as well. Then the big event, the *Mosoq Karpay*, will happen.

There will be many powers available to us tomorrow, *atiy* (ability), *munay* (selfless love and compassion), and *kausay*. *Atiy* has to do with your resilience, with your stamina, with your vitality. *Kausay* is life force. *Munay* has to do with the power of love abundant to us.

So tomorrow, when we do the big celestial *despacho* and the individual *despachos*, it is your time to speak to God and the mountains. Your faith, intent, and Heart are necessary in this transaction. Everything we are going to do is for our families, our health, our bodies, and for our journeys. We still have many other journeys to undertake for the work that we do in the world and for the vision of the world. There is nothing that the *apus*, mountain spirits, and the land cannot give us. Everything is possible. May your visions, purpose, and dreams come true throughout these days of ritual. That is all I can tell you, brothers and sisters.

After Adriel finished, Don André spoke:

Brothers and sisters, may this evening be blissful. May the love of Pachamama embrace you deeply. I would like to express my gratitude to Jose Luis for enabling all of us to work together at this time. I would like to thank the mountain spirits themselves for bringing me here, and I would like to thank the current God we have, Jesus Christ that watches over us. You have shown tremendous effort. You have done this strenuous walk that is very difficult. These mountains will provide you with the necessary blessings.

So, the powers of this land will convene here in this ceremonial place. I know in my Heart that Q'ollorit'i is the boss of everyone and will be here providing you with blessings and with gifts. This is true for all the other mountain spirits, as well as Ausangate.

The others have spoken sufficiently about the work we will do tomorrow and about the beauty, powers, and gifts of Sigrena Cocha, the spirit of this lagoon. I want you to take that medicine back to your homes. You owe that to your community and your families. You need to bring this medicine to them. Ausangate will come and your *mesas* will never be the same. Your *mesas* are going to be set into a motion entirely different from what you have known. The right hand of Ausangate will be gifting you those *khuyas*.

Your prayers should be for yourselves, your loved ones, your families, your communities, and for your nations. I admire your effort dealing with the suffering that this elevation and difficult terrain has tested you with, but you will take good medicine for your families. Apu Señor Q'ollorit'i, Snow Star, will give you a new vision, *estrella*. It is the new vision of the time to come.

We have a long journey ahead of us. Our lives will provide other venues of learning with new challenges, but with the medicine of Q'ollorit'i, the vision, the *estrella*, the guiding star, and the presence of all these *apus*, you will be successful. Tomorrow, we will call everything around us and everything above us — the sun and the moon, the stars and superior presences, and all the features of power of the land to come into our ceremonies.

Brothers and sisters, that is all I can provide to you. Thank you. Sweethearts, doves of my Heart.

Asunta was the next *paqo* to speak:

What a place to come together, brothers and sisters. So, we are here on the Belly of the mother with a wonderful, wonderful sacred lagoon surrounding us and all we have to do is ask with love all the

Figure 26. Don Hilario (photo by Flora Meyer)

santa tierras, all the spirits of this lagoon, and all the mountain spirits, the *apus*, Ausangate, *santa tierras*. The elder mountains have been around for a long time and they provide the best *khuyas* a medicine person can earn. The spirit of this lake, Mama Cocha, located in this place of high energy will surely clear and cleanse anything that needs to go.

So make tomorrow the best day ever of your lives to meet the spirit, to meet God. Make your prayers include all the different powers that dwell in these territories, in these mountains, the *apus*, the *santa tierras*, and higher spirits — whatever your belief system, that you source from — even the Christ. The Christ is known to give us great blessings as well. Call him into your ceremonies.

You will return home with this newly emerging empowered *mesa* and will walk in the world as *hanaq qawaqs*. A *hanaq qawaq* is a sage, teacher, or a master that understands the ways of the land and articulates the medicine of the land though chewing like a condor chews, half-chews, and gives that knowledge to their children, to their people.

It is an honor to have met you. My name is Asunta, and I know you are the lineage of my father, Don Manuel Q'uispe. I am very thankful to see how this lineage is also affecting my life in such wonderful ways. I am very privileged to be with you. Thank you.

Don Hilario was the last *paqo* who spoke:

So, how is everyone doing, brothers and sisters? Tired, looking tired. So, let's talk about the power of this place. I recognize and I honor how far away your homes are and recognize the effort you have given to make this journey, to arrive at this place. The endeavors that you have in your personal lives brought you to this place. Now that you have reached this point, this is a different territory as well. I am sure it is challenging, but those endeavors need to be brought into a faster delivery line, so that this medicine can push those mementos and fuel those endeavors.

I know some of you have walked this path of life, this journey, and have met great places of power. I am sure there is great power in your places as well, in your lands there. There are holy places and sages and great information. And yet you have come to this distant place, to learn from our sages, from our holy places, and from our body of knowledge. I admire you. The journey itself is sometimes difficult. There are challenges and heartbreaks, and sometimes we experience being in the void of the unknown.

Life is a wonderful event. Whether it is there or here, we must come out victorious in this personal journey that we have embarked upon. We must emerge victoriously as individuals of power. Life is a challenge. We have physical and emotional things going on. At elevations like this, our bellies may not work properly, etc. We bring those things to *despacho*. Those are the challenges that we must overcome. These are little metaphors. But the journey itself, when taken with great Heart, is a lot easier to embrace. So, little steps, big steps, cycle after cycle, *pacha* after *pacha*, year after year, we have to get to that plateau. I see you arriving into that plateau. There are individuals here with great power, with accumulated experiences — sages, and there are the young *paqos* as well.

It does not matter where you are in your journey. What matters is your Heart and how you provide power to your families. We are coming into a time and place when we no longer embrace the theologies given to us by our ancestors. Our eyes are opening. We want to create a new way to speak to the land that supports spirit and us. We have reached a time in our journey, or in life, when we can no longer embrace the old theology. Time is accelerating. We have bigger cities, bigger populations, and bigger needs. With this come different entrapments. We have entered a time that requires us to have a different discourse for our journey that pertains to spirit and that pertains to us. It is important not to become entrapped by what is happening in this rapid time of change.

Above everything, we are children of the land. The basic understanding is that we have always been children of the land, and as children of the land we need to remember the old way of dialoguing with that that supports and nurtures us. Everything around us has *kausay* and is infused with life force.

If that living energy permeates every aspect of life and can come actively through us, then everything is possible. This is the time for us to bring *kausay* forward. It is the time because of the rapid changes that are happening in the world, and because this life force — *kausay* — is particularly abundant in this place. The new mainframe that is being established in our Hearts and vision is bringing life force and creativity into reality, with unlimited possibilities. Walk in the world as *paqos*, empowered. Bring the bread of God, bring the bread of the *apus* into healing, into your transactions, and everything will offer you great results, results for you and results for your people.

I've seen many of you have great hands for healing. I see many of you with the capacity to carry great knowledge to become wonderful sages. I see in you that you have been blessed by God in so many ways. So, this path of empowerment is for your people, for your loved ones.

This journey that we have all undertaken is one of service, of embracing our loved ones. Everyone should have an *ayllu* and should be the engine of those *ayllus*. My vision is that all of these *ayllus* will weave themselves together, creating a bigger *ayllu*. There is an *ayllu* of mountain spirits as there is an *ayllu* of medicine people. This interaction is one of service, of embracing one another in love. You need to assist and attend to those individuals in your villages that perhaps are straying off from that right relationship with the spirit of the land. You need to bring them back.

The *apus* have always said to me that this journey is about speaking your truths and walking with truth, with elegance, with resilience, with strength, anchored in the land. One should live that way, the way one should journey with the blessings of the creator.

"The *apus* are assistants, the *apus* are guardian spirits. They are under the command of the Great Spirit. In our great place here in this latitude, those guardian spirits walk among us, they take care of us. They love us, hold us, and show us the way.

Now everything has to be in proper exchange. You need to provide the blessings, prayers, and offerings to them as they provide blessings and gifts to us. There is a saying in the Andes that everything you do — right or wrong — will come looking after you. I learned that from my grandmother as a young boy. I learned that everything not done properly — in *ayni* — will come looking for you to set the record straight. You need to be in *ayni* with Great Spirit, in *ayni* with our verbiage, in *ayni* with the land. So, improperly asking, improperly calling, improperly using our verbiage will always be addressed. Thank you.

It was time for us to pick up our belongings and begin hiking. As the trek for the day began, I was pleased to discover that my physical energy had returned and that I could move up the mountain at a faster speed with less effort than I had been able to

Figure 27. Sigrena Cocha (photo by Devin Arnold)

the day before. Perry and I settled into a pace together that was comfortable for both of us. I was glad that I was keeping up with him and not slowing him down.

After crossing another summit with an elevation of about 15,000 feet, the landscape opened up on the other side and the beautiful lagoon of Sigrena Cocha appeared, stretched out in the distance ahead of us. The contrast of the color of the aqua-blue water beside the stark white snow-capped mountain glacier set against the blue sky was striking. As we hiked further, the glacier of Ausangate to the right of our path became increasingly prominent.

It suddenly occurred to Perry that this was most likely the closest we would come to the glacier ice. He informed me that this was his chance to collect the blue glacier ice that he had seen in his dream vision. Wanting to support him in the spirit of the moment,

I decided to check with Jose Luis to see if climbing the glacier was a possibility.

As we discussed the options with Jose Luis, it becomes clear — at least to me — that we were not carrying the appropriate gear with us. We were dressed fine for the midday temperature, wearing long-sleeved shirts with a light vest, but neither of us was carrying a heavier jacket, or gloves and hats in our daypacks. Jose Luis said that he thought it would be better for us to return on our own the next day, equipped with gear and horses. Perry and I both agreed with the plan and kept walking toward the lagoon where we were camping for the night.

After we reached the camp and unloaded our gear in our tents, the group met during a late lunch in the communal tent. As Perry and I were discussing preparations with Jose Luis, it abruptly occurred to me that the journey to the glacier would take an entire day and I began to feel conflicted. I wanted to encourage Perry to follow his vision; however I realized that if we went to the glacier on our own, we would miss the ceremonial preparations for the high *Mosoq Karpay* rites — a primary reason I had returned to Peru. The idea of Perry going to the glacier on his own made me incredibly uneasy. This was a rugged and challenging landscape and people had died in these mountains from causes including hypothermia, landslides, and avalanches. Although rationally I knew that Perry was much more capable than I was of successfully accomplishing the glacier mission, I was adamant about him not going alone. Jose Luis looked at me and raising his eyebrows said, "I guess you will have to make a choice."

A couple of our friends suggested asking Don Hilario for a coca reading. Each *paqo* has different abilities to look at what might happen, something the *paqos* call tracking. Don Hilario was well respected as both a healer and a tracker. Earlier in the day Adriel, who is also an excellent tracker — probably the best regarding personal future — informed me that he was returning to Cusco the next day but had agreed to give us a coca leaf reading before leaving.

Outside of Peru, I do not ask people, other than Perry, to track for me. I prefer to rely on my own relationship with the spirits, my ally the Birdman, and Perry's connection with his guides. Nevertheless, I have always had great respect for Adriel's abilities in reading coca leaves, and having an annual reading with him when I am in Peru has become a ritual. However, in this particular situation we were advised to consult with Don Hilario.

Perry agreed we should meet Don Hilario together so that he could read our coca leaves and track the potential success of our climbing to the glacier the next day. Our guide Hamilton had kindly agreed to interpret for us and was now sitting with Perry, Don Hilario, and me in our tent.

Don Hilario laid his *mastana* cloth down in the center of the small circle we had formed, all sitting cross-legged on top of duffle bags and sleeping bags. He reached into the *ch'uspa* bag that he was carrying at his side and took out a handful of coca leaves. Don Hilario quickly sorted through them all, inspecting each to make sure it was whole, and arranged them facing up with the stems pointing downward. Then, while holding a small stack of leaves loosely between his index finger and thumb, with a quick flick of his wrist he scattered them on top of the *mastana* cloth lying between the four of us. I watched the leaves fall, trying to guess if there was anything unusual in the configuration they had landed in by closely watching Don Hilario's facial expression. I realized that Don Hilario was probably a good poker player, judging from his ability to maintain a straight face and give nothing away. However, Hamilton looked noticeably worried.

Even before anything was said, I knew it did not look good. I saw that a couple of leaves had landed upside down and were overturned. Hamilton and Don Hilario quickly exchanged words in Quechua and Hamilton began shaking his head. In English, he told Perry and me that if we went to the glacier I would not make it back.

For Perry's benefit, Don Hilario threw the leaves three times and each time the results were the same. Although Perry was disappointed, we all agreed that it would be a mistake for us to make the trip to the glacier. I thanked Don Hilario and Hamilton for their help as they were leaving the tent.

Perry and I remained in the tent. I could tell that Perry had many thoughts running through his mind. He said that he was reluctant to give up the idea of going alone. I began to feel increasingly more anxious and unsettled. About ten minutes later, Adriel suddenly showed up at the entrance of our tent for the reading we had discussed earlier in the day.

Initially I had wanted Adriel to track the course of the upcoming year, but now we had more pressing matters at hand. I was hoping that he would say something that would convince Perry not to go to the glacier. Adriel sat down cross-legged and took a handful of coca leaves from the small green plastic bag he carried in his coat pocket, sorting them into the proper position. I offered him my writing journal to use as a surface and the reading began.

After examining the tossed leaves, Adriel smiled. He said that this year, unlike the year before, looked auspicious. Nodding, Adriel looked directly at each of us to make sure we understood before he continued speaking:

"You are both healers. You love mother earth. Your spiritual path is open. You will get money to build your house."

Looking at me, Adriel continued:

"You are teaching, writing, showing your work — very successful. You and your husband working together is a good union and you will both return to Peru many times. There is a publisher for your book — excellent. The book will expand beyond the USA. At first there may be problems with Colorado but do not fear. Success will come in the second wave. An *apu* will appear in a dream. Obstacles will be overcome with faith.

"Your son is okay. Your husband is a protector of your sons. Bring your son to Peru to overcome addictions. He has to walk the path. Show him the spiritual path — he is a good healer. Show him natural medicine. He is going to travel to South America."

Looking at Perry, Adriel said:

"An authority will be interested in your invention. You are going to make money with this work and people are going to visit. The *apus* are waiting for you."

After Adriel had finished, he said goodbye and left the tent. Adriel's reading generated a renewed burst of enthusiasm from Perry. After Adriel had left, Perry explained to me that Adriel's reading was an indicator that it would be okay for him to climb the glacier if he went alone. My anxiety ratcheted up again and I reminded Perry that both Don Hilario and Hamilton had strongly advised him against making the trip. Perry tried to reassure me that it would be okay because we had asked Don Hilario if we could both go and had not asked specifically about him going alone.

The tension between us began rising and an argument began brewing as I felt own my internal temperature quickly going up. I felt panicked, fearing for Perry's safety. Perry told me that I was encroaching on his vision. Our exchange of words sped up as our dialogue bounced back and forth.

Suddenly, Adriel reappeared at our tent and we invited him in. Looking at Adriel's face, I could see that he was worried. Adriel intently looked at Perry and said, "The *apus* will meet you from above. You do not need to climb the mountain. Do you understand?"

As Perry reluctantly nodded, I reiterated what I heard Adriel say to make sure that his message was clear. I asked Adriel, "Are you are saying that Perry does not need to climb the mountain, even if he goes alone?"

Adriel repeated, looking at Perry, "Yes, you do not need to climb the mountain."

I thanked Adriel profusely for coming back to explain his words. He smiled at me and bowed, before quickly disappearing down the path to where all of the *paqos* were meeting.

I began to feel slightly relieved, hoping that Adriel's words would carry more influence with Perry than mine had. Looked over at Perry, I could see that he was visibly annoyed. I decided it was best to leave him alone so that he could think about the information that he had been given.

Both of us were tired and grumpy. Perry said that he would not go but I know that he was not happy about it and there was nothing left to say. We had gone over the matter several times. The temperature had dropped considerably in the last hour since we had been in our tent and the sun had set. Soon it would become even colder, reaching freezing temperature by morning.

We agreed to skip dinner and go to sleep. I was drained by the events that had transpired between us and was worried, annoyed, and frustrated. I put on a couple more layers of clothing and burrowed deeply into our sleeping bag, hoping to shut the world out. I went into the inner world to visit the Birdman and Ausangate before entering a dream state. Even though I was irritated, Perry's body heat was comforting and my anger began to dissipate. I wrapped my arm around Perry snuggling closer for both comfort and warmth and closed my eyes. As I began to relax into the stillness, I hoped that not climbing the glacier would be easier for Perry by morning. Unfortunately, that was not going to be the case.

At some point in the middle of the night, I felt Perry gently shaking me, calling my name. Although I really had no idea, I guessed that it was around about 3 AM. I took an earplug that I was wearing to block out the sound of snoring out of my ear so that I could listen to what he was trying to say to me. Even before I could comprehend his words, I heard the tone of his voice — and I felt a sinking sensation in the pit of my stomach. The glacier predicament was not behind us. It was looming right in front of us at three in the morning.

Perry told me that if he left for the glacier now, he could be back before the *Mosoq Karpay* rites began. I was mad that I had been woken out of a sound sleep and that my nervous system — and state of mind — were being hijacked. I could not believe that this was actually happening on the day of the initiation ceremony. Instead of moving into a meditative state of union to prepare, I was preoccupied and worried that Perry would disappear and not return if he decided to climb the glacier — especially in the middle of the night. Emphatically, I heard myself loudly whispering "NO!"

Now I was wide awake. The fight had started and I was ready to confront him head on — over what I perceived was an issue of life and death. I informed Perry that I resented his need to follow his interpretation of every vision at the expense of everything and everyone else around him — including himself. I reminded him that visions could be metaphorical and that the meaning was not always literal. I also communicated that I was royally pissed off that this was happening the night before the major initiation rites that we had both committed to, together. I grew angrier with Perry as I grew angrier with myself for allowing myself to enter this state of mind. As it was happening, I was also aware that my anger was only making things worse. I recognized that the source of my anger was fear — from the knowledge that even though Perry was an experienced outdoorsman and capable of handling harsh elements, he could die.

Perry lacked equipment, did not know the terrain, and was planning to go without assistance. I was determined to do anything I could to stop him. I wondered if this was how spouses of soldiers, fire fighters, racecar drivers, and mountain climbers felt.

I fortified my conviction with anger by telling myself that I had not signed up for this. Perry was — again — making my life unmanageable — and I was assisting him. As I heard myself using Twelve-Step language, I remembered to surrender. It then occurred to me to ask Ausangate for help — so I did.

In my Mind's prayer, I asked Ausangate to protect Perry. I explained that I knew that I was miserably failing, in my current state, to prepare for the initiation. After a short while, deep in my body I sensed an inkling of a solid, stabilizing presence that began to grow. I recognized Ausangate's powerful anchoring presence and started to calm down.

I acknowledged my commitment of service to Ausangate and focused my attention on realigning my will with clear intention. Suddenly a wave of tranquility washed over me. I gently asked Perry not to go to the glacier and to stay for tomorrow's initiation with me. I promised him that I would return to Peru, or go to Alaska — or even Telluride — to support his vision with the glacier, and added that we had come to Peru to complete these rites together.

Perry was not happy — but he agreed. I thanked him for listening to me and we both fell back to sleep. The next thing I knew it was morning.

16. Sigrena Cocha

It is knowing what to do with things that counts.

—Robert Frost

July 13, 2011

When I slowly opened my eyes and looked through the nylon tent fabric that was backlit by the early morning sunlight, I could see that that the condensation on the outside of the tent had turned to frost. Even though it was comfortably warm inside our sleeping bag, it was time to get up. My body was stiff. I had been restless throughout the night, shifting and turning. I looked over at Perry who was already awake and in the process of putting on a sweater over his long underwear. Perry appeared to be in a jovial mood. He said that he had dreamed that Ausangate had told him that I could not soar yet but that I could flap my wings. I decided to move forward with my plan to pull myself out of the sleeping bag and into the cold air.

After climbing into a couple of layers of clothing, with mittens, a scarf, and a hat, I unzipped the flap of the tent and looked out. Doña Bernadina was sitting on a rock washing and combing her long hair. Stationed next to her was a yellow plastic bucket of water that she had presumably drawn from the stream a couple of yards away. Doña Bernadina's slender four-and-a half foot frame was perched agilely on the rock. I was happy to see her. I

223

Figure 28. Sigrena Cocha (photo by Frances Marron)

wandered out of the tent and over to the large thermal container that had been strategically situated in the middle of the common area of the camp. I picked up one of the reusable plastic cups on top of it and poured a cup of hot coca tea. As I tentatively walked toward Doña Bernadina, she looked up and smiled at me. I asked her if it was okay if I sat down near her. She nodded and continued running the comb through her hair. Unbraided, it fell down past her hips.

I found a neighboring rock a couple of feet away from the one she was sitting on. I enjoyed watching her efficiently perform her morning ritual and was struck by the beautiful sheen of her thick, smooth black hair as it captured rays of sunlight. She was, as usual, wearing her traditional outfit and, as always, she looked clean and well-groomed. I asked her if I it was possible for me to spend a couple of months studying with her. She looked at me with a penetrating stare that was direct but not unfriendly and said, "First, you must learn Spanish."

I nodded, acknowledging that she was right. I made a commitment to both of us that this year I would seriously work on learning the language. I was slightly annoyed with myself that I had put it off until now — I should have begun a couple of years ago. If I wanted to be an apprentice, I needed to commit to learning their language — the same way I needed to learn the technology of ceremony and ritual. I began to recognize that I had reached a point in my training that I couldn't fall back on expecting the energetic connection to carry me. If I wanted to be taken seriously I needed to demonstrate that I was taking the practice of walking a medicine path seriously — with respect. Doña Bernadina appeared to be having similar thoughts. After the grooming ritual was finished, I walked with Doña Bernadina to the designated community-eating spot.

Sitting in breakfast circle with the others, I decided to not focus on the undercurrent of low-grade irritation that I was still feeling toward Perry — an emotional hangover from the night before. I wanted to put the thoughts out of my Mind so that I could mentally prepare myself for the approaching ceremony.

The year before, I had allowed myself to become annoyed when someone had haphazardly bumped into me while I was in a vision state during an initiation ceremony. My internal reaction had pulled me immediately out of the experience and I did not pass the test I was being given. At the time, Ausangate had sternly advised me that I needed to overcome this aspect of my personal

Figure 29. Lagoon (photo by Frances Marron)

shadow. I wondered if what had happened this year with Perry was another test.

Now that I knew Perry would be okay, I focused on shifting my mindset. I was back in Peru with the beloved mountain who had helped me to open my Heart. My irritation was a petty distraction — miniscule in contrast to the presence of this powerful light being. I reminded myself that this was a sacred pilgrimage and giving energy to anything that took away from the connection with the sacred mountain was disrespectful. Ausangate deserved more.

I put my hands on top of the *mastana* cloth of my closed *mesa*, feeling into my connection with Ausangate with my Heart — not my Mind. I looked up directly in front of me and saw that the mountain was surrounded in vibrant sunlight. I could see waves of energy emanating off the top of the snowy mountain peak into the radiant blue sky. I loved this mountain from my soul. Feeling back in my body, I once again remembered why I was here — and I felt centered.

When breakfast was over, we collected *mesas* and ponchos and left for the purification ritual in Sigrena Cocha, the sacred lagoon that was about a mile away.

The mountain air was growing warmer as the sun rose higher in the sky. One by one, the women in our *ayllu* walked quietly down the narrow dirt path, single-file between small sage-colored bushes.

The trail was situated on the side of the hill that bordered the rocky shore of the lagoon. Meanwhile, the men had gone off in a different direction to perform their own ritual. The energy of Sigrena Cocha felt very feminine to me and I was happy to be sharing this moment with the community of women.

As we continued walking, I looked across the glassy, aqua surface of the water to the left of me and suddenly became overcome with its magnificence. In that moment, I was overwhelmed with feeling the powerful silence that comes with the absence of sound. It occurred to me that this kind of silence is louder than noise. My psychologist brain wondered if this was the result of growing accustomed to the daily bombardment of sensory input in the modern world. I noticed that being in the silence was pulling me into an altered state. Particles of light were dancing off the glassy surface of the water and were growing more distinct. The atmosphere around me was vibrating.

After about a mile, we reached a lower clearing area nestled between shrubs along the shore of the lagoon where we would conduct the ceremony. After placing our belongings off to the side, the group of women joined and called sacred space following the direction of the movement of the sun. We asked the *apus* to bless us with their presence.

Doña Bernadina and Asunta stripped down to their underwear and waded into chilly, three-foot-deep water on top of a bed of river rock. Before the cleansing ritual began, Doña Bernadina expressed to us that each drop of lagoon water carried a spirit that was giving its life in service in exchange for our cleansing when we entered the water. As I looked around into the faces of my female companions, I could see we were all feeling the powerful impact of Doña Bernadina's message. I accepted that we each had a personal responsibility to make this ritual meaningful, by holding the life of the water spirits that were being sacrificed on our behalf in reverence. As I read over these words now, they sound metaphorical to me; however, in ceremony the energy behind them was very real, not only symbolic.

In the process of the sacred ceremony, one by one, we entered the shockingly cold water naked. Doña Bernadina was singing and calling on Ausangate for assistance, to help bathe and purify us. She intermittently rang a bell while verbally administering the rites, making sweeping movements around our shivering bodies as we knelt in the water. We stayed in the kneeling position long enough for her to blow energy into the top of each of our heads. Next, we stood up so that Doña Bernadina could hit us — vigorously but lightly — all over our body with a straw whip that she had dipped into the freezing water. This was done to clear away the *hucha* that we may have been carrying with us in our luminous bodies. Although I noticed my physical body trembling in response to the cold temperature, I tried to stand still in respect for the water spirits and *paqos* and for the sacred gifts we were being given.

After all of the *hucha* had been beaten out of our energy fields, Doña Bernadina grabbed an individual bundle of fresh mint from the pile that she had carried all the way from Cusco in her *manta* and patted our entire body with it to help us restore alignment and balance. We then carefully placed the small white flower that we had been holding in our hand since the ritual began into the water as an offering, blessing it with our prayers and intentions.

After all of these steps were complete, Asunta smudged our bodies with smoke using the burning incense container that she was holding. Asunta ended the ritual with the purification practice of taking a swig from a bottle of rose water. She then lightly showered each of us with a mist of water from her mouth, using her breath to propel the liquid as a spray.

After the water ceremony was performed individually on each of us, we found comfortable places to sit and work with our *mesas* in meditation and prayer, connecting with Ausangate and the other mountain spirits in silence. When the sun was almost at its high point in the sky, we folded our *mesas* inside the *mastana* cloths. We collected our belongings and walked back along the path to reconvene with the men in the *ayllu*.

Quietly, the men and women in our *ayllu* assembled in the opening on top of the hill overlooking the lagoon to prepare the *despachos* for the coming fire ceremony. The *pampamesayoqs* created a large celestial *despacho*. They began by first placing wood kindling under the large sheet of plywood that the packhorses had carried from the base of the mountain. The rest of us began constructing our own individual *despachos* with ingredients included in the celestial *despacho* kits that we had purchased in Cusco at the shamans' market. We added to our creations by embellishing the mandalas that we were making with natural materials we had found nearby, such as dried plants and bird feathers that we had collected along the way.

While climbing around the adjacent rocks, Perry found a large eagle feather that he placed in the center of his *despacho*. We quietly became engrossed in our sacred ritual, praying to Ausangate and asking for the *apu's* blessing. I began transferring

230 Lessons of the Inca Shamans, Part 2

Figure 30. Perry's *despacho* (photo by Perry Edwards)

streams of prayers into the form of leaves I put together to make *k'intus*. After the last *k'intu* had been strategically added to the circular flower formation of leaves, I repeated the same process again, searching and sorting through the pile of coca leaves. I fished through the pile, pulling out whole leaves and combining them in groups of three to create more *k'intus*. After I had placed as many bundles between my fingers as I could hold, I added another layer of leaves on top of the circle that was already formed. When I finished wrapping the *despacho* by tying it into a package with string, a couple of hours had past.

After each of the members of the *ayllu* had finished making their own individual *despachos*, we all gathered around the fire that the *paqos* had built for the ceremony. Following the normal tradition of fire ceremony, in groups of four we approached the fire. We faced each of the four directions and performed the cleansing ritual in each of our three energy centers, Belly, Heart, and Mind, before placing our individual *despacho* offering into the fire. When we finished, we turned our backs and walked away.

In *despacho* ceremonies, once the offering has been placed into the flames, *paqos* say that it is important not to look at it again because this undoes the intention of the energy that has been imprinted into the offering. At the end of the ritual, a few of the *paqos* stayed to tend to tend the fire while the rest of us returned to camp. Later, I would learn through assisting Adolfo in this practice, that in addition to tending the fire, a *paqo's* role is to hold space in service of the ritual by asking Pachamama and the *apus* to receive this offering being made by the group. The *paqo* functions as a conduit between the spirits and the people.

Perry and I made a beeline for our tent to drop off our *mesas* and packs and add a layer of clothing before meeting for lunch in the large communal tent. To reach open seating spaces, we all had to carefully climb over legs and feet, stepping cautiously to avoid knocking over a cup of tea or falling into someone's lap and ending up in a plate of food. I was happy that I happened to land next to the bowl of popcorn, which was my favorite part of the meal.

The atmosphere seemed quieter than usual. There was noticeably less conversation and laughter. Most of us were in our own states of reverie, playing back the events of the day in anticipation of the ceremony that evening. After eating another light midday meal of quinoa stew and bread, we wandered back to our tents.

Lying down on top of the floor of sleeping bags, clothes, and packs that Perry and I had haphazardly distributed across our six-foot square suddenly felt very relaxing. Both of us dropped almost immediately into our own interior worlds. As soon as I closed my eyes, in my Mind's eye I could see my ally, the Birdman, and felt the company of Ausangate.

In this instant I perceived Ausangate as a formidable tower of light. I concentrated on aligning and harmonizing my luminous body more fully with the frequency of the *apu's* energy vibration. I will try the best way I can to describe what "aligning more fully with the frequency of an energetic vibration" actually felt like. Please keep in mind that the examples are only words to describe something that happened in my Heart and Belly.

Somatically it feels like I tune into and "reach" toward the higher energy vibration through my temples. The vibration registers in my body as an energetic "humming." The sensation in some ways is similar to yawning without opening your mouth — when you are trying to hide from others that you are yawning. There is a mild pressure.

The sensory experience of harmonizing the Mind with a higher energy vibration also reminds me of what it feels like to imagine hitting a very high musical note without actually making a sound. Although the experience of temple pressure is comparable to attuning to an energy frequency, it feels like hooking into something with substance but yawning discreetly and hitting a high note internally does not create the impression that anything is "there."

With my intention to connect in the inner world with Birdman and Ausangate, I tuned into their higher energy frequency. As is usually the case, I saw a very bright white light radiating from the Birdman and the column, which intuitively I understood to be Ausangate. I stated that my intention was to become an open channel to serve by bringing Ausangate another connection into our physical reality, by aligning my will with the will of the *apus* — for the highest good.

Beyond these words, the rest of the experience was an energetic connection that does not translate well contextually — because there were no additional images. I had the faint impression that activity was going on in the uppermost region of my psyche or energy body. A part of me felt that I was waiting at the gate of a lower level, while another part of me passed through. All of it was beyond what I could consciously access.

About an hour or so later, as the sun was approaching the horizon, Jose Luis called us to begin the first phase of preparation for the *Mosoq Karpay* rites. With *mesas* and extra layers of warm clothing, we climbed up the base of the steep hill on the other side of the camp away from the lagoon. Perry had stayed behind the group to finish working on the crystal invention he had begun putting together in our tent over the course of the last couple of days.

When we reached the top of the hill, I could see a valley hidden from the camp. I lingered behind, hoping that Perry would catch up with us. After a while, I realized that I would need to make another decision — either wait for Perry or stay with the *paqos*. I made the decision to move on. I realized that it was important for me to focus on getting ready for the ritual. Later, Perry told me that it was not hard for him to track us. However, at the time, I was caught up in reliving the memory from last year, when I had been in another a situation of being forced to make the choice to leave Perry behind at the airport when he did not have his passport, and returned to Peru alone.

As feelings of sadness tied to the past became stacked on top of what was happening now, I tried not to let myself become sidetracked by apprehension or annoyance. I wondered why I seemed to keep finding myself in the position of needing to let Perry go. Perhaps I was still learning the lessons of the Black Snake.

Meanwhile, the *ayllu* was in the process of creating another celestial *despacho* for a second fire ceremony. When this *despacho* was completed, it consisted of seven sections, formed by each of the seven *pampamesayoqs* who were with us. Each of us created 144 *k'intus*. I was a little surprised to discover that I still had an abundance of new prayers for more *k'intus* — even after what had been downloaded earlier in the day.

A cycle of collecting and sorting *k'intu* leaves into groups of three started again. Some time after I began placing prayer bundles of coca leaves into three stacks for the different stations of *paqos,* I noticed that each of my piles had become about an inch thick.

Perry had still not arrived. I directed my prayers to Ausangate and the other *apus,* asking Ausangate to help me release my attachment to Perry's current whereabouts. The thought again crossed my mind whether this was a test to determine if I could focus myself and not allow myself to become distracted. If my purpose was to serve as a conduit, being distressed about something I ultimately had no control over limited my availability and demonstrated a lack of commitment on my part. My determination to focus on why I was here gathered a second wind. My Heart was opening in response to an incoming wave of love that was washing through me, linked to the strong sense of devotion I felt toward Ausangate. I became realigned in my connection with this amazing *apu,* remembering that I did not need to try to control the situation — or Perry. I could let it go.

It was almost dark when we handed our *k'intus* to the *paqos* to be blessed and incorporated into the celestial *mesa* that now covered the 4-foot by 5-foot sheet of plywood — while we had filled individual *k'intus* with our prayers, the *paqos* had skillfully crafted an exquisite piece of art as a ceremonial offering to carry these prayers. One of the shaman's responsibilities is to create *despacho* offerings by making them aesthetically pleasingly to the spirits while at the same time feeding and fortifying them with powerful prayers through clear intention, thought, care, and love. After each of the *paqos* had blessed all of the *k'intus,* they were added to the configurations of multiple mandalas on the table. We each individually scattered the remaining kernels of corn and

Figure 31. Perry's sign for Deborah (photo by Deborah Bryon)

pieces of colorful candy evenly across the top. At the end, we dipped white carnations into the small wooden sacramental goblets and sprinkled drops of red wine over the entire *despacho* to feed it with fertility. The *despacho* was complete.

Perry suddenly appeared out of nowhere wearing a sign about 8-1/2 inches by 11 inches in size, on which he had written in large bold letters, "Pachamama loves Deborah and I do too!" Underneath the text, Perry had drawn a large heart with an arrow through it and had written "my heart" inside of the heart. He had collected plants and had woven them into the card.

David, the kind man sitting next to me, smiled and said, "I like the sign!"

Everyone smiled. Although I felt a huge wave of relief that Perry had arrived — along with feeling a surge of love — I was slightly annoyed that I had been derailed because I wanted to remain focused on Ausangate. Although I recognized that I was feeling loved by Perry's declaration, a part of me also felt that Perry had hijacked attention away from this important event — which he had promised to share with me. Perry continues to be one of my greatest life teachers — especially in teaching me to give up my need to try to control, which is pointless and never works anyway.

Perry sat down next to me and put his arm around my shoulders. I decided to let go of the irritation I felt, since connecting with Ausangate was ultimately why we were here. I remembered our original intention of bringing the energetic connection between us into the energetic bond with Ausangate.

While the *despacho* was burning, we sang songs for the *apus*, who are known to appreciate singing. We started with "Amazing Grace," followed by the Beatles' song "All You Need is Love," followed by a series of other songs that we each took turns initiating. The mood of the *ayllu* became increasingly jovial as we tried to sing in harmony while, at the same time, to remember the words to the tunes we were singing.

The tone of the *ayllu* became more serious after the celestial *despacho* had finished burning and the fire ceremony ended. We each approached one of three dyads of *paqos* who were administering the first phase of the initiation rites. Lying down on the blanket between Don Hilario and Doña Bernadina and gazing upward toward the expansive sky, I saw hundreds — maybe thousands — of stars peering down and surrounding us. The sky seemed to stretch on endlessly.

In Peru I have witnessed vast star constellations that I have never seen at home. Besides the fact that Peru is in the southern rather than the northern hemisphere, the sky is exceptionally clear and it is possible to see much greater distances. The mountains and Pachamama have a relationship with the sky. They function as an integral part of each other and belong together in the formation of the vertical world. This is a sharp contrast to the modern world where man-made urban skylines have been placed between the earth and the stars.

As I closed my eyes, I heard Don Hilario chanting sacramental words in Quechua. Out of my three energy centers a vortex of white light emerged and intensified. I was aware of falling into a deep altered state hovering on the edge of consciousness. At one point I noticed that one of the *paqos* had placed a *khuya* in my hand, which I was holding over my Belly. The next thing I knew, Don Hilario was trying to help me sit up. We sat in stillness for a while, reorienting to the physical world. When we were reasonably back into our bodies, Perry and I trekked down the hillside, back to camp.

The starlit sky provided ample light for us to see as we walked back to our tent in silence. Perry showed me what he had been working on for the ceremony. He had created a vacuum inside a plastic coke bottle that contained a battery-powered device he had purchased on our shopping adventure in Cusco. In addition to the vacuum, there were two large crystals inside the bottle. Perry told me the vacuum protected the power of the crystals from outside interference and then said, "Wait till you see what happens." He was clearly excited about it.

Perry carefully placed his invention outside of the large communal tent. Then we went into the tent wearing several layers of clothing underneath wool *mantas* (ponchos) and clustered closely together for warmth.

The night temperature had dropped significantly since the sun set and was approaching freezing. The familiar weight of my *mesa* bundle sat comfortably on my lap. We spoke softly among ourselves as we waited for the entrance of the *paqos*. A while later, they entered and formed a half-circle facing us. I could feel a subtle current of *kausay* energy humming through the energetic field. A silence fell over the tent as the lanterns were put out and there was no longer any artificial light.

I have learned that an environment without light makes the veils between worlds more permeable so the *apus* can enter into this dimension. In the past, *paqos* have told me that developing the ability to see in the dark helps to facilitate the development of psychic sensitivity because of the effect it has on the way our brains process incoming sensory information. By eliminating incoming stimulation via our ordinary senses, our perception through other channels becomes more acute.

Sitting in the darkness, I could make out Don Sebastian's deep voice quietly calling the winged beings into sacred space. I sensed that an energetic shift was occurring in the room, as I experienced the vibrational current building. In the pitch-black space surrounding me, I could see specks of white light swirling and forming a luminous vertical column of white light in the center of the tent. Although I could not make out the boundaries of physical forms, energetic beings in shades of golden and white light without defined edges were beginning to materialize and fill the tent. Their shapes had a curious texture of dimensionality and depth, with fluctuating shadows and light that did not appear solid. There was a great deal of intricate detail but I was unable to register exactly what I was seeing. Whatever I was seeing lacked any context in my physical reality. It looked like there were openings that were not exactly doorways because they kept shimmering and fluctuating in and out of my perception. The variations seemed to be delineating some sort of energetic space in an unfamiliar realm. They were subtle and hard to make out — yet in fleeting moments more defined shapes emerged and they became easier to register.

I was viewing an alien world for the first time and I wanted to make visual sense of what I was seeing so that I could process the sensory information in a way that I might better understand it.

The energetic formation I was witnessing was too ephemeral for me to capture with my Mind. I was left with vague fleeting impressions that I later attempted to draw. However, what I was able to commit to paper was only an elusive approximation of a transitory mood.

As I write about my memory of the experience now, it seems like I am trying to access a dream experience that is only lightly brushing the brink of consciousness. It seemed very strange to be seeing all of this with my eyes open in complete darkness. At the same time all of this was happening visually, the room was full of a strange orchestra of sound. I could hear bells ringing, Adriel's whistle, and other eerie reverberations that I had never heard before and cannot describe. The sounds were not exactly melodic, but I could detect a range between high and low resonance. It reminded me of the sound an electric guitar makes when an object is moved across the strings. As I think back on it now, it strikes me that there were more dissimilar varieties of somewhat harmonious, free-form noises emanating in the room than there were people present.

Sitting bunched under my *manta* next to Perry, I oscillated in and out of varying degrees of consciousness. I fluctuated between a more conscious state of taking the sensory experience that was happening all around me into a very deep place that I was only vaguely aware of and have no words for — I only knew I was there. It felt like I could have been asleep but I was not. I noticed that it made no difference if my eyes were opened or closed — I was still seeing the same thing.

The column of light in the center of the room had grown more pronounced and the depth of the shapes in the room had deepened. I saw a path through three doorways. Psychically, I stretched and passed through the doors. I could now see multiple layers that reminded me somewhat of the emanations seen in

Tibetan prayer paintings of Bodhisutras extending from the earth into the sky.

The *Mosoq Karpay* rites had created a quantum shift and time and space were being redefined. By the time I received the actual rites I was in a deeply altered state. Past memories of how to source from the energetic collective that had been stored in my luminous body were reawakened. Beings were flying around the room in simultaneously elliptical and diagonal paths. I heard rites being given to me in a language I could not understand. I could feel energy flooding my body. I was intuitively reaching up into a column extending above my body into a realm in which I was on the verge of being unable to maintain consciousness, and then I was experiencing coming back down. This happened twice. Perry told me later that while I was receiving rites, twice he saw my spirit rising up beyond my body on wings. He said it became twice as tall as my physical form as it towered over my body while flexing white transparent wings. What I was experiencing may have corresponded with what he saw, but I cannot be sure. A crystal that had been imprinted with these rites was put into my hand by one of the *paqos*. As I sat down, I heard a voice in my Mind say, "You passed."

Perry received the rites immediately after me. The beings of light continued to fly around the column of light that extended through the top of the tent into the sky with specks of light moving everywhere. The sounds I was hearing stayed the same. I could not see anything beyond what I have described — including what was happening to Perry. Later, Perry told me he felt tingling and beautiful ringing sounds coming down and going up through his body at the same time and had arched his back and opened his mouth to receive the intense channel of energy flowing through him. Perry said that while he was experiencing the energy transmission he had not known where he was or how long it lasted.

Sometime after the ceremony had ended, we all stood up in the tent. Jose Luis told Perry that it was okay for him to put on his demonstration with the crystals. Perry asked the group to form a circle in the tent, holding hands while we all stomped our feet in unison. Once we all got on the same beat and were stomping in a steady rhythm, Perry stepped outside the tent flap and grabbed his crystal-vacuum coke bottle.

He moved inside the circle and began circling in front of each of us as we continued holding hands and stomping our feet. A loud rattling sound emanated from the plastic bottle he was holding as he continued walking around the inside of the circle, and a glow began to appear as the rattling sounds being generated in the bottle continued to increase in strength. The sounds accelerated as a powerful glow began to radiate out about a foot beyond the bottle. Then it all stopped and it was over.

We all stood in silence inside the circle, knowing that something had happened, but not really knowing quite what. Perry explained that the rattling of the crystals inside the battery-powered coke bottle vacuum had produced a very bright light.

The group started breaking up and leaving the tent, and several people thanked Perry for his demonstration. Perry told me later that after leaving the tent, he had thanked Jose Luis for allowing him to make the demonstration. A little later, we wandered back to our tent and fell into a deep sleep until morning.

17. Down from the Mountain

That religious experiences exist no longer needs proof. But it will always remain doubtful whether what metaphysics and theology call God and the gods is the real ground of these experiences. The question is idle, actually, and answers itself by reason of the subjectively overwhelming numinosity of the experience. Anyone who has had it is seized by it and therefore not in a position to indulge in fruitless metaphysical or epistemological speculations. Absolute certainty brings its own evidence and has no need of anthropomorphic proofs.

—Carl Jung

July 14, 2011

The next day, after receiving *Mosoq Karpay* rites, we completed the pilgrimage ceremony as the Apu Huascaran had instructed by making an offering of corn to Pachamama. Then it was time to make our descent down the mountain toward the Urubamba Valley. After performing a ritual to thank Sigrena Cocha for her assistance and saying good-bye, we hiked along the mountainous shoreline above the turquoise lagoon for several hours. Eventually the landscape changed and we crossed regions of rocky terrain speckled with small farms. We clambered down steep hills, walking on the patches of short rough tufts of grass commonly found at higher altitudes in the Andes. Several times our path crossed the tiny stream flowing down from the mountain lagoon.

The stream kept disappearing and reappearing as we forged ahead.

At some point, we realized that the path that we were supposed to be following was on the other side of the rock-strewn bank of the stream that had gradually grown wider in the descent. The trail that we were on disappeared and we saw that the horses carrying the gear were on the opposite side of the watercourse.

We decided to continue walking downhill, with the hope of finding a point where it would be easier for us to cross. Eventually we found ourselves on the outside of a stone fence surrounding a small farm. Anticipating that we could cross closer to the stream, we arrived unexpectedly in a pasture with a large bull. Luckily, the bull was not concerned by our presence. As quickly as possible, we climbed over the rock fence into a green field with more animals. The llamas and chickens did not appear as menacing as the bull and were equally oblivious to our existence. We made our way across the grassy meadow that was apparently their home and arrived at the edge of the rocky stream, which was flowing about fifteen feet below. We were expecting to find a bridge of some sort — and we did. However, the bridge consisted of four pipes approximately three inches in diameter that were bound together with wire. I considered trying to wade across the stream but that would have been even more precarious. I was appreciative when one of the horse wranglers who had escorted us on our journey appeared out of nowhere to help. He nimbly convoyed us, one at a time, across the makeshift bridge while holding our hands.

Meanwhile, Don Sebastian had decided on another tactic. He trusted his equilibrium crossing the rocky current and went into the water. Don Sebastian's sturdy frame was larger and more surefooted than the rest of us — even in his plastic sandals. He was also more appropriately dressed, wearing the traditional

Q'ero trousers that were cut above the knee. Fortuitously, we all made it to the other side safely and our journey continued.

A couple of hours later, while we were still hiking through wet grassy landscapes, Perry abruptly stopped and excitedly shouted, "This is the pink and the green from my dream!" We were in a place where mossy stones were scattered across the landscape. In his dream from a couple of years ago Perry and I were on a hillside. Perry was driving a bulldozer towards where I was standing. He was pushing dirt ahead and I was waving my hands, guiding him toward the pink and green. In the dream, the pink and the green represented a vision of our new home.

The dream had felt big at the time and had continued to hold meaning for Perry. He had talked about the pink and the green off and on for the last couple of years, wondering what it meant. Now, standing at the base of Ausangate, facing the glacier in the distance, Perry was struck with by a burst of intuitive insight that what he was seeing correlated with the images in his dream. He said, "Look at the moss on the rocks — it's pink and green."

Later, I asked Perry why this was the pink and the green — it was not the first time he had seen green moss on red rocks. Perry explained that this felt different — somehow he knew that this was the pink and green.

As we followed the rediscovered path, the terrain eventually changed again. The green tufts of grass gradually disappeared and the route turned into a rocky trail that traversed the side of the mountain. As we forged on ahead, Perry spotted unusual looking rocks that he identified as remnants of dinosaur bones. Our other *ayllu* buddies became excited with Perry's novel sightings and began inquiring about what he was doing. As the discussion grew more dynamic, I dropped behind to spend my last minutes with Ausangate in silent appreciation and reverie. Out of the corner of my eye, I noticed Adriel perched quietly behind a rock, his jet-black eyes darting quickly back and forth as he surveyed the landscape. His manner reminded me of a scavenger bird like a raven. I wondered what he was doing and when he had arrived but did not ask since he seemed engaged in his own activity.

I passed him, mutely trudging up the path by myself. Doña Bernadina caught up to me, prancing and skipping with what appeared to be an unlimited source of energy. She grinned and playfully grabbed my hand. We marched on together until we could see the wranglers in the distance ahead. The horses that had carried our bags had stopped and were grazing near the temporary camp that the wranglers had assembled for our lunch stop. The cooks were preparing the meal. We had come to the end of the trail. When I looked up the side of the mountain at the right, I could see a road.

I poured myself and Doña Bernadina cups of coca tea and plopped down on a large rock next to her. The two of us leaned our backs up against each other for a minute or two, relaxing in the noonday sun.

Doña Bernadina pretended she was tired and feigned a huge sigh of relief while dramatically drooping her head and shoulders in an exaggerated movement. I shook my head at her knowingly and we both started laughing. Doña Bernadina climbs mountains as swiftly as a frisky young mountain goat. I was fully aware that today's hike had not been a physical challenge for her. A minute later she jumped up and began singing, making circular motions and gestures as she danced around the circle of people who were sitting on the ground eating.

18. Conversation with Jose Luis

About forty-five minutes later we packed up and climbed on the bus that had arrived to take us back to Cusco. I had asked Jose Luis if we could discuss the manuscript for the first volume of *Lessons of the Inca Shamans* and we found a seat together in the back of the bus. This chapter is a slightly cleaned-up version of our taped conversation that day.

DB: Jose Luis, what do you think is important to explain more fully?

JL: In the Andes Mountains today, there are only four remaining active lineages. There used to be twelve. Each of the four surviving lineages has different regionalisms and ways, because of their respective traditions related to their topography. For instance, here in the highlands of the Q'ero, trading of wool, alpacas, and llamas is very important in their economy. In the case of Vilcabamba, coca leaves provide their livelihood. They are merchants of fruits and tropical stuff. They do not have llamas or alpacas.

The Q'ero have become popular because of the wonderful, colorful, living traditions that they have — particularly around carnival and fertility, etc. But there are other groups that you have been exposed to. For instance, the people of Vilcabamba. The *altomesayoqs* whom you have worked with — they all belong to the lineage of Vilcabamba. It is important to clarify this. The *altomesayoqs* come from Vilcabamba and their *mesa* belongs to the Vilcabamba lineage.

There are different groups and one of the groups that probably nowadays is being exposed to this new spiritual lens is the Q'ero. But it does not mean that the Q'ero are the ones that hold the whole context of cosmology, not at all. They have a version that is pure, beautiful,

Figure 32. Jose Luis and the altomesayoq Santiago creating a despacho (photo by Brad VonWagenen)

fantastic, and it works for their environment. If you are a herder, it works.

What I teach is a hybrid of the different groups. I have learned a lot from the mountain spirits, from the Vilcabamba lineage. So I think what you also need to give yourself credit for is not only the Q'ero that you are working with but other systems as well.

You have not been to all of the territories in the Andes Mountains and have not met people from all of the villages yet. There is also a rich cosmology and body of knowledge that comes from the lineage of Lake Titicaca, known as the island people. They are the people of the sun, living on the shores of Lake Titicaca with spectacular medicine traditions. Another region in the Andes is the lineage of Surimana. Wonderful traditions.

The mountain traditions differ among regions in their approach to shamanism and have some unique regional deities. These regional deities really have to do with the nature, the quality, and the type of the region's topography. For instance, at these elevations you need to be in right relationship with the *apus* from the get-go. For example, the little plants are at the mercy of frost. They receive either too much water or no water at all so their lifeline is frail. Yet, when you have a strong relationship with the mountain spirits as we have here, people can flourish tremendously. They are able to raise great herds and great potatoes because they live in *ayni*, in right relationship with the *apus* of these mountains.

The common denominator between all of the different villages living in these Andes Mountains is the Quechua language. One of those groups, which you have worked with, are the Q'ero who live in this highlands. The Q'ero have been exposed to the church as well, but because of their isolation and their lifestyle as herders and farmers, they have remained insular. Interestingly, their farming tradition is altitudinal. They have different ecological levels that they farm at. They chose to live at high elevation because the grass for the animals is very good. You have seen all those llamas and alpaca herds. They thrive in these elevations. The animals do not do as well at lower elevations because the grasses are different. The grasses that are growing here are the grasses that they love. They have the build for this type of elevation.

So in the case of the Q'ero, the Spanish conquest did not push them into isolation. They have stayed here because they are herders and this is where their animals thrive. In regard to farming, they have a range of

Figure 33. Alpacas in the high Andes (photo by Tom Blaschko)

different ecological-level farming — from corn, chili peppers, to sweet potatoes, to small potatoes way up — dehydrated potatoes, etc. They have at least six or seven of those ecological levels.

The Q'ero have been legendary, particularly in the last 20 years, because they have been able to keep their traditions pretty much untouched in comparison to other groups of Quechua people. Groups from other topographies and regions, living in areas that are more accessible, have adopted more of the modern ways. In the case of the Q'ero, they have not adopted too many of the Christian traditions. The little bit of the Christian tradition that they have developed centers around the mountain Q'ollorit'i, or Snow Star, which has become a symbol of Christ.

You could say there are three basic domains of shamanism in Peru today. What I have just explained to you is about mountain shamanism. There is also coastal shamanism, with San Pedro traditions. Those *paqos* are amazing healers. And then the jungle *paqos*, the Amazonian shamanism — the jaguar *paqos*. That is a different ball game.

So you have three realms, three regions of consciousness, consisting of different approaches, cosmology, belief systems, iconography, and mythology. For instance, Sachamama is the mother of the rain forest. You do not have trees at this elevation so what is important here are the mountain spirits. In the jungle, Sachamama translates herself in the big, mighty trees such as the *lupuna*. These enormous trees stand 60 meters high and the thickness of these trees is the length of this bus! Just the trunk! The jungle has a different ecosystem from mosses and orchids to parrots and everything. It is a whole living system out there where the spirit of the rain forest lives.

The three systems of shamanism, the jungle, coastal, and mountain approaches, are based upon their specific regions and geography. They are very rich in their own unique settings. For instance, the jaguar imbibes the plant medicine of *ayahuasca*. The spirit of *ayahuasca* comes and reveals to you what needs to be done in the moment, right there on the spot. You do not have to be throwing coca leaves, or have your *mesas* — none of that. So that is what Peru is. Peru is not only the Q'ero.

DB: Well, I would like to support what you are doing in your work and wondered if there is anything that I may be misrepresenting.

JL: The rich diversity is one aspect. The other point I would like make clear is the importance of the vision of Don Manuel Q'uispe. The individual Don Manuel had great vision. Before his death, Don Manuel had come into a place of deep awareness that his people were not going to have the strength in the well-rooted traditions to be the conduits of the old tradition. For many of the Q'ero today, shamanism has become an economic adventure. Does that make them *paqos*? Perhaps to some extent. They still live in the tradition of honoring the land, but does that make them masters? The old masters are gone. No one has been fit in the village to become the next *altomesayoq*. Why is that? It is like, you have a class of students and nobody will go for a Ph.D. Nobody has the drive, stamina, focus, that guiding light within.

The reason is simple. The Q'ero have come down from the mountains and have become acquainted with modern ways of living. Their homes no longer have to be little places made out of stones and thatch. Now they can have gas stoves and glass in their windows. They can educate their kids in schools. A lot of the Q'ero do not want their kids way up there. It is a lot easier for them to buy a little piece of land and live here — and educate their kids. Education is important.

Don Manuel Q'uispe said, "When I come down from the mountains, I am going to do what is needed in my power even if my own village does not agree with this, which is fine." He disseminated his knowledge to a few people. One of them is me, and the other is Alberto Villoldo — there is no other — that's it.

I am not Q'ero. I am from the city. The new *paqos* are individuals that need to integrate the old and the new at a higher level. The new *paqos* have to be educated and have an understanding of existence, the journey itself, and of their current cosmologies. They need to have developed an awareness of how life is, with aggression and violence, nowadays. You know the type of life. We have electronics and information and room service, etc. A lot of us do not want that. We want to source from primary things, from life, from light.

We no longer abide by the old theologies because in the Christian tradition, for instance, God created the universe and left. He left his creation and we are waiting for his return. Come on — right?

Don Manuel's vision was that his people needed to merge with the city, with the process of industrialization, with the process of culture. He believed that perhaps a few survivors along the way, if their medicine or their calling was strong, would be able to integrate the new and the old at a higher level. Meanwhile, there are not too many of them.

Maybe the people from the West are the ones, individuals who have gone through the dark night of the soul and have come to understand their personal and collective journey. Perhaps, these individuals are highly educated and have already healed individually. They no longer source from the cultural paradigm but from a different context of reality. These are the new *paqos.*

This is the reason Don Manuel started giving away this medicine free to people. In my case, I worked with him for a number of years, since the early 1990s until he died. He lived in my house. He was like a grandfather to me. His stories, teachings, traditions, and his way of seeing the world had to be learned from a Quechua context. How a Q'ero person sees the world is different from how you see it or how I see it.

The words are one thing, but to eat, to be, to live inside the culture and understand is another. There is an old saying, in order to learn a language you need to source from that culture, or you need to live in that culture so you know the language. Otherwise, it is just a translation. I had to learn to see. I had to learn how he thought, how he felt, how he saw the world. It was not an easy task. We traveled to the States together a number of times. We did a number of demonstrations, presentations, ceremonies, and healing ceremonies — particularly after 9/11 and all of that.

So, in Peru the vision of the medicine tradition is a hybrid. The new *paqos* have to be cross-pollinators. You cannot just use one system, one tool, one approach. There are many approaches. Because of progress, because of communications, you cannot just use the mountain system. I love the mountain system because it does not rely on any psychotropic medicines whatsoever. It is clear. Getting to that level of clarity is a different ball game. It is an uphill battle for a lot of us to be living in that energy, with that degree of serenity like the *paqos* do here, with a degree of clarity as well.

DB: So, for Westerners who are willing to make the commitment to learn the medicine traditions, what do you tell us to do?

JL: As the medicine people say, it takes Heart, real Heart. The approach is very simple. You begin with the collective and through the collective, you heal the personal. In the West our approach is, heal yourself first and then you can heal the others — which also works.

DB: Yes, in Jungian Depth Psychology, it is the latter approach. I believe that this occurs for Westerners because the West does not have the same kind of support system. A lot of what has been published has focused more on a new-age, metaphysical, ego-based philosophy, based on the premise "you can have anything you want." I wanted to write about the shadow side of it because it is not talked about or understood very well. Writing is a vehicle to serve the collective.

JL: Right. Um, I like that. You know, I think we need to. Since you are speaking about the collective, why not speak about the shadow of the collective? And why certain approaches and theologies are not working for us.

DB: Isn't the collective goal to try to save the earth and to work on connecting the energy?

JL: No, I think the collective goal is that they need to save themselves. We have a deep shadow aspect in our lives that we need to save ourselves from.

DB: Isn't that what Castaneda wrote about with sorcery?

JL: I read that a long time ago. Ultimately, what is it that you want out of this whole adventure, this epic journey? You have to come into a place of self-awareness per se, into a place of right relationship. All of the aggression, violence, or whatever is the lion that is lurking out there. We are all in that big vessel. So, we want to either save the earth or save ourselves. I think in the case of the Q'ero, what I love about them is, why not live life to the fullest? We do not need to save anything. Water the land, feed the land, and walk in *ayni* with the land. It is not that your goal is to save the land or to save yourself. Your goal is to live life to the fullest.

DB: So it is no longer a hero's journey.

JL: Absolutely. You don't need to do suffering. You do not need to fight certain beliefs and positions. No, create meaning from how deeply engaged and meaningful your life can be.

DB: Isn't it about connection?

JL: It is always about connection because we have a cultural makeup in which everyone has been disenfranchised from life, from happiness. We must change that. In the case of Christianity — we have been kicked out of the garden. Even if there is a new God hanging on the crucifix, he seems to be doing the same things as the *apus* by providing us with safety, fertility, abundance, etc. The job description of Christ is pretty much the same as the *apus* except that there is a lot of agony and pain in his ways. We do not need to have the same agony, the same suffering. Maybe Christ is the embodiment of our own suffering, believing that is necessary, but we do not have to do it this way.

DB: So, everything is about living fully.

JL: Right. Bringing, transporting the energy of that collective state, of numinous experience. The *altomesayoqs* take it a step further by aiding the *apus* in physical manifestation. The *altomesayoqs* are highly specialized. They have developed the ability to create the doorway between realms, between worlds — whatever that is. The cool thing about this is that these spirits — all of them — are benefactors. All of them are in charge of providing comfort, safety, guidance. They make sure there is life force in the little plants, life force in the makeup of the village so that everything flows in right relationship. Their job description pertains to guardianship and stewardship of humanity.

The *apus* obey as well. Within their realm of consciousness, there are also hierarchies of power. There are little *apus* that are probably more lost than you and I, and there are the big *apus*. Through the *altomesayoq* tradition, particularly in this area, these spirits have fused themselves so much and so well to our human cultural paradigm that they have even learned our language. They have learned to speak, think, feel, and validate exactly the same way we do. That is outstanding. That is phenomenal. What is the principle that guides the little potato to become a full-blown potato?

The *altomesayoq* brings the voice of spirit. Simple as that. For us individuals that live in this realm of consciousness, you know it is like wow! This is because we live in a culture in which we are separated from the universe. We are people that no longer speak to trees, or mountains, or anything — so this is phenomenal. But for individuals such as the Q'ero, you, and I, spirit is something to us.

DB: So, the prophecy is that the next group of medicine people will come from the West. The people coming from the West will be bridging both, through learning the Incan ways. Then, will the next phase of the vision manifest in the form of the old traditions or will it morph into something new?

JL: The next step is cross-pollination. You can embody the Q'ero teachings, the Vilcabamba teachings, but ultimately it is your voice. Ultimately, it is a new, evolved culture. This has to do with a paradigm shift. This has to do with an entirely new cosmic vision, a different understanding of the universe, and a different vision. You know, a cosmic vision of Western people is different than the cosmic vision of the mountain people. The new *paqos* have to realize that the current cosmic vision in the West is something that creates that separation. They need to embrace the cosmic vision that we have here, and then take it and carry it forward.

DB: Then once you get past the question of whether you believe that *apus* can materialize or not — the vision becomes a reality. So, in the West, besides working with clearing the shadow to become a living embodiment of the energetic collective and of *kausay*, it also requires learning to trust intuition. It is not going to come from the old ways, but rather through the energetic connection — by having the fire ignited from the rituals and technology of the old ways. Once the flame is lit, then it needs to be brought forth in a way that can be assimilated in our culture.

JL: Yeah, because in the West we do not have herders and farmers. People buy their stuff in supermarkets. So, you have to adapt the old into the new setting in a way that is meaningful, and in that process of adaptation you need to bring other elements.

In my case, I cannot just stick to Q'ero cosmic vision. It is too rigid and naïve, in a way. I love the approach of jungle *paqos*, their way of seeing and understanding energy. So going back to your question, it really has to do with becoming a global individual. But if you are like everyone else, dedicated to your sense of self and the old salvation — then that is not going to do anything.

DB: So serving the collective is not collective in terms of the culture, but rather the energy, the higher vibration of the collective.

JL: Yes, collective does not necessarily mean that it is your group of people, your family, or your country. It doesn't mean that you need to understand how they live and deal with each story, or draw conclusions of all the common denominators between everyone, no. Collective means living a life in which you are no longer your own person but you are collective. You are the land, you are the people. Sourcing from this other entirely different way so you do not have to deal with the shortcomings of the personal, which is your self frame or your sense of misfortune, love, money, or work. Collective means the makeup of light and life and fertility. Can it support you? Can you grow corn with it?

DB: What I often see us doing as Western analysts and psychologists is to get stuck in our heads. What you and I are talking about now involves making a shift from using our heads into experiencing the collective energetically in our Hearts and bodies, by becoming an expression of the experience.

JL: Yes, it occurs as a mythic understanding of reality that has moved beyond the symbolic or literal domain. The mythic element gives you one thousand and one ways to understand it. One thousand and one ways to express it— and all of them are valid. For example, as a literal construct, if I give you a fork, it is only a tool to eat. However, it could also become a tool to dig.

DB: To paraphrase this, in Jungian language, what you are describing is called the archetypal realm. The energy of the archetype is expressed and manifests through various symbols. I believe this was one of the places where Jung fell short. There is another realm that goes beyond the archetypal, the essential level of the energetic collective.

JL: ...energetic, absolutely. Absolutely. The collective is energetic, and it depends on our perception and way of engaging in our capacity to create meaning. There are many ways of creating meaning. There are layers of understanding in the way to create meaning.

DB: And maybe that is how we grow corn with it, by putting it into a language that people can understand and access within the context of their lives. Coastal and jungle shamanism would be other ways of making meaning.

JL: Those are approaches. Everything is just an approach. Ultimately, the greatest capacity for human beings — through intent, through love, through all those wonderful virtues, passion, dedication, focus, or stubbornness, whatever — those are just a plethora of adjectives describing your capacity to create a meaningful life. We play with different approaches, decoys. It is about learning to function outside the norm and the traditional cocoon of understanding. Through ritual — particularly ritual — new pathways to understanding are created. Through these pathways of understanding comes the capacity to create more meaning out of life, out of love for life, love for families, and love for loved ones.

DB: This is all an expression of the energetic collective.

JL: Absolutely. But the collective is all over the place — it is just a function of how our perception engages with it. Our perception has to do with our capacity to create meaning in any given exchange. What I am saying is, there are many ways of creating meaning. When you see beyond the symbolism and the archetype, it comes to you and you understand the technical language, you can see the protagonists of this kaleidoscope of occurrences out there that you are calling energetic. It is out of this energy that you can pass through all these different filters, layering of understanding, and still have a way to create meaning. It is all about how you create meaning. There are different ways of creating meaning. The more ways you have to create meaning, the greater the understanding. You cannot just go into one channel of meaning. There are multiple channels.

DB: Are you referring to intersections of time and space, like *pachas*...?

JL: It is not necessarily an intersection. The intersection is the beginning of a moment, rather it is an allocation of time and space. That is the *pacha* in which events, themes, directions, everything has a momentum, is going someplace — a tree, a dream, this bus, etc. Anything that has not been, that has not come into *ayni*, or has not been fulfilled will always try to find a *pacha* to fulfill itself.

DB: Maybe that is why there is a need to create personal stories.

JL: So what is fulfillment? For instance, the seed creates and brings forth the greatest meaning — in the expression of fruit — with the wonderful smells, textures, and forms. Out of this tiny little thing, it develops into color, exuberance, and aroma. Ahh, the miracle of life!

This is not a religion. Mountain spirits are wonderful. I love them dearly. They're great, great points in my journey — or in anyone's journey. And that's what they do. But there's even more — life itself. Even the mountain spirits are gravitating towards the fulfillment of life because through service they fulfill themselves. Even Christ had to die for our sins and so he could fulfill himself and be embraced by God. That is the hero's journey — but we do not have to do sacrifice.

DB: The journey provides the traction to discover meaning.

JL: The journey is the scenario in which you develop your own understanding of your footsteps before and of your footsteps after, being your own witness as much as your own protagonist. That is the journey.

DB: Maybe the purpose of going on the journey is to learn how to step outside of your own paradigm.

JL: You have to step outside of your paradigm. There is no other way. You cannot utilize the given paradigm. We are gifted with intent, with faith, with dreams, with visions, with Heart, and everyone is a co-creator. Everyone has the faculty and awareness of being an active participant in the creation of life. It is probably the greatest awakening. With that comes responsibility, and with that comes awareness and a vision. You have to have a vision.

DB: Maybe that is why religion does not work for many of us, because it is plugging into somebody else's algorithm versus creating and embodying our own.

JL: I think so, too, yeah. Theology is great when you are naïve and just coming out of the cocoon. You need certain directives, certain parameters for character, personality, focus, etc. — to contain all that energy.

DB: Well, all of these experiences are metaphors, expressions of the energetic collective anyway, aren't they?

JL: Pretty much, yeah.

DB: I think it's important for those of us in the West to realize that this is not just about "love and light" or that we can just plug into somebody else's algorithm — that's religion. To do this we have to feel it with our Heart and we have to be able to use our Minds in ways that enables us to work with it, to metabolize it.

JL: I would say the same thing but in different words, you know. Everyone has to have a code.

DB: That is unique to the individual.

JL: Yes. Well, there is the collective code, which is cultural or religious. In addition, you need to have your own code for life, of what is valid for you, empowering to you, and what is sacred to you. Everyone should have a code, and that is the first thing that we teach in cosmology classes, you know? What is important in life? Is it family, love, vision, God, your wife, or is it your Heart? A code has to do with behavior and how you walk in the world. A code has to do with your sense of balance, your sense of love, your sense of equilibrium as well.

DB: It gives structure for people to develop or unfold.

JL: You have to have structure. People need structure.

DB: They need a container.

JL: Exactly. And that is the code.

DB: So, Jose Luis, is there anything else that you would like to see included?

JL: Well, I want people to live fully. I want people to live in right relationship with themselves, with God, with the world, even with their governments, whatever that is. I want people to truly follow what their Hearts are here to do, are here to embrace. That's what it is. This is nothing more than celebration of life, the celebration of your passions — whatever that is. Digging for dinosaurs, or gardening until 1:00 in the morning, so be it. It is not as if you have to save the world in any particular way. It's how can you live life to the fullest? Then comes the realization that this is my way, you know? Now can I integrate into the bigger picture? Through this process, can I find out what my coordinates are in the tapestry of this universe? Where I am in all of this? What is my legacy? I believe in that. It is finding that internal memory, that internal guidance system within us.

At the beginning it is the form, it is the structure. You have got to do this; you have got to follow these three steps. But once you embody that, you need to take that to the fire so it does not own you.

DB: One of the ways this may manifest is through creativity or creative acts, whether it is writing or it is looking for dinosaurs. It is about having some sort of a dialogue with what is living.

JL: Absolutely. I believe in that. You have to have that creative capability every day, every breath. You cannot follow the footsteps of other creators. At the beginning perhaps, but then you just have to actively participate in creation through active creativity.

DB: So, learning the practice, learning the rituals, is not about the specific structure. It is about creating the intention to be in right relationship with the world. Sometimes the *apus* seem to become upset if a ritual is done wrong. Are they reacting to what they perceive to be a lack of respect versus an absolute, concrete, definite procedure?

JL: Well, let me use this metaphor. In any transaction, in order to be in right relationship with a dream, with a universe, with God, whatever, there is a process of healing. There has to be healing. After the healing takes place, there is transformation that is structural. Once you are done developing the transformational and structural parts, then there is free flow. That's embodiment. Embodiment is not just in your Mind like a piece of knowledge — you already know it.

DB: You have to feel it. I love the way this experience corresponds to alchemical symbolism. If you look at alchemy, which is the shadow side of the Catholic Church, it is all about transformation. Every time you go through a cycle, you go through the shadow — the *nigredo*. Then something living emerges and grows, and there is life and fertility. Then there's the coming together, the union, the transformation, the conjunction, through what Jung called holding the tension of opposites — and then the cycle starts over again with the *nigredo*...

JL: Right. It's structuring — every relationship has a structure. Whether it is diametrical opposition, as you say — or similarity — it does not matter, there is always structure.

DB: Or masculine and feminine qualities.

JL: Yeah, but those are just aspects, you know. True embodiment is both.

DB: And that is where it becomes the energetic.

JL: And it is no longer based on structure. Whenever you talk about an energetic construct, an energetic construct is sequential and random. But the structuring itself has to be sequential for us in this plane of reality. This structure has to be sequential. There is nothing random in this.

DB: Isn't that what an important part of this whole process is? Accessing the energetic connection and finding a way of bringing it back into this dimension by creating structure, by finding a way to assimilate it within this culture. The energetic collective itself is outside of time and space. But the expression of it is the way of growing corn with it, bringing it back into the day world.

JL: Right, but it has to do with an inner understanding. I mean true inner understanding that even defies your own account of it.

DB: There are no words for it, are there?

JL: There are no words for it. It is the experience itself. There is a difference between, serving yourself from the experience — which is that structure. It is so different from serving the experience itself.

DB: I love that.

JL: So, the experience is the event, the experience is in the engagement. You can call it anything, serving the relationship more than anything does. It is how you relate and the many other ways you could relate by serving the relationship itself. The experience might be the past, the given, but the relationship is endless. The relationship is always timeless.

DB: Because it is outside of the paradigm.

JL: It is outside, exactly. So, even though I love serving the experience, it has to do with a reenactment in a way. It has to do with coming into a place in which you give fuel to your thoughts and your Heart, to provide new ways of relating to that experience, new ways of creating meaning out of that. But if you change that into a different context, serving the relation, whether it is God, whether it is loved ones or your garden, first of all the awareness of the relation.

DB: And is that through your Heart?

JL: It is your whole being. It is not only mental, or how your garden feeds you, or how God holds the mystery for you — that's embodiment. In order to understand relation, you need to have a structural understanding so there is a receptor that sends the signal per se. So there is similarity, there is dissimilarity — whatever, right? At the end of the day, you have to make *ayni*. There comes a time when you no longer even have to check your *ayni* because you have always been in *ayni* all along. That is the relation.

DB: So, by showing up in our lives we have an engagement. We show up at a certain allocation of time and space — whatever we happen to be living at any given moment. So by living, there is an enactment going on. Being in physical reality is an enactment. Going through the enactment is the way we create meaning to transcend, to get to the next level, if we choose to do that — otherwise we just keep looping in it.

JL: Exactly. In my own understanding, life moves through periodical cycles, and out of these periodical cycles. Through maintaining continuity, it acquires momentum. A eucalyptus has been a eucalyptus for ten years, and then somehow because of environmental cues — less water or Darwin's survival of the fittest — it must undergo a quantum shift into a bigger eucalyptus tree in order to survive. What I am saying is that life has all these momentums. Awareness has to do with how these momentums are pushing your vehicle, and which momentum is making a loop.

DB: It is not necessary to come back to Peru to be on a specific mountain to experience connection. You have the awareness, you go to Peru, you make the connection, you feel the *ayni*, you go through whatever change you go through energetically and you live in this body, living to the fullest wherever you are at — and bringing it back to the collective in whatever you do. It is being in the present moment in whatever capacity. Maybe a potential fallacy for some of us is believing that we can only have an energetic experience when we're in a remote place.

JL: True.

DB: You may get the awareness from having the support of the Q'ero and the *apus* — and experiencing it.

JL: Right. It has to do with our way of managing life, micromanaging life, exercising control. When people find themselves in environmental situations in which they exercise no control whatsoever, they become more available and more aware, more present. When we feel that we are safe, in control, and that we are with all that equipment and technology of the modern world, we go into automatic pilot.

DB: This is why the hero's journey is an enactment, we do not have to do it — but it can be a wakeup call. I have noticed working as a psychologist that people are the most accessible when they are in pain, what is bringing them into my office for the first time. I have learned that with some people, if I am not able to connect with them right then and there in some capacity, and work with them to help them shift into an energetic experience that they can feel and that registers with them, then once they start to feel better — I cannot, it's gone.

JL: True, true. And, you know what the cure is for that? Ritual. Not ceremony but ritual itself — there is a difference between those two. Ceremony is the landscape, but ritual is the enactment. Tapping back into those sources, into those places where that awareness is raw, is primal. We do not have ritual. We have customs and certain traditions, but we do not have an enactment of those principles that you feel — good or bad.

DB: Well, maybe part of it does not know the outcome.

JL: It does not matter what the outcome is. For instance, being in control, in that automatic pilot we always want to know the outcome and the outcome is regulated. But here, you do not need to know the outcome, but rather the event, rather the protagonist, rather, the feeling, the emotion.

DB: May I give you an example that I think illustrates this?

JL: Um hmm.

DB: I had this dream at a crossroads in analytic training, a time when I faced a conflict between studying shamanism and pursuing analytic training. There was a time conflict and at one point, I was in a position during which I had to make a choice of which road I was going to follow. So in the dream I was standing and on the left was a series of judges who were Jungian analysts. They were in a courtroom wearing wigs and robes. Analytic training was a big deal to me at that point in my life and I was very concerned whether I would be able to move forward and complete it. In the dream, on the right, was a cliff looking over a large valley that was far below. In the dream, I was forced to make a choice. I had to either show up for the trial or jump off the cliff. So I jumped off the cliff. I flew and soared, and thought, "Ah, this is so wonderful." I landed and said to myself, "Ah, I'm going to do that again!" Then in the dream, I heard a voice say, "You can't do it again because now you already know what will happen. What gave you the freedom in the experience before was the willingness to jump."

JL: The exercise of innocence. That is what you are saying. In innocence you are dealing with the unknown, you are taking risks. That is what ritual is about. It takes you to that place of innocence. It takes you into that place of not knowing.

DB: Jose Luis, I would like to donate part of the profits from the sales of this book to support the *paqos* and their community in some way.

JL: ARI would be fantastic. The nonprofit that we have is called the Andean Research Institute (ARI). And ARI is doing wonderful things. Really wonderful things. Now we have the social program for kids and mothers and the impoverished. We have the *paqos* program, which has to do with collecting information. It has to do with creating a nice sizable library in different media formats. We have interviews, we have recordings of healing approaches — everything that has to do with the medicine traditions, so that it is not lost. A lot has been lost. There are technologies on the verge of extinction that we're trying to collect in video, voice, and writing — all those technologies, all those mythologies, stories, legends, about transformation, the human condition, and the spirit. It has to do with how we bring the necessary elements of our cosmology to fulfill ourselves in life.

In addition, the second goal of ARI is to promote environmental protection. I am so interested in the rainforest. I would like to spend the rest of my life trying to protect the rainforests in whatever way I can. We are purchasing pieces of land, pieces of land here and there, for the sole purpose of preservation. So animals, ferns, mosses, trees, and whatever stays there unaffected by humans.

This is for the world, this is for everyone, and everyone has that obligation. I think in the case of the environment, everyone is part of this. Everyone. In the case of social outreach, there are people who care about poverty. Our students of shamanism, they care about shamanism.

You know, they want those traditions to be alive. So, there is room for everyone.

We took a break for water here.

DB: I have a lot more I'm interested in. One of the areas is about how to combine these experiences in Peru with living a life in our modern culture.

JL: So, ask me questions.

DB: Well, one of the things I want to ask you about is my current conceptualization of the reentry experience. I guess I understand two things about reentry. There is a creative aspect and there is an aspect of recapitulating. It begins as a somatic experience — that is then recapitulated — first by working with images and then language. I think is very exciting about how shamanic processes correspond to new findings in the field of neuropsychology. There is so much support.

JL: Umm.

DB: And I believe that the stages in early-child-development experiences are relived while going through reentry. We don't have words for it.

JL: Um hmm, um hmm. I am following you.

DB: Well, coming back from Peru after my first intense initiation, what I found most helpful in gaining insight into the energetic experience surprised me. First, I read Castaneda, and then I started reading psychoanalytic material on Object Relations Theory. I discovered that some of the earliest, most primitive psychological states that occur during infant development seem to correspond to what happens after having an intense energetic experience. You come back and you try to make meaning — without a language or context for understanding.

I am also noticing that people have different and unique reactions in reentry. I observed that Perry and I handled it very differently.

JL: Um hmm.

DB: It seems that one of two things happen for people in the reentry struggle. They can become inflated with the energy and feel manic — or highly energized — and have to learn how to contain and harness it in a way that's productive. Alternatively, some people become very introverted and feel alienated because the experience is so difficult for other people who have not been through it to understand — and there are no words for it. Creativity is one way of channeling the energy. I am giving you a summary of what I observed in my own process. I would appreciate hearing what your thoughts are.

JL: All of them are accurate. They are very well depicted, by the way. I think it is what feels right in your Heart. When you find what is right for you and you produce that internal change, then your environment will change as well. That's the key.

DB: It's about sourcing.

JL: Yeah, exactly. That is what I am talking about. Whatever it is that you find deep within you that makes you comfortable, gives you a smile, makes you passionate, makes you creative — gives voice to that environment and produces transformation that heals Hearts and Minds. It is a matter of cultivating. It has to do with cultivating within. And the ritual, time for yourself, and crafting ways how you nurture that finding within you.

DB: Another thing I found coming back was that working with clients was healing. I discovered that my practice was a place where I could work and meet them in those deep, deep states. It became very real.

JL: Um hmm.

DB: When you are working with people, you have to know those places within yourself to work with them.

JL: So you can relate, absolutely.

DB: You learn to source from the mountains instead of people. The mountains are always there. There is an idea in Jungian psychoanalysis that you work through the personal mother, and then you get into the archetypal connection. In Jungian language, it would be that at the core of every complex there is an archetype, the archetypal energy is what heals.

JL: Um hmm.

DB: So if you get to a point where you work through this and you have that connection, then that's the place that you source from. It is that sense of having that inner sense of knowing — and that is what happens in shamanism. The experience cannot be verbally articulated because it is experienced through the body, but it is the same process. I see many parallels between psychoanalysis and shamanism. Psychoanalytic work goes into earlier states, which is what happens in this work, because you have to go to primitive places.

JL: You have to go to those primary places, definitely. You have to figure them out and bring them out into the light. They have tremendous potential. It really deals with not only your capacity to exercise well-being. There are key aspects that remind you of potential, remind you of gifts.

DB: Yeah. I could not work with someone if I could not envision wholeness for them, if I could not see that.

JL: Healing, has to do really, you should underline this, healing or the healer needs to be able to ignite, turn on the switches in a person's body, whether the situation is physical, nonphysical, whatever, right, and reactivate the memory of their healed state. That is all they need. As human beings, our bodies have memory of our healed state, so it is accessing that healed state and turning on those switches. Making that memory active. That is what healing is about.

DB: We need to have and hold that vision for the people we work with. As healers, we need to see, sense, and understand what the healed state of the individual is. A lot of the new research that is coming out in psychology and in neuropsychology is about what is happening in the energetic field between people and what gets co-created in the field. Now in western science, there is support for it.

JL: Right, yeah, right. Great, great.

DB: Maybe part of it is putting it in a language that is not too foreign or frightening for the Western collective.

JL: Right, yeah. Everything in the universe has a healed state. Everything. Everything. So the *paqo* has to access that memory. The *paqo* has to see, sense how, where the technical state is and bring that into the healing by moving energy using *mesa* stones — or whatever — to remember and hold that healed state. Once the body recognizes the healed state, aligns itself with it, that is it. The healing is done.

The healed state, it is a degree of awareness, the capacity for seeing and sensing. Not everyone is able to see that because there are guiding principles, their deep mythic construct of realities and so for those individuals — particularly in this cosmology that we live in — everyone sources from the scarcity.

DB: When I am sitting in the room with somebody working through past trauma, if we end up in a very dark spot, I am continually sourcing and pulling in energy. I often feel myself returning to Ausangate or Alankoma — when I was blasted with energy — and that is what I source from. I function more as a conduit. Do you think that is what usually happens in shamanism? We get our memories awakened and when we are working as healers, we are able to pull from that place?

JL: Absolutely. You have to, and healing is a non-personal state, by the way. It could be personal but it's not. It's a non-personal state. So in this case, you clearly delineate the frontiers of your clients and your energy, and none of your stuff passes on to your clients. Conversely, your clients' energy does not pass on to you either. So, a good healer understands what is personal and non-personal. And healing is a non-personal event but it sources from tremendous unconditional love that sets the pace. Love is not directed towards this individual — none of that. Rather, it is an energetic shift and transaction that imbibes the land, imbibes the spirits, imbibes codes of this individual's memories, to come up to be seen.

DB: So, when we are working that way, aren't we all just being channels for the energy?

JL: Yes. The medicine people from Bolivia look at the body of a person like a hydraulic system. They believe that you just need to move energy. They find the places where the river of light is backed up, where there is nothing flowing. They go at it with a big roto-rooter or plungers and get it moving in a non-personal way. Furthermore, they do not even see the dramas, dilemmas, or whatever of the individual. They only see energy, and that is why ritual is necessary. To be in that deep state of ritual where you are no longer your own persona. You are, animistically, the guide, the benefactor. You are the voice to the soul's memory. You are a conduit, you are a channel, and let the body express itself.

DB: Yes, it always comes from the body. How are we doing on time?

JL: We are doing great. The city of Cusco is right there. Way in the distance. We are doing well.

DB: You know, meeting and developing relationships with the *apus* has been an interesting process. I noticed that the first time I met with the *apus* — the first time I came here, I could not believe what was going on. Then, I looked at the *altomesayoqs'* faces. I trusted their faces, but I thought, "This is really weird!" My understanding of reality had to stretch in order to begin to accommodate the actual experience. Then, the second time in Peru, I was still confused and trying to make sense of it all. Then the third time I was here, meetings with the *apus*, I was not even listening to the words. I was just feeling the energy. This time, I have observed that I fluctuate between taking notes and feeling the energy, but I am noticing that when you look at the notes, the words themselves are not that profound; it is the energy behind it.

JL: It is a transaction. In my case, I go into this trance state of sorts. The information comes in as Quechua and comes out as English. Because it's — exactly — this energy, this transaction. Then comes the humor, and then comes the feeling good.

DB: The life.

JL: Yeah, the life. And that for me is medicine. Yeah, sometimes they have amazing things to say, but most of the time it is the energy.

DB: So, for you last night, during the initiation ritual what was that like for you? That was so powerful.

JL: For me, personally, I was held by the *apus*. They were all over me. They were talking in my head. It was like, "A little bit to the left." I hope that I know that those voices in my head are the *apus* so I am not going ballistic or crazy. It's fun, it is really fun. It energizes me. There is always reciprocity. They fill my Belly and they fill my Mind with, you know, I am an information junky. I love knowledge. So it comes and I learned a lot, so they have been great in that regard. Physically sometimes, it is taxing. But in dreamtime, I am embraced by their presence and I sleep well. These rites of passage take a lot of you, everything of you. That is the only way to do it. It is integrating. It is right. It is the way to bring people into a better place.

DB: Well, after experiencing a rite of passage, perception changes, the jungle did it for me.

JL: The jungle is a different gorilla, isn't it? Yeah.

DB: That jaguar, wow.

JL: Oh, those cats, yeah. I love the jungle. I am empty with my realm and then the voice of the animals will come. They help me find the rhythm, and the song comes, and the song is spectacular. As it comes, I am having this, uh, this climatic, orgasmic, ecstatic flight, and all I am doing is providing the voice for their love, their words with their wisdom. Sound does amazing things. I fly, take off... Many of those songs I do not remember when I am in this other reality.

DB: Those are beautiful. That is another way of holding space, isn't it?

JL: And the songs, I love those songs. Those songs have to do with healing. It is all about healing, and tapping into the souls of everyone and whatever is coming up at that time. It comes through sound.

DB: So, do you understand the words or do you feel it?

JL: I do not even know what they are saying.

DB: Do you recognize sometimes what you are saying?

JL: Occasionally I recognize, but much later, I am like, "Oh, it's about this, oh, it's about that, oh, wow!" Many of the words, the language, is not even Quechua or Spanish, it belongs to different native groups out there. I have learned a little bit so I am able to recognize that. It is a weird combination of Quechua and something else, so that gives me a little door of sorts to peek and just understand what is going on. But with medicine songs, in many instances I do not know what they are about, but it does the healing. It brings the vision.

DB: Do you find — actually, I already know the answer, but I will ask you anyway — that your song changes between the mountains and on the coast?

JL: Totally, totally. Different systems, yeah. I love the coastal *paqos*. They're wonderful. Their *mesas* are huge. It's all about healing. It's all about extractions. And their medicine, San Pedro, gives to your visions. I mean it is not as drastic as *ayahuasca*, you know, boom, you are seeing. Rather it gives a halo to everything, fuzziness to everything, and a deeper understanding of whatever you are seeing. Ah, a eucalyptus tree. You see the glow of life. That's the beauty of that plant. You can snap in and out. It's very gentle. I have not worked with San Pedro medicine in a long time. I feel that *ayahuasca* has chosen me even though I trained with the masters. One time I was in the Amazon and this wonderful *paqo* said, well, you have to choose, you cannot have both. *Ayahuasca* is very jealous, you should know.

DB: Yeah, you do not want to mess with that.

JL: Yeah. *Ayahuasca* chose me. I tried to do San Pedro ceremonies, and I could not even lift my limbs for takeoff, nothing. Just sat there. Nothing. Nothing. So in the case of *ayahuasca* I do not do it that often, maybe once a year. It is like learning to ride a bicycle, you know.

DB: You know what I liked about *ayahuasca* — besides the fact of learning how to give up physical form? I do not like hallucinogenics because my brain travels fast enough anyway, but I loved learning how to transfer out of my head by shifting my assemblage point and move into my stomach, it was like diving under a wave. I never had that experience of having a consciousness outside of my Mind — having it in my Belly.

JL: Um hmm.

DB: *Ayahuasca* forces you into places.

JL: Yeah, yeah, *ayahuasca* has a mind of its own. As much control as you want to exert, you still have to go into your own visions, your own resistance, or your own fears, *ayahuasca* just uproots you and takes you into what you need to see. It is the vine of the soul.

DB: If this ends up in the next book, I think that it is important to clarify that the way to go about participating in an *ayahuasca* ceremony is not by going out and finding *ayahuasca* on the street. That would be the Western way of having a drug experience.

JL: Yeah. *Ayahuasca* is not for everyone. There are people with very fragile psyches, and these poor people all they do is resist, resist. It becomes a survival thing.

DB: You have to give up. When I was being eaten by the anaconda, I learned you have to give up your body.

JL: Absolutely.

DB: And then you are fine. Thank you for doing this, Jose Luis.

JL: No problem, my pleasure.

19. Temple of Pachamama

Upon arriving in Cusco, we grabbed our gear from the bus and headed into the lobby of the hostel where we would be staying. After obtaining our room keys and the luggage we had left behind, we made a beeline for the showers. After a couple of days of not bathing, rooms with showers that had warm water and comfortable beds felt like a luxury. The room where we were staying looked out on a Spanish courtyard of flowers with a view of the city in the distance. The wooden floors and staircase that led up to a small loft with a bathroom had a patina that made the chilly room seem warm and inviting.

After a shower, Perry and I dumped our luggage on the bed and began sorting through it to find a clean set of clothes. With a new set of multiple layers on, Perry and I made our way through the courtyard to the cobblestone street to find something to eat. We walked several blocks down the steep decline and wandered into the main plaza. We decided to eat at the first pizza restaurant that we encountered. The appeal of quinoa was long gone and I was craving something less healthy — with cheese, flour, and seasoning. Perry raised no objection and enthusiastically began ordering a large quantity of food off the menu. In a peaceful satiated state, stuffed with coca tea and carbohydrates, we returned to the room where we were staying. We climbed into bed under three extra wool blankets and promptly fell asleep.

July 15, 2011

This morning after a quick breakfast, we joined Jose Luis in the lobby. We exchanged good-natured small talk about a comfortable night of sleep before heading off for the Temple of Pachamama at Moray. Moray is considered one of the places where the ancestors broke through the veil. This sacred spot is understood by *paqos* to be the mythic Belly of the Andean Mother, Pachamama.

The temple was surrounded by large fields of grass with a view of the Sacred Mountains in the distance. The temple consisted of several large concentric circles that were carved in the highland topography. It is regarded as a place to adjust one's medicine body using the *wakas* as the "tuning fork." Jose Luis explained that the *wakas*, hosting unique vortexes of different vibrational energies, had been marked by boulders at the bottom of the round amphitheater formation fixed in the land.

Wakas are "power spots" infused with energy linked to *ceke* lines, the energy lines that connect the energies in the earth. In areas where these *ceke* lines have been activated, such as Moray, the veil is more transparent, allowing for a greater flow of energy and communication with the collective.

Being in these places helps to induce heightened perception and expanded states of awareness. Sourcing from these spots enables the *paqos* to draw in the energy from the earth to facilitate well-being and healing.

Jose Luis said, "We are here to connect with this mountain spirit to do healings and rites of passage. This is Doña Bernadina's favorite place so she is going to lead us."

We followed Doña Bernadina down the spiral dirt pathway and onto the steps of stone pegs jutting out from the wall. When we reached the bottom, we found places to sit at the individual

Figure 34. Temple of Pachamama at Moray (photo by Carol Dearborn)

wakas that we each had a natural affinity for. We opened our *mesas* and invited the presence of Pachamama and the mountain spirits.

Don André rose to a standing position and extended his arms out in a motion that encompassed the landscape around us. He began speaking:

Embrace this valley and the meaning. For me, individually, this has been the most extraordinary journey. You have not received the old, traditional rite of passage. You have been given the new rites of passage. This is a new *pacha*, a new way of being, and a new medicine people. Now, you have to walk in the world like a big *paqo*, a *hatun paqo*. It is not that you are going to walk in the world with a big banner on your foreheads. *Soo-si-koo-yow-un* in Quechua is a metaphor. It means it is not that you have a title. *Soo-si-koo-yow-un* is not something that you traditionally wear as an outfit. It's a way of being.

Little by little, this, this seed has to grow. This is about our performance as individuals of service. This is about how the energy, the medicine, flows and becomes articulated — how it is manifested through you. There will be people in your village that might need your assistance, people that require healing. Since you are now equipped, all you will need to do is call the mountain spirits. This must come from your deep, very clear intent. When your intent is clear, the medicine will be with you. The *apus* will dispense medicine and healing for those in need. Your *mesa* now includes a crystal that has high value, tremendous value. It is not only a crystal *mesa*, but a condor *mesa*. It is a visionary *mesa*. And that is what the *Mosoq Karpay* is about — a new vision.

It needs to start with you. You need to engage in your own healing — through your own healing, through your own discovery.

Jose Luis interjected:

What he is saying is do not miss out on this opportunity. Maybe this is the only one left. Do not miss out on this opportunity to bring healing to your lives. When that healing gets done, then the manifestation of this energy that you have received will be more visible, more palatable, and your way of being as you walk in the world will entirely change. It will change you and change the ones around you.

Don André then continued:

What I know from this *mesa* is that your intent now needs to be your banner. Your intent now needs to be your vehicle. Your intent needs to be clear, absolutely clear. And with that, you can mix your faith, your will, your want, your need; your visions — whatever — and healing will take place. Anything will come into manifestation.

So, brothers and sisters, I ask you from the depth of my Heart — you need to weave your *mesa* now composed of that crystal, into your lives. You have to take care of it. You need to feed your *mesas* with love, incense, candles, aromas, smells, and love.

The *mesa*, as you know, is a living entity. It is not a rock. It is a living entity. So as you get tired, the *mesa* too might get tired. You need to feed yourself as much as you need to feed your *mesa*. This *mesa* that you have is connected to those powers, to those mountain spirits, those spirits that we have talked to, woven in this land, so you need to feed and maintain that relationship. Keep it alive and fed.

There are so many endeavors you have in your lives — journeys, health, relationships, projects, etc. — that need to come into fulfillment like a flower. You need to see the fulfilled state of all of these endeavors. There is so much assistance that you have. We have cited a few things such as the rainbows and the different elementals. All of them are connected to your *mesa*.

The land itself can perpetuate field energy in a place, in some location of people. The powers that direct all those energies down in the land obey the directives of mountain spirits, the directives of God. When that *mesa* is connected to those higher powers, nothing in the land will touch you, it will always protect you.

The *apus* have all these directives, all these principles, and their job description is health. Their job description is vision. When yours and theirs are in alignment as you walk in the world, as you find challenges, they will unfold. They will open up and always create opportunity for you so nothing will challenge you in the way of not having a *mesa*.

You are stewards of the land. You are stewards of those mountain spirits. You are the voice of the land. You are the voice of those spirits. All of these people that I work with, Doña Bernadina, Jose Luis, or whoever — we are stewards. We bring the voice of the land. We must be open conduits of those spirits and bring well-being in whatever situation we may have in front of us. We need to step away from the personal. My only recommendation is please take good care of that *mesa*. You should understand how valuable that *mesa* it is for you. Take care of it, nourish it, and, and embrace it. May this be a great day like all the great days we have had together. That is all I have to say. Happy journey!

Don Hilario spoke next:

I do not think I have greeted you, so good morning to you. I would like to say a few things about the *karpay* rites and the *mesa*. We have encountered wonderful experiences, and gone to wonderful places, with great teachings and great rituals. Even though the experience might have reset your medicine bodies, and even though the experiences that we have had in the mountain have revealed wonderful gifts for you, your steadiness and your resilience is what I would like to talk about. You need to work in your deep states of clarity and deep states of serenity, so this medicine not only accompanies you but grows with you.

Your consistency of connection, your consistency of feeding this *mesa* and feeding yourselves will create a more active companionship and more tangible power available for you. The possibilities are endless. If you want to be an *altomesayoq*, there is the possibility. It is up to you. It is up to you how you can harbor that power and grow that power. You have to feed that *mesa*. You have to empower that *mesa*, and you should know that the crystal you are carrying now in your *mesa* is not just any other crystal. It has high value. I like to emphasize that. With that, the possibilities are endless. The crystal is also a metaphor to find within you your crystal state.

How you find your crystal state is by finding yourself in the collective. When you have gotten the blessings of Apu Ausangate, for instance, there are different expressions, different versions of that mountain that are common. However, there is one version that has to do with that crystal, with that crystallized collective. You need to recognize and find yourselves in that place. This is like a mother crystal that can grow other baby crystals. And, let me warn you that are you are going to be tested on your performance, whether you are fit and worthy of that medicine. You have to show power. You have to show teeth. You have to show resilience. You have to show presence. This is the first day of your lives as medicine people. So again, I want to emphasize that this particular *mesa* needs a lot of care. It needs to be fed. As you are thirsty, your *mesa* is thirsty. You need to have an altar at home, you need to smudge it. And with that there is the understanding of how you take care of yourselves, how you feed yourselves as well.

I am sure there are great power places where you live, to connect, cleanse, and to do ritual. So, walk in beauty, walk with strength, and walk with clarity. Brothers and sisters, thank you for listening. That is all I have to say.

Jose Luis spoke last:

I would like to say a few words about this new era, this heralded stage of life. We are emerging into a new place, into a new platform, into a new time continuum. You look at the Mayan calendars, their accounting of time is ending next year and there is a new beginning, an entirely new reset. It is a *pachakuti*. *Pachakuti* has to do with the allocation of time and space, in which visions become seeds. As seeds become the vehicles of transformation, that transformation leads you into a healed state, into a fulfilled state. *Phukuy* refers to the process of germination, moving into states of fruition, to change some of our guiding mythologies. Don Manuel said we need to change them all. We need to be spearheads. We need to be mavericks. We need to be the ones that journey into those places in memory, into those foreign new topographies of cosmic vision, where no one has dared to journey before.

So creation is an ongoing, wonderful thing that revisits itself as it fulfills itself — time after time. Yet, even at a state of such high continuity, of healed and fulfilled states, there is always a quantum shift. There has to be a quantum shift. As human beings we have been locked in a particular way of being with common denominators: fear, loneliness, feeling disenfranchised, wanting to belong. So we belong to our belief systems. We belong to our affinities. It has to break. Collectively speaking, as this new era is dawning on us, some of the *paqos* I know say we are emerging into this other fifth dimension. A fifth dimension, in which the laws of physics, the progress of science, and the technologies of spirit, also, are becoming more accessible.

As we are emerging into this place, through this new rite of passage, we become global. This is what I call collective. You have to become collective. Of course, you can choose to live under your rock if that is fun, if that is fulfilling for you. Why not? However, being a person of power, being a shaman, being a *paqo*, you need to live life to the fullest. Moreover, in living life through those different venues, opportunity is created through envisioning.

You have to create opportunity. This is your capacity to create meaning. This is what living life to the fullest is. You cannot just follow the creation of meaning of some cosmology like the one we have here. Meaning that is engaged with life! Meaning that is engaged with spirit! Not the other hero's way of finding meaning in that epic journey through suffering. It is not about belief systems either, it is about leading, it is about existence and bringing life into your entire body, entire Mind, entire Heart. The *Mosoq Karpay* has to do with envisioning. It has to do with claiming yourselves by the vision, sourcing from the vision. You have to have a vision. A vision that is collective. In that state of collectivism, one that pertains to your health, your love, your well-being, and your safety.

Mosoq Karpay has to do with emerging into a new state of communion. This is what the new map is about. *Paqos* are mapmakers. We have to bring new coordinates, new landmarks, new topographies, and we have to test them ourselves. We have to half-chew them, like power, like knowledge, and then feed it to our loved ones, to our people. At this stage in time, in space we cannot sit comfortably just watching the world go by. We have to participate, co-participate.

One of the main tenets of shamanism is co-participation. Co-participation calls for understanding, stewardship, responsibility, such high degree of responsibility. We are responsible. You cannot let life happen out there. We are responsible for how we are going to engage. If you engage in a literal or symbolic way, you are not going to create a big ripple to produce that change unless you become collective and unless your own dialogue becomes mythic. A mythic way of walking in the world is the key aspect of *Mosoq Karpay*.

It is no longer your personal identity or persona. I am no longer Jose Luis, no longer my own history. I source from my lineage. I want to become the voice of each one of these individuals, while at the same time remaining non-personal. Mythic means nonpersonal, and overly personable, and entirely collective. These tenets, these points are the new coordinates of your new map. We have to do it. There is no way around it. We have company, we have great allies, we have the mountain spirits, we have the whole lineage behind us, and they are accessed through ritual. Mythic engagement is the technical language of spirit. Not English, not Spanish, not this cause and effect type of descriptive language-based reality. Metaphorically speaking, it is the way of the Heart. The way of the light. The way of being. The way of releasing yourself from doing into the state of non-doing, collectively, not personally.

So, emergence is that big thing for all of us. We cannot be cast adrift in these waves of change out there. We need to raise our sails and choose direction. We need to make maps, not only secure ourselves in certain harbors of safety, but also set sail into the unknown. Go into the places where no one dared to sail before. We have to do that. There is so much possibility in this adventure. So, the *Mosoq Karpay* — besides vision — also has to do with becoming the anchor of your own *ayllus*. The steward of your *ayllu* — even if your *ayllu* is only composed of you and your pet. That is the entryway. When you go back home, hopefully you will find a medicine *ayllu*. I hope that you will be the conduit for this new weaving, network, relationships, vision — a steward of a vision that can bring people together. This is about *ayllu* making and this about being stewards of *ayllus*.

You cannot walk in the world like the old Lone Ranger hero, riding into the sunset after good deeds, on your own, on your horse. It is about collectivism. It is no longer just *ayni*, but *mink'a*. *Mink'a* means collective *ayni*. This new *Mosoq Karpay* is really about *mink'a*. This new *mink'a* is neither cultural nor spiritual — it has to do with a non-personal way of being with one another. From there stems the personable, the commonalities, the relationship. When we find a relationship out in the ordinary world, it is because of commonalities. Is that right? Of interests, of attraction, etc. This is different.

This is about map-making. So the basic question is what is your map, how should your map be. Is it a contingency plan? Is it a new vision that might have to deal with absences, scarcity, your longing, or what has not been fulfilled? Those are questions that you need to answer for yourselves. The *Mosoq Karpay* has to do with an entirely new cosmic vision with different principles, with different guiding mythologies, with a new identity in the world. So this identity that you are bringing from the mountain has to do with your soul's construct, with your soul's vision, with your soul's journey. Part of the memory resides in that memory bank, your soul. The soul has come here into your bodies, into the current themes, situations, landscapes, relationships, geographies to fulfill itself. Simple as that. A cosmic vision, a cosmology is nothing more than the processes that lead life into fulfillment.

20. Making the Paradigm Shift

Returning from a spiritual journey requires finding ways of "growing corn" with the knowledge we receive from the experience. It is important for us to ask ourselves: How do we hold space in the world in order to upgrade our lives and make a difference in the lives of our families and communities? If we call ourselves healers and shamans, what is our relationship with healing and what are we doing? What is our purpose and intention?

During a conversation I had with Jose Luis, he commented:

I used to do healing and, client after client, the outcome was tremendous. Then, the person would come back with the same situation. When healing took place, we were just shedding healing layers and layers and layers. Anyway, to make the story short, it seems like a lot of us in this society loop a lot. We just go back and repeat the loop. I do not want to keep doing the same thing, healing. It could be profitable because I was good at that. But, how can we assist in improving their lives?

So, I went into teaching and I did a lot of teaching. I still teach, always trying to find ways to articulate bodies of knowledge, technologies. I have been doing a lot of research. I am going to turn 50 and I have been directly and indirectly involved since I was 20, very actively for the past 20 years now — or 25 that I've been teaching. We change. We advance our body of knowledge — we evolve our vision of the world, our understanding of the world. This panorama of narrative, the sense of self is not only for us humans. It is also happening in the world of spirit.

I realized that I would rather invest a lot more in the human mind. Our human mind, the capacity particularly of, of imagination is tremendous. We can imagine a great Christ celestial, with a thousand angels with big trumpets. Alternatively, we can imagine Dante's inferno. It is our choice, right? I think we are on the right track, as far as how we not only help and empower individuals but how we can bring more shamans into this beautiful setting and how can we make all the shamans change their own narratives and cross-pollinate.

I agree with Jose Luis's thoughts about looking at our choices. Often when we become healers and spiritual seekers, we think we need to fix things, find what is missing, what has been broken, what piece needs to be brought back to the wholeness. To do this we may focus on a past imprint, situation, or event that has taken place in a person's life. Yet, perhaps looking at those broken pieces — at what is missing — is not really what is needed. Perhaps we need to begin to see ourselves differently in the world so our narratives change as well.

As a psychoanalyst, I am aware that the energy of the past often lives in the present — and that it manifests energetically in the field. By working with the lingering "charge" of the energy from past events, we can affect how the present is experienced. Yet, we can lose our energetic connection to what is happening by remaining attached to a past narrative. By making assumptions about what we know, we lose the ability to perceive what is alive as it is unfolding.

The survival of our planet requires us to be in relationship with the natural world. Today, the ancient knowledge of Andean medicine tradition is being woven together with the technology of our modern world in the new age of collective pluralism. The ancient traditions are merging with what is happening now, combining with the expanding frontier of science and technology. We are learning to embrace the wisdom of the past as we grow and transform in every moment.

When we walk a spiritual path we experience various projects, visions, activities, etc. that become vehicles for us to participate in assisting in the world. We find balance by being in a reciprocal relationship with our families, friends, and communities while at the same time maintaining the awareness of ourselves as individuals. The energy that feeds imagination and visions comes from us, through our connection with Pachamama as an endless source.

So how do we participate in the world and at the same time live in connection with the natural living world? How can we become collective individuals? We need to give ourselves time and space to actively listen with our Belly and Heart — as well as our Mind. When we only listen with our Mind we are more likely to hear what we already know. When we pay attention through feeling with our Bellies and Hearts, we realize that our universe is layered and multidimensional — extending far beyond the temporal, physical reality we live in. When we listen with our Bellies and our Hearts, we can live in all of the universe.

The paradigm of the modern healer is shifting. The new medicine people are creating opportunities for healing through finding new ways of bringing deeper connection. The old identities of being in the role of caregiver and patient are fading as movement is made into a relationship of *ayni*, of reciprocity and right relationship.

As *paqos* we are conduits, connecting the physical and spirit worlds, by bringing ancient wisdom into the modern world. The shaman's purpose is not to have mystic visions living alone on the mountains — it is to serve the experience of the collective by growing corn with it — bringing it back into the day world in a useful way.

One of the changes that comes from being in *ayni* that time is no longer linear. New stories are being written. As we move away from pursuing the "hero's journey," with a goal of reaching an evolved state, a shift occurs between figure and ground. We can participate in completing a hero's journey, but there is an opportunity to deepen our spiritual connection — by dropping our old narratives and guiding mythologies and making ourselves available to a relationship with collective experience.

Being in a state of collective connection expands our consciousness in a way that involves our entire being. This expansion is much greater than the old identities we have carried through our subjective narratives — based upon assumptions about the world we inherit from our immediate families. The opportunity exists for us to grow beyond — as Jung said — our personas into the numinous experience of the Self, and even further into the objective reality where everything is connected. With this new awareness it is possible to bring the collective memory of our experience — the history of the world, the village — into a deeper understanding. The history of the world is who we are. We are collective.

In conversation Jose Luis has said:

One of the wonderful effects that comes from becoming a shaman is that, if you are going to serve, it means that you need to be a collective individual. The collective of the land, the collective of those spirits or power are now your identity. You are a messenger, you are a conduit. So we need a rite of passage, a social rite of passage. That has to do with that paradigm shift in the sense that it could be more enduring, more fun, and more productive to source from that collective identity. At the end of the day, you have to go home. You have to carry your body. You have to carry your experiences that are personal to you, but it is not necessarily primary anymore, but secondary. As the scenario indicates, you source from a grander collective in which all of the participants of that collective know your Heart, know your Belly — there is no opinion, no judgment. It is doable. We spend a great deal of time here, so for me, let us just do it and perhaps we do not have to think too much about it. It will give us so much more meaning but so much more separation as well.

My intention in writing this second book was different from the first book, *Lessons of the Inca Shamans, Part 1: Piercing the Veil.* In *Part 1*, I was sorting through things, trying to understand the process that had taken place in my personal journey. As my writing continued, I became more focused on the perceptual changes that take place in moving from matter into spirit and into energetic connection.

Words are important because they provide context and a bridge toward understanding. Living in this culture requires cognizance. This is necessary to organize and make sense of our experience. But the essence of living comes from the energetic experience — where we feel alive and find meaning through connection.

As a psychologist and Jungian analyst, I have found that I can use language in my work with clients — yet the energy I work with in this process comes from someplace else — a place bigger than me. I happen to be the vehicle that is holding it.

As *paqos*, we become conduits serving through manifestation. As healers, we are metabolizers. Living in temporal reality requires us to use metaphor to make meaning in our world. As Jung said, we need symbols to hold the energy of the experience, a psychological space can be described — and people can say, "Oh, I get it!" My friend Robin Robertson, an excellent writer, has said, "I try to make what I write so clear that when the reader finishes, they *think* that they already knew it. But actually they didn't."

Stories provide context because narrative is sequential — it offers structure. The stories we tell can be anybody's story. The stories need to be told in a collective way that we can relate to. Perhaps that is the purpose of cosmology — and ceremony. Universal myths hold the essential energy, the *kausay* life force.

They are emanations, expressions of something greater than we are.

> *At the end of the day, you have to use your intuition, your Heart. It is an act of love. It is a tremendous act of love. It's the reciprocal effect of your efforts and identity as a way to participate in this global vision. You have to use what feels right for yourself. That's the bottom line. This little conversation — it's how you see it and how I see it. At the end of the day, it is irrelevant. What matters is what rings truthful in your Heart and you should follow that gut feeling. It is usually right.*
>
> —Jose Luis Herrera

Appendix. List of Despacho *Ingredients*

alabaster man and woman figurines — duality, serving in reciprocal unison

alphabet noodles — communication and the ability to use language

anise seeds — sweet fragrance attracts spirits

bread — in this tradition binds the family together. It is commonly used in soul retrievals.

candles — used for light and illumination

candy — represents harmony and attraction. Harmony in an environment occurs through sweetness, especially flower shaped candies. The candy represents germination, fulfillment, and fruition. Every *pacha* brings fruition.

candy house or car — the metaphor is for success, as you define it

candy man and woman — symbolizes harmony in the couple. The element of two is very important because it not only symbolizes right relationship among humans, but also between humans and the collective.

chocolate frog — harmony and the cycles of water

coca leaves — primary ingredient of *despachos* that prayers are blown into. Coca leaves are frequently replaced with bay leaves in the West.

cotton — symbolizes purity on which you lay all the gifts by placing it on the top of the other ingredients. Symbolizing clouds, it can also be cycles of water and rain. In a *despacho* for Pachamama, it represents water. In an *Apu despacho* it represents heaven and purity.

corn (*maize*, or *sara* in Quechua) — production and abundance crackers / wafers — flour products represent your *anima* (spirit)

dough wafers — with a picture of St. Nicholas it is given to the *Apu* spirits who bring good news; with a picture of a cross it symbolizes health and is used in health *despachos*

incense — attracts Spirit

llama fat — (*untu* in Quechua) the act of bringing forth through vision. Coca leaves and llama fat are combined. They are basic to calling the *Apus* and bringing them.

llama fetus — to give birth and bring potential into manifestation, to get rid of sadness

lima beans —because of the color, they harmonize the *despacho*. Sometimes we give a positive and a negative ability in different *despachos*.

loadstone / magnetite — brings attraction. It is a favored item when doing business *despachos*.

metal frog — attraction. The frog is the one that calls. The messenger.

metal hand — friendship. The hand is flanked by symbols of winged beings, and is the dynamic nature of all relations that must be served.

metal moon (*luna*) — symbolizes the agricultural calendar. The spirit of the moon is feminine and referred to as Mama Killa.

metal sun (*sol*) — symbolizes the social calendar, social interaction. The spirit of the sun is masculine and referred to as Inti.

metal star (*ch'aska*) — protection

mica — represents silver, and maintaining the integrity of the soul as it grows stronger

molasses candy — harmony

papel de regalo — decorated wrapping paper used for *despachos*

pewter horseshoes — fluidity in business and good fortune through "right relationship" and reciprocity pewter left hand — receive, you must give and receive — a circular process

pewter right hand — positive, giving, welcoming

qori — gold, symbolizing spiritual wealth and solar energy

qullqi — silver, symbolizing spiritual wealth and lunar energy

rods — amplify sound

sequins — ornamental décor to provide decoration

shell — the womb of the heavens and the container in which creation sits. Sometimes you pour some wine inside. It is also the spirit of the waters. This is a metaphor for creation. We are creating a venue. *Despachos* are traditionally mediums to propitiate right relationship. If you put items into the *despacho* that you are missing, you will propitiate lack. It needs to be an open and active dialog of creation.

seeds —the basic complement that the land needs so the land can bring abundance back to you

sugar — sweet to attract spirits

tacu (red clay) — can bring positive or negative outcomes and is often used in *despachos* that protect against psychic attack. It can wash off negativity or repel what is sent to you, depending on affinities.

thread — white and yellow, gold and silver thread binds and brings wholeness

tobacco — attracts spirits of North America. Tobacco is also used to attract the spirit of the plant in *ayahuasca* ceremonies.

wayruro — a small red and black seed representing the masculine and feminine principles that brings protection. Two of these seeds are often placed in the center shell for good luck.

wine — red wine for Pachamama, the earth, and/or white wine for Viracocha, the heavens.

winkiki seeds — a seed that grows underground and has a supernatural presence. Used to attract. It also has the ability to bring together polarizing energies, such as man and woman.

Glossary

Most paqos in this book are referred to by just their first names. The glossary reflects that usage. Many paqos have the honorific title of Don (masculine) or Doña (feminine) added to the front of their names. The glossary reflects what Deborah Bryon calls each of these paqos. A new student of Incan medicine should find out what each of these paqos prefers to be called.

Mountains and *apus* are related to one another, but the best interpretation we have is that an *apu* is a spirit living on (in?) a particular mountain. This distinction means that the glossary has entries for both the spirit and the place. The spirit entries start with Apu.

Another excellent and more extensive source for the meanings of Incan words is www.incaglossary.org.

Adolfo— altomesayoq, mentor and teacher; his full name is Adolfo Ttito Condori

Adriel — Andean paqo and coca leaf reader

agua de sangre — sacred water, literally water of blood

Aguas Calientes — the town closest to Machu Picchu; literally hot waters

Alankoma — a sacred Andean mountain; keeper of the eagle's nest, the place where eagles, condors, and falcons reside on its summits

Alca Cocha — rainbow lagoon, below Sigrena Cocha

ally — the intermediary or necessary conduit between the ego and otherworld experience *almakispichi* — a disincarnate soul that has not been purified and is still wandering in the middle world

altomesayoq — the most highly respected of the *paqos* or *mesa* carriers, with the capacity to serve as gateways between ordinary and nonordinary reality. They each have membership with a particular mountain and speak directly to spirits of that location. These *paqos* source (derive) energy from the directors of the holy mountains, the *apu* spirits, by engaging in an active exchange with the energetic collective. Also called *hatunmesayoq*

Amaru — the mythic snake being of the lower world, Ukhu Pacha

Amaruina — literally serpent of fire; ancient spiritual lineage of wizards with special visions

anamisma — an energetic state where power implodes

Anasazi Indians — ancient Native American culture in Four Corners region of the United States and throughout all of Southern Utah

Andean Research Institute (ARI) — a non-profit organization in Maras, Peru, that supports the Andean and Amazon cultures and the wisdom keepers of those cultures with the intention of preserving the practices and technology of ancient Peruvian medicine for existing generations and for all those to come

anima mundi — Stanislav Grof's term that describes the universe created and permeated by a superior creative intelligence

anthropos — the ancient idea of an all-extensive world soul, a kind of cosmic subtle body

apachetta — a pile of rocks built with prayers and intention to form a structure for healing

apu — the winged beings, the great collective mountain spirits. The *apus* of a mountain are an expression of the collective composite of Pachamama. The collective has different creative expressions that mirror the people of the land.

Apu Alankoma — the *apu* who provided Deborah's first major experience of piercing the veil

Apu Aspo Kenta Rebacha —the *apu* that ensures the proper flow of water allocated to animals, plants, and people

Apu Ausangate — the observer that has the power to multiply alpacas, sheep, faith, health, intent, and power; second in command after Apu Salcantay

Apuchin — the mythic condor being of the upper world; the energy center of the Mind

Apu Chupícuaro — a collective mountain spirit from the mountains of Bolivia, the director of the *altomesayoq* Juanito's *mesa*

Apu Corrichaska — from the fourth level, in charge of registering the stars in the sky. One star belongs to each individual that incarnates.

Apu Cruz Pata — an apu that visits Juanito's mesa

Apu Everest — a sacred mountain that keeps the light of the world

Apu Huanacauri — an apu that visits Doña Alejandrina's mesa

Apu Huascaran — the powerful benefactor of *altomesayoq* Doña Alejandrina's *mesa*

Apu Kaylash — an apu of initiation bringing initiates to enlightenment

Apu Machu Picchu — a 1500 year old apu that visits Doña Alejandrina's mesa

Apu Mama Simona — a feminine apu, located near Ausangate; involved with fertility and healing, married to the sun because she is the first peak in the region to receive the sun's rays

Apu Misti — an Andean apu that visits Juanito's mesa

Apu Nuevo Mundo (Apu Mundo) — an apu that visits Juanito's mesa

Apu Pachatusan —the axis of local and collective *pachas* near Cusco; the axis for happiness, the energy that moves human lives

Apu Patapac — the *apu* benefactor of cattle thieves that takes the animals into an underground hiding place with large interior spaces

Apu Picol — the herder of people

Apu Potosi — an apu that visits Doña Alejandrina's mesa

Apu Pukeen — in charge of constructing housing; brings the earth up to build a home

Apu Qariwanaku – an apu who visits Doña Alejandrina's mesa

Apu Q'ollorit'i — "Snow Star," gives vision, symbol of Christ

Apu Qullqi — an *apu* benefactor of Deborah's mesa from the city of Cusco, close to the sacred mountain Pachatusan; an accountant, in charge of records of all births and deaths in Cusco

Apu Sacsayhuaman Cabildo — the keeper of knowledge and wisdom

Apu Salcantay — directs all mountains and holds the power of life and death, with power over the four elements

Apu Sawasiray — embodies the power of "eternal youth" through dreaming and brings dreams back into reality

Apu Senqa — the keeper of water of Cusco. He rules all rainwater, lagoons, and rivers. When this *apu* is cloudy, it rains in the city.

Apu Sinaq'ara — an apu that visits Doña Alejandrina's mesa and directs the soul at death

Apu Sokllacasa — an apu that visits Doña Alejandrina's mesa

Apu Towianami — honored in traditional Q'ero villages

Apu Wanakauri — an apu that visits Doña Alejandrina's mesa; associated with a mountain in the area of Cusco

Apu Waquay Wilka - provides physical *mesas* for individuals to become *altomesayoqs* per Apu Salcantay's instruction archetypal or mythic realm — the third level existing outside of linear time, where synchronistic events are connected

assemblage point — a point of perception in the subtle body responsible for shifts into different states of heightened awareness

Asteonoku — the first peoples in the Americas that built the first temple cities and pyramids

Asunta — a female *pampamesayoq* who is Don Manuel Q'uispe's daughter

atiynioq — feminine energy

atiy — ability

Ausangate — the mountain considered one of the holiest mountains in Peru, connected with one of the most evolved of the collective mountain *apu* spirits

Ave Maria Purisima — the ceremonial salutation to the *apus* during ceremony; Spanish words from the Catholic religion

ayahuasca — hallucinogenic medicine and the related ceremony of taking the medicine practiced in the Amazon basin; the jaguar who imbibes the plant medicine as the spirit of the Amazon

ayllu —community; may refer to a person's village, group of *mesa* carriers practicing shamanism, or any other group formed for a common purpose

Ayllu K'anchaq Qoyllur (AKQ) —group formed to transmit the ancestral knowledge and the spiritual legacies of the Andean medicine people with the purpose of recovering, interpreting, and promoting spiritual treasures of the Andes in other parts of the world

ayni — the balanced state of reciprocity between all living things; being in right relationship

Birdman — Deborah's spirit ally

Black Snake — the mythic being symbolizing the shadow period

brujo (feminine is *bruja*) — Carlos Castaneda's term for a medicine
man that follows the path of sorcery to gain personal power
and knowledge; generally regarded as causing harm to others

Cainan — the powerful black jaguar ally Deborah associates with
Chocachinchi and the Amazon jungle

Calas Asiah — an ancient pyramid in Asteonoku

cayangate — the two types of energy that are masculine and
feminine, *yanantin* and *masintin* and of opposing dualities;
fertility, fecundity, and multiplicity

ceke lines — existing energy lines that connect the energy
meridians in the earth. These *ceke* lines intersect at *wakas*,
places that are power spots infused with energy. By activating
ceke lines in areas such as Peru, the veil becomes more
transparent, allowing for a greater flow of energy and
communication with the collective. Being in these power spots
heightens a person's perception, and it becomes easier to
achieve expanded states of awareness. The Peruvian
altomesayoqs enter into dialogues with the *apus* and work to
open *ceke* lines in the mountains to promote healing in the
earth.

celestial *mesas* — *mesas* bestowed directly by the *apus* upon the
highest *altomesayoqs* with the greatest capacity to hold the
power

ch'aska — star

chi — life force energy

Chincheros —an Incan village between Cusco and Urubamba
known for weaving, also a sacred site with *wakas*

Chocachinchay — the commanding jaguar spirit of the Amazon;
in Incan cosmology, governs the middle world of Kay Pacha
and is the symbol for physical manifestation

Choquetacarpo — a mountain in Vilcabamba; a plant that is good
for lung ailments, growing at same level as the short grasses

ch'uyanchasqa — the shedding of what is

ch'uspa — a small woven bag with a strap used for carrying coca leaves

collya — queen, moon spouse of the sun king

conjunctio — the phase of union and transformation in alchemy, through what Jung called holding the tension of opposites resulting in the transcendent function

Cusco — the site of the historic capital of the Inca Empire

despacho — an offering to Pachamama, given through fire or buried in the earth. It is an arrangement of coca leaves (bay leaves are used in the United States), resembling a mandala — embellished with grains, candy, and other colorful objects that symbolize gifts to the upper, lower, and middle worlds. After carefully separating the coca leaves or *k'intus* into groups in three, the shaman transfers intent into the leaves using breath, and each group of leaves takes on a specific prayer or pattern to be let go of and given to the fire. The leaves surround a central symbolic object that is determined by the type and purpose of the *despacho*. Most *despachos* are gifts to Pachamama, although some are for releasing *hucha* or negativity, and some are visionary *despachos*, requesting blessings from the *apus* before initiation ceremonies.

Don Alberto Villoldo — the other person, besides Jose Luis who was taught by Don Manuel Q'uispe

Don André — a male pampamesayoq known for his big heart

Don Francisco — a male *pampamesayoq* who was president of the Q'ero nation

Don Hilario — a male *pampamesayoq* who is known for his skill at healing and reading coca leaves

Don Manuel Q'uispe — the great *altomesayoq* who prophesized that the next paqos would come from the West

Don Sebastian — a male Q'ero *pampamesayoq* who heals through *despacho* offerings

Doña Alejandrina — a female *altomesayoqs*. Apu Huascaran is the benefactor of her mesa

Doña Bernadina — a female *pampamesayoq* who works with herbs

Doña Maria — a female *altomesayoq* who works with an *apu* called Aspo Kenta Rebacha from the village of Kico, a remote area of the Andean mountains

dreamtime — a time and experiences experienced outside of ordinary reality; a term probably borrowed from Australian aborigines

energetic collective — the fourth level, the essential or energetic level of spirit or collectivity, corresponding to the *unus mundi*

Engady — the return of a new Incan order

estrella — the manifestation of an *apu* on a sacred path; receiving a summoning or calling to follow the path of an *altomesayoq* or *pampamesayoq*

faramya — the Quechua word for "pompous asses."

Florida water — used for purification in ritual; flower essences in alcohol

fuego sagrado — "sacred fire" in *despacho* ceremony

gamen — merging that occurs when spirit enters the body

hallpay — ritual for coming to unity, to *ayni*; bringing conflicting elements into sacred space; types of *hallpay*: *sapan, yanantin, masintin, yaqui*

hampuy — the Quechua verb "to come" used by shamans when calling sacred space

hamut'ay — practice of connecting with the land and *apus*

Hanaq Pacha — the upper world

hanaq qawaq — a sage, teacher, or master that understands the ways of the land and articulates the medicine of the land though chewing like a condor half chews and gives that knowledge to its children

Hatun Karpay — the Great Initiation — collective sacred lineage of the Q'ero shamans passed down is the fourth level of initiation, which comes with the understanding of numinous experience and the energetic collective

hatunmesayoq — see *altomesayoq* and *hatun paqo*

hatun paqo — literally, big paqo; *hatunmesayoq* is another word used to refer to *altomesayoqs* that emphasizes multi-dimensionality

Huanca — a Quechua people living in the Junín Region of central Peru, in and around the Mantaro Valley

Huascaran — the tallest mountain in Peru in the Vilcabamba region; the home of the *apu* who *is* the director of the *altomesayoq* Doña Alejandrina's *mesa*

hucha — negative energy

ikaro — words spoken by shamans during ceremony and ritual

illa — creation

Inihuatana — Hitching Post of the Sun entrance to Machu Picchu

inkari — the right side of the body governed by the masculine principle of linearity

Inkari — first man created

insuflar — literally "to blow"; that which something, such as energy, is blown into

Inti — the sun

Inti paqos — wizards, visionary paqos

Jose Luis Herrera — student of the high mountain, Amazon, and coastal medicine traditions of Peru who has studied under the most respected medicine people of Peru; leader of the trip to Peru described in *Lessons of the Inca Shamans, Part 2*

journey — shifting into an otherworld state of consciousness to retrieve information

Juanito — a male *altomesayoq* whose benefactors are from Bolivia

Kabbalah — a set of esoteric teachings meant to explain the relationship between an unchanging, eternal, and mysterious Infinite and the mortal and finite universe (God's creation)

karpay — the shamanic initiation rites given when the shaman's body of knowledge and the power of the shaman's ancient lineage pass to the apprentice through the *mesa*. The *karpay* is integrated by the *paqo* into conscious awareness through a process of recapitulating and remembering through the body by working with the *mesa*.

kausay — the energy of creation that is often experienced in the body as a vibration or in the heart as a feeling of universal love towards everyone and everything, not attached to any person or outcome; life force

Kausay Pacha — collective energetic realm; spirit world

Kay Pacha — the middle world, the world of consensual reality

khuya —a rock, crystal, or stone that is part of a shaman's *mesa* that energetically carries the shaman's medicine body or capacity to hold power. (sometimes spelled *q'uiya)*

k'intu — a group of three coca leaves carrying the energy of direct intent

Kujawami — an apu mountain in the Q'ero region of the Andes

Kundalini — powerful fire energy; the serpent goddess at the base of the spine

Lake Titicaca — the largest lake in Peru, in the Andes on the border of Peru and Bolivia

lipka — linden tree or basswood; sometimes translates as lime tree, but it is not the same as the citrus lime; an alkaloid obtained from the tree that increases the effectiveness of the coca leaves when they are chewed for energy and to mitigate altitude sickness at higher elevations

literal level — the first level, normal awareness and existing in the concrete world of every day, out-in-the-world experience

llank'ay — the energy center located in the Belly, anchoring in the body

luminous body — the energetic container that holds the totality of psychic experience, between consciousness and the collective unconscious, that extend beyond the physical body

luminous energy field — a record of personal and ancestral memories that surrounds the physical body; an archive of past life events, including former lifetimes

lupuna — teacher tree; a giant tree found in various parts of the Amazon; one of those beautiful giants of the Amazon, grand, imposing, and well rooted in the jungle's soil

Machu Picchu —"ancient peak;" the Lost City of the Incas in the Cusco region of Peru

Madonna of Candelaria — Black Madonna

Madonna of Copacabana — the Madonna shrine located in Bolivia near Lake Titicaca; "one who looks at the precious stone."

Mama Cocha — mother of the waters

Mamacha Virgin Mary — the healing water emerging from the earth at Pachatusan

Mama Quilla — mother of the moon

manta — cape or blanket

Maras — a town in the Sacred Valley where ceremonies with the *apus* took place

Mariano Turpo — the late transcended paqo whose spirit will return on June 24, 2014, to Sigrena Cocha

masintin — the *hallpay* ritual of bringing similar energies together

mastana— a traditional cloth that holds the *mesa*

mesa — a collection of individual stones (*khuyas*) assembled over time, a living representation of the paqo's medicine body. A full *mesa* is usually comprised of about twelve stones, wrapped in a *mastana* cloth, which is a square piece of material that carries the stones. The *mesa* is the carrier's connection to the collective energetic realm and the world of consensual reality. It serves as a bridge or gateway, linking the paqo to lineage of ancestors from the past and children of the future. (Spelled *misa* in Quechua.)

mesa carrier — a person who works with a ceremonial medicine bundle consisting of sacred objects that are usually stones or crystals that have been collected and worked with over time; the objects that hold energy for that particular individual in Q'ero shamanism

Mesa Verde — archaeological sites of cliff dwelling homes and villages built by the ancestral Pueblo people, sometimes called the Anasazi

mesayoq — paqo who acquires power through a mesa

mijo — a term of endearment for a son

mink'a — communal labor done for communal good; service; mutual work given for returned work; collective *ayni*

misa — see *mesa*

Mocha — a culture of people in the region of the Pacific Ocean

mona — herb that brings clarity and vision

montera — wide-brimmed hat

mosoq — a stone or crystal that holds energy for vision; a new rite of passage that occurs through reconnecting with ancestral lineage and the cosmos

Mosoq Karpay — "new initiation"; the inscription of code from sacred crystals given by the *apus* into the luminous body, creating a shift from physical to energetic expression at the fifth level of sacred work

munay — the universal feeling state of love connecting us to the land and every living thing around us

naranga water — purification water used for clearing *hucha* energy

ñawin —"the eye"; a fountain in nature that is a place of manifestation from the energetic into physical

nigredo — an alchemical term that applies to the shadow phase of transformation that occurs at the beginning

Nilam — the name Mocha people use for Tanopa, the child of the sun and the moon

nivela — level

numinous experience — an energetic state of ecstasy and connection to all living things

Ocongate — a district in the southern highlands of Peru

oferendas — present for fire ceremony

Ollantaytambo — an Incan archeological site in the Sacred Valley of Peru

pablitos — from *ukukos pablitos*, the "bear people" who carry out sacred pilgrimages for their villages on Snow Star

pacha — a period of time and space; an era; a world, as in the upper, middle, and lower worlds; an Inca map of consciousness referring to the structure that contains *kausay* in Andean cosmology. In every person's life there are significant events occurring at specific times and places that shape personal fate and destiny. These pivotal points on one's life journey are considered to possess greater amounts of *kausay*.

pachakuti — a time of upheaval and transformation, such as we are living in when visions become seeds

Pachakuti Amaruina — Doña Alejandrina's child

Pachamama — Mother Earth

Pachatusan — a sacred mountain on the outskirts of Cusco

pampamesayoq — "keepers of the earth"; paqos who are in a reciprocal helping relationship with Pachamama

paqarina — feminine place of emergence associated with water and caves; a fountain of manifestation from the lower world into the middle world of Kay Pacha

paqo — a *mesa* carrier following the Andean medicine tradition

parlero — a midwife of the dead who moves souls from one phase of time to the next

phukuy — the ritual act of blowing an intention three times into the leaves of a *k'intu* in order to establish an energetic connection linking the three worlds; the process of germination, moving into states of fruition

Pisac — "Temple of the Visionary;" a village in the Sacred Valley on the Urubamba River

Pocatan — the lineage of the Polcatambo nation whose role is to clean up after the Q'ollorit'i pilgrimage

Polcatambo — (see Pocatan)

Pomacanchi — the village next to a sacred lagoon that is Adolfo's birthplace; a place of ceremony next to natural sacred fountain of energetic manifestation

poq'po — energy body

Punko — "silver doorway;" the ancient name of the Apu mountain Qullqi Cruz

phururuna — sentient beings who watch over birds and animals; perhaps from the Purun Runa, an ancient people who were one of the first civilizations in South America

qantuta — national flower of Peru; *Cantua buxifolia*

Qariwanaku— the place where you set the record of cumulative effects of reenactments straight; the fifth level of the sixth mountain equal to the sixth brother of Ausangate; a healing place with underground springs

Q'ero — one of the lineages who are descendants of the Incas in the Andean mountains

qollari — the feminine principle governing the left side of the body associated with formlessness

Q'ollorit'i — an annual sacred festival overseen by Apu Q'ollorit'i; (also spelled Q'oyllur Rit'i)

Quechua — the language spoken by the descendants of the Incas living in the Andean mountains

Q'uispe Conchi — the village where *paqo* Mariano Turpo was reborn on June 24, 2014

Qullqi — the night quality of silver, a place of mystery in dreamtime

Qullqi Cruz — "silver doorway"; changed to "silver cross" by Spanish culture; has to do with abundance; a highly regarded mountain in the third dimension

recados – items placed in a *despacho*

Rio Vilconata — a segment for the Urubamba River in the Sacred Valley

romero — rosemary plant

rose water — water used in purification rituals associated with heart feeling

ruda — rue; a plant used in ceremonies to change luck

Sachamama — Mother Tree, the rainforest counterpart of Pachamama

Sacred Valley — also known as the Urubamba Valley; in the Peruvian Andes

Salcantay — the mountain associated with the most powerful sacred *apu,* where a celestial *mesa* is buried

salka — wild and undomesticated

sami — the refined light energy of plant spirits

saminchasqa — the act of blowing prayers into a coca leaf in order to establish an energetic connection linking the three worlds

Santa Catalina — the sacred mountain of the shepherds that deals with abundance; the keeper of wild and domestic animals

santa tierra — a feminine spirit that works with Pachamama; comes up from the earth through the floor during ceremonies with *altomesayoqs*

Santa Tierra Belen — a *santa tierra* that visits Doña Alejandrina's mesa

sapan hallpay — a ritual with coca leaves between an individual that involves opening the energy centers as a means of connection

Sawasiray — also known as Qullqi Cruz. A sacred mountain near Chincheros

sayak — benefactor

Señor de Huanca — a spirit associated with the chapel on Pachatusan; the Christian manifestation of Pachatusan

sephiroth — one of the 10 attributes/emanations in Kabbalah, through which The Infinite reveals himself and continuously creates both the physical realm and the chain of higher metaphysical realms

shadow —Jung's term for hidden unconscious aspects of one's self; sometimes refers to the "dark" elements

shamanism — Eliade described shamanism as a "technique of ecstasy." Webster's dictionary has defined it as "excessive joy" and a "kind of cataleptic trance." Michael Harner described shamanism as "a great mental and emotional adventure" and wrote, "Ultimately shamanic knowledge can only be acquired through individual experience (pp. xiv-xv)." These definitions reflect that understanding energetically beyond words does not occur in the Mind, it can only occur in a state experienced through the body, primarily the Heart and the Belly.

Sinaq'ara — mountain in Peru that produces the Sinaq'ara Glacier

Singrena Cocha— a sacred lagoon on Ausangate

Snow Star — the mountain *Q'ollorit'i,* which has become a symbol of Christ

sonqo — Heart center

Surimana — a lineage of medicine people living in the Andes

symbolic level — second level experienced through dreams, metaphors, and images. This corresponds to Winnicott's transitional space of the imaginal realm between fantasy and reality. Jungians have described this as the imaginal realm where inner dialogue using the technique of active imagination can occur.

Tanopa — the child of the sun and moon in the Incan creation myth who founded cities and taught the people how to live

Taripay Pacha — encounter with the universe, a new era of human experience, the age of meeting ourselves again when humanity will have the chance to consciously evolve in an era of harmony; a time of choosing that the individual can choose for himself or herself

Taytacha Temblores — lord of the earthquakes: refers to the Black Christ icon paraded through Cusco believed to have had the authority to stop powerful earthquakes

temenos — sacred psychological container that holds experience

Temple of the Winds — (Ollantaytambo) sacred Incan site overlooking the Sacred Valley

the land — what the Q'ero shamans refer to as the collective expression of Pachamama

Timolina — marketed in English-speaking countries as Thymoline, a commercial alkaline mouthwash and gargle containing thyme oil, eucalyptol, menthol, and pine oil, dissolved in alcohol, similar to Listerine. Used as a liquid with a very pungent smell that you rub on your body to ward off evil spirits, particularly when you are panicky or you are in distress.

Tinqui — a city near Cusco in Peru

tinquy — the first level of relationship in touching energy bodies

Titicaca — lake in the Andes on the border of Peru and Bolivia

tukuy — complete

tukuy munayniyoc — all-encompassing unconditional love from the third level of energetic relationships

tupay — a warrior's way to resolve conflict through working with the *mesa*, the one who challenges and is willing to meet one's Self; the second stage or relationships

Ukhu Pacha — the lower world

ukukos pablitos — the bear people, half bear and half man who make the sacred pilgrimage to Snow Star

unkuna — traditional blankets that hold the mesa medicine bundle

unus mundus — the deepest level of the collective unconscious and the place or state in which matter and psyche merge into one world; a composite universal Self that exists beyond time and space

urpichallay — "sweet dove of my heart"

Urubamba — the river valley in the Sacred Valley of the Andes

Vilcabamba — one of the two sacred mountain areas where a celestial *mesa* is buried (also spelled Willkapampa)

Viracocha — the great creator god in the pre-Inca and Inca mythology in the Andes region of South America

waka — a power spot in nature

Waquay Wilka — "sacred tear" one of the seven sacred mountains in the Andes

wilka — sacred

yachay —the Mind, one of the three main energy centers; clear vision and wisdom

yanai — clear vision

yanantin – balancing masculine and feminine energy

yaqui hallpay — the energetic connection in community

yarrow — sacred

yuya — the organizing principle of wisdom

Index

vision, 17, 260
  Perry's view, 17
vision state, 44, 46
waka, 109, 276
Waquay Wilka, 107, 114, 118,
  122, 173
water, 42, 73, 99, 174, 176,
  202, *See also* glacier water
  Florida. *See* Florida water
  holy, 113
  naranga. See naranga
    water

rose. *See* rose water
water flute, 203
water of blood. *See agua de*
  sangre
wedging, 51
wind, 173
yachay. See Mind
yanantin, 14, 101, 111, 135,
  158, 159
yanantin despacho, 183
Zero Cola, 186

About the Author

Deborah Bryon's journey on the Andean medicine path started over a decade ago when she began having dreams that led her to Peru to work with the Andean paqos. As a Paqo Yachacheq, her vision is to bring the wisdom and practice of the Andean medicine people back into the Western world with the intention of building communities that practice what she has learned about the healing of people and spirit of the land.

Deborah is a graduate of UCLA and received her doctorate in Counseling Psychology from the University of Denver, before becoming a diplomate Jungian analyst with the Inter-Regional Society of Jungian Analysts. She has authored several articles on Andean medicine, the mesa, and Andean teachings for spiritual magazines and Jungian publications. She frequently lecturers in the analytic community on healing the "whole person" with a focus on conscious integration, creativity, and spirituality.

In addition to writing, teaching, and seeing clients in private practice, Deborah is a painter and member of Spark Gallery. She uses painting as visual language to describe her experience of spiritual connection with the Apus and Andean Cosmos. She currently spends her time between her private practice in Denver and Capital Reef Utah, with her husband Perry Edwards, and their two dogs. She is the mother of two sons, Devin and Colin Arnold.